Growing and Learning in Rural Communities

A professional development manual for facilitators of community engagement towards sustainable futures

Revised edition

Helen Sheil (Dr)

Centre for Rural Communities Inc.

Author: Helen Sheil

Artist: Anne Lorraine

Desktop Publisher: Filomena Lea

© Copyright 2003, Revised edition 2024
The Centre for Rural Communities Inc.
Toorloo Arm 3909, Victoria, Australia
https://ruralcommunities.com.au

ISBN 978-0-9943393-8-6

This publication is copyright. The Copyright Act 1968 of Australia allows a maximum of one chapter or 10% of this book, whichever is the greater, to be copied by any educational institution for its educational purposes provided that that educational intuitions notice to Copyright Agency (or the body that administers it) has given a remuneration to Copyright Agency Limited (CAL) under the Act. For details of the CAL licence for educational institutions contact: Copyright Agency Limited, (02) 9394 7600, info@copyright.com.au

With thanks:
To the many elders and educators
who generously and patiently shared their
'practice wisdom' and stories.

To the academics who respected and
affirmed the value my work.

To my partner Neil Smith for being a
co con-spirator in this journey, and
my sister, Val Growcott for financial
support in publishing.

Especially to those who welcomed
a collaborative way of working.

Helen Sheil

I acknowledge the Traditional Owners of Country throughout Australia and recognize their continuing connection to land, waters and culture. I pay my respects to their Elders past, present and emerging and thank them for sharing their stories and culture and friendship.

CONTENTS

Introduction	7
Acknowledgement: The motivation, journey and potential	9
The reality, then and now	13
Beyond knowing to implementation	15
Why study circles?	16
Facilitator's professional development manual	19
Why a regional approach?	19
For a time the stars aligned	21
Opportunity for involvement by tertiary partners	22
Change initiated from within communities	23
Who is the manual for?	26
Important role for regional institutions	27
Partnership with Regional Universities….	27
Why community knowledge informs regional development	28
Further references	29
Chapter 1: Personal and Community Development	31
Focus of this chapter	33
Useful practices	34
Questioning	34
1. Introduction to community development	35
2. Role of the community development worker	49
3. State of our communities: Conceptual tools	53
4. Locating learning within communities	59
5. Changing roles of Government/Community/Market Place	63
Further references	68

Chapter 2 : Strength in Diversity — 71

    Focus of this chapter — 73

    Introduction — 73

    Strategies: beginning the practice — 74

    1. Challenges of change — 74

    2. Beginning: the important first step — 76

    3. Community development workers role — 77

    4. Same but different — 79

    5. Opportunities to learn together – unpacking the myths (lies) — 82

    6. Resilient communities: a dynamic quality — 83

    7. Why and how people change — 87

    8. Reframing through legislation and policy — 89

    Further references — 92

Chapter 3: Safety and Respect — 95

    Focus of this chapter — 97

    Introduction — 97

    1. Principles for regional community development — 98

    2. Involvement and Participation — 100

    3. Safety — 102

    4. Practice and Reflection — 104

    5. Healing divisions and damage (between people, communities and nature) — 105

    Further references — 109

Chapter 4: (The Model) Collaborative Engagement for Transformation Goals and Implementation — 111

    Focus of this chapter — 113

    Collaborative Engagement for Transformation — 116

    1. Dialogue — 116

    2. Time — 124

    3. Visioning — 128

    4. Local community ownership — 130

5. Action	136
6. Networking	141
7. Co-operative Culture	146
8. Transformation	152
9. Reflection	172
Further references	176

Chapter 5: Bio-regional Approach — 179

Focus of this chapter	181
1. A bio-regional approach	181
2. Role of Community Development Worker	183
3. Finding out	185
4. Working with Government	191
5. Learning about learning	193
6. Networking	199
7. Rural Communities, regional groups and peak bodies	201
8. Communications: Social media and platforms	206
9. Establishing structures and financing projects: regional economics	207
10. Rural Trusts and Foundations	213
Further references	218

Chapter 6: Continuing to Develop — 221

Focus of this chapter	223
1. Narrative as a tool for change	225
2. Use of media	239
3. Continuing to affirm	242
4. Walking away, knowing how, when and why	243
5. Continuing to learn	245
Further references	246

• INTRODUCTION •

ACKNOWLEDGEMENT: THE MOTIVATION, JOURNEY AND POTENTIAL

I write this update from Gunaikurnai country on the edge of Bung Yarnda (Lake Tyers), the site of the first Victorian landrights title for the Lake Tyers Aboriginal Trust in 1970 and on the edge of Bidwell-Maap country (National Museum Australia 2021). I acknowledge the Elders past, present and continuing who have hung onto their culture under constantly changing policies that have discriminated and controlled them. Many have been my teachers in finding ways to reconnect across divisions. I thank those who gave generously of their time. Talking with me, affirming that sitting together and listening to each other was their way of doing business and from whom I learnt the words 'educate don't hate' (Uncle Albert Mullett who like Oodgeroo Noonucaal worked to transform relationships between black and white Australians).

'educate don't hate'

I thank those who spoke to students, community groups and in recent years *Stories of Influence* gatherings at Nowa Nowa and Lake Tyers Beach (Sheil 2019): Bruce Pascoe, Dr. Aunty Eileen Harrison, Wayne Thorpe, Grattan Mullet, Ray Thomas, Leane Edwards, Aunty Phyllis Andy and Uncle Herb Patten.

Dr. Aunty Doris Paton affirmed my use of study circles as a practice approach she had used in her work with Australians for Reconciliation (1993). Marjorie Thorpe became friend to all my family, adding richness to events with ceremony of country. Those like Kevin Murray and Lennie Hayes who always made me welcome.

Other elders, colleagues and custodians included Uncle Max Dulumunmun Harrison and his daughters. It was a humbling experience to be welcomed into a healing ceremony and to sit and share stories of survival on a massacre site while an eagle flew overhead. To walk with Aunty Marion Pearce and local women while she burnt gum leaves in her beautifully carved coolamon and a black snake slide through the grass. Stories educate us to understand how to live in this country with respect for the earth and all species. An invitation to become custodians, to care for country together.

practices that bridge conflicting world view

The motivation to introduce facilitators to practices that bridge conflicting world views originated from the devastating experience of living and working in rural Victoria, Australia in 1993. At this time, urban decision makers, influenced by policies of privatisation, chose to centralise services and infrastructure across the state, sell natural resources and state-owned enterprises. Communities of under 3,000 people were considered problematic and local ownership of services cumbersome.

The outcome was compulsory amalgamation of local governments. Council staff were dismissed and with them went important local knowledge of infrastructure, landscapes and populations. Neighbouring communities were 'invited to choose' which schools and hospitals stayed open. Housing, health and welfare organisations doors were closed when the need was greatest. Rural networks were terminated.

To rural people who knew the vibrancy of community life and were aware of the dependency of urban communities on food, water, natural resources and recreation generated from within rural communities, the policies made no sense. I was one of many people impacted.

It took time to move beyond our own grief

I had moved to Mirboo North in 1992 and been impressed by how people worked together. Mirboo North is situated on the edge of the Latrobe Valley coalfields where many local people worked for the State Electricity Commission. With privatisation of the power stations 6000 workers lost their jobs. Centralised market systems took precedence over quality of life for those who produced food and fiber, worked in mines and the power industry, took care of local waterways, fund raised for local schools and hospitals, organised sporting events and generally took care of each other and welcomed visitors. Banks adopted similar polices and closed in rural areas. I was a Community Development teacher at Central Gippsland TAFE and my partner worked for Rural Enterprise Victoria. Both positions were terminated. The scale and speed of the imposition of polices was traumatic.

It took time to move beyond our own grief at the loss of income, and the removal of democratic forums and organistions. It took time to face the challenge of connecting with urban decision-makers across divisions legislated into practice by every level of government.

Concerned people from regional educational institutions and those who had been employed in regional development across Gippsland began to meet. We shared a vision of a Centre where rural communities are the primary focus for resourcing, research and learning, rather than the lower echelons of a confusing range of portfolios and departments across multiple layers of government. The Centre was established in 1995 as an alliance of post-compulsory regional education institutions: Adult Education, the TAFE sector and Universities in partnership with rural communities of up to 10,000 people.

The mission statement reflects the Centre's approach.

- *The Centre for Rural Communities (Inc) will accomplish its Vision of rural communities that are socially, environmentally and economically sustainable by enhancing the capacity of rural communities to provide for their own optimal wellbeing.*

- *The Centre will assist these rural communities by working with them on social, economic, environmental and education issues through networking, acting as a clearing house for information, collaborative action research, partnership projects, training and other methods where appropriate.*

- *Methods of assistance will primarily be aimed at increasing the knowledge, expertise and skill levels of rural communities and will emphasise and encourage collaborative and empowering approaches* (Smith and Pearce 1995:2).

Work by the Centre paid attention to programs that stood out for their capacity to work in partnership with rural people and relevant institutions.

There was an awareness that communities with a history of co-operative ventures were stepping up and taking ownership of services and industries but in the absence of networks and resources other communities were in decline with people moving away (Smith and Pearce 1995).

As a rural woman, I had experienced the transformative impact of the Rural Women's Program in Gippsland introduced by feminist educator Helenė Brophy (1985-86) and the Victorian Rural Women's Network, facilitated by networker Jenni Mitchell (1986–1999). In both initiatives, issues of concern to rural women and the status of rural women shifted from margins to mainstream. The collaborative process began with us. Facilitators

There was an awareness that communities with a history of co-operative ventures were stepping up and taking ownership of services and industries

invited our involvement, listening and affirming, organizing network events and creating opportunities for us to be heard by decision-makers. Encouraged to find out more and to speak about our experiences we began to lead and shape change in our communities. We were not alone, but centrally resourced with regional structures. The active presence of rural women discussing and initiating changes invited new partnerships and greater awareness of the benefits of challenging and transforming 'accepted truths'.

We were not alone

The myths of the uniformity of rural life began to be unpacked, enabling the reality of diverse lifestyles to be visible. In the process a pattern of discriminatory language, lies (myths) and legislation that placed one group as superior and others as inferior became evident in layers of classification of women, of rural people, of Aboriginal people (Rose 1997/Sheil 2003).

By understanding ways to challenge the colonial pattern that regards some groups as expendable, replicated to create multiple and overlapping divisions across gender, race, ethnicity, geography, ability, and nature, a way to find connections emerged.

Nine strategies were common to both the Rural Women's Program and the Victorian Rural Women's Network and became a guiding framework of Collaborative Engagement for Transformation. The strategies are introduced in Chapter 4 providing a process to change understanding, challenge destructive practices, expand opportunities and transform relationships. The motivating focus was to reframe understanding of the status of rural communities in the national wellbeing, and facilitate the establishment of partnerships with and between rural communities. The strategies proved transferable to sectors experiencing the status of 'other', men/women, wealth/poverty, First Nation/Second Nation, Ethnic/European, rural/urban, nature/culture and the multiple overlapping barriers that silence and discriminate.

A place-based approach can factor in the regional reality of population and landscapes,

This is the time to invite hierarchical institutions to invest in mutually beneficial partnerships with communities. When we listen to local people opportunities for all levels of government along with private and public sector organisations to contribute an enabling role to regional development becomes evident. A place-based approach can factor in the regional reality of

population and landscapes, facilitating engagement with those closer to the heart of changing conditions. Communities cannot achieve this in isolation.

The manual names nine strategies that contribute to long term change, introduces theories that inform the value of each strategy, ways to implement relevant practices and stories of outcomes. Those with responsibility for community engagement can utilise this approach to improve opportunities for community members to add their unique knowledge to decision making processes (Sheil 2014).

While the combined impact of centralised and privatised policies and practice enshrined in legislation continue to transfer assets away from rural to urban centres and corporate entities, the strategies within the model of collaborative engagement continue to be relevant. The approach has relevance to diverse sectors and urban communities.

Two decades after writing *Growing and Learning in Rural Communities* (Sheil 2000), Gippsland, Victoria, where I live, has experienced three years of drought, the most intense fires in our history, followed by lock down on economic activity, particularly tourism, to prevent the spread of the global COVID 19 pandemic. Isolation has limited the contribution of recuperative gatherings for bushfire impacted communities at a time when they are most needed. For those of us less impacted there is an urgent need to collaborate, to rethink how we connect in communities and act responsibly for the catchments we inhabit.

to rethink how we connect in communities

During this stressful time the shooting and protests in the United States of America over the police killing of George Floyd (2020) in public, in the day time, focused attention on the state of First Nations people in this country. There is an increasingly public voice for a treaty and the need to acknowledge and heal the harm of our past destructive history. https://www.firstpeoplesvic.org/treaty

THE REALITY, THEN AND NOW

In the absence of an Australian rural policy, three factors dramatically impacted on the wellbeing of remote, rural and regional communities in the 1990's that radically altered relationships between government at all levels, industry, community organisations and community life. By 2020's there has been a whole generation who have lived their lives and taken on management and practice roles under this culture of market dominated thinking. It is timely to reclaim theory and practice that embraces reintegration with all aspects of community life.

1. The innovation and availability of technology in its many forms, and the speed with which 'information' can be processed and transmitted. 'The globalisation of communication: computers, multimedia, satellites, of finance: trading stocks, bonds, currency, commodities, future options and derivatives' (Henderson, 1999:1).

   By 2020, crypto currencies, 'fake news' the election of populist leaders running their agendas on multi-media backed by increasingly wealthy and powerful individuals and industries are evident. Media platforms such as Crikey, Get Up and a myriad of civil society, humanitarian and citizen science activist organisations facilitate people organize and take action to challenge destructive practices.

   For many regional people experiencing the impact of multiple disasters of drought, fire and pandemics of Covid 19 and variants the barrage to support issues they care passionately about is exhausting in the absence of civic leadership.

2. The second factor is the continuing wave of deregulation, privatisation, liberalisation of capital flows, opening of national economies, extension of global trade and [the] export led growth (ibid). Access to technology enables market driven economics to dominate decision making in all spheres of life.

   By 2020 these policies that have now been in place for lifetime of many, legitimize an increasing powerful consortium of corporations whose business is the continued extraction and burning of coal, oil and gas. It is estimated that 100 corporations are responsible for 70% of the world's greenhouse gas emissions since 1988. These firms and all of the smaller fossil fuel businesses are enmeshed with lenders, insurers, lawyers, accountants and service providers of all kinds. Known in some sectors as the Fossil Fuel Order they comprise an array of power that functions to maladjusted Australian politics, economics, law and society (Ritter 2021:10-11). An institutional corruption that shackles Australia moving towards the target of net zero emissions by 2035 despite the policy and technical solutions being in place to achieve this goal with massive social and environmental benefits (Garnaut 2019).

3) The third is the continued dominance of economic interests above all others. Our once plentiful resource base in this country is diminished as it has globally. Many nations have reached the point where increased rates of extraction and production impoverish the land and the people who depend upon it. It is a concept of development that has passed its use-by-date (Manfred Max Neef, 1991/Sheil, 1999).

By 2020 the combined impact is evident in the experiences of rural and regional life globally and regionally. In South-Eastern Australia the 2019-2020 bushfires destroyed 35million hectares of land, over a billion animals died in New South Wales fires. The secondary impact of smoke resulted in 445 deaths and thousands hospitalized costing $274 million, the total disaster recovery budget and this was prior to the impact of longer term recovery and trauma from bureaucratic processes. Insurance claims of $2.2 million stretched capacity and is challenging for insurance companies. The Bushfire Royal Commission is drawing on this summer's experiences to prepare for predicated future disasters if business as usual continues to be the norm (Hitch, June 2020).

Our once plentiful resource base in this country is diminished as it has globally.

In the increasing divisions between excess wealth and increased poverty those with money move for comfort and lifestyle to regional paradises displacing those who created and cared for environments and communities. Maleny in Queensland or Byron Bay in New South Wales are becoming the choice of location for supermarket chains and home of millionaires and billionaires (Lesser, 2021).

Tracking the source of wealth, who profits and who pays requires a radical rethinking of policies and practice as global pandemics and disasters drive home the reality that we are in this together.

BEYOND KNOWING TO IMPLEMENTATION

While my research of the rural women's programs gave insight into ways of working (the what) and gave visibility to groups that had been silenced and marginalized, the next challenge was how to introduce this approach to regional workers. In Australia regional responsibility is fragmented across four levels of government and multiple portfolios (Sher and Sher 1994). While every level of government and regional authority affirmed the value of the approach, each recommended another organization until we were back where we started with local government. At the time, local government lacked the resources, capacity and motivation to initiate change.

Philanthropic groups funded the production of a study circle kit, *Building Rural Communities through Co-operation* (Sheil, 1999) featuring stories of co-operative ventures in power, health, agriculture, media and forestry. Skill development in facilitation, sufficient consensus decision making, networking, co-operative culture, visioning, local community ownership, action, transformation and reflection. This experiential learning introduced learners to sequenced practice.

WHY STUDY CIRCLES?

The process – democratic discussion among equals is as important as the content.
(Study Circle Resource Centre Guide 1997)

find common ways forward

At the time of writing *Building Rural Communities through Co-operation* (Sheil, 1999) I was aware that study circles have a history in adult education and civic engagement in USA. In Australia they were used by church groups, unions as well as tackling dry land salinity or other agricultural issues too large for individuals to deal with in isolation. The Aboriginal Reconciliation movement had chosen this approach to bring landholders and Aboriginal people with diverse interests and economic foundations together to hear of each other's views of the world and find common ways forward.

Study Circle Guidelines introduce a participatory culture that invites people to rate the importance of each guideline and the significance for the current groups.

As the vision is to expand resilience not divide communities

These guidelines establish an inclusive process of asking and listening, essential to establishing relationships between people with different life experiences. Each person takes a turn facilitating sessions experiencing the challenge of ensuring everyone is heard and respected. As the vision is to expand resilience not divide communities study circles appeal.
https://ruralcommunities.com.au/publications/ or https://ctb.ku.edu/en/table-of-contents/advocacy/advocacy-research/study-circles/main

In later years I became aware of the international extent and transformative capacity of study circles. While terminology differs, the value of small democratic discussion for self-determined education is a consistent elements throughout the world. In Sweden, Study Circle Associations receive national funding and are familiar to the majority of the population (Larsson and Nordvall, 2010). I was invited to visit Sweden and meet facilitators implementing community study circles to envisage the future of rural areas. In Chile, they are known as Mesa de Unidad (table of social unity). In the United States of America study circles and citizen forums have a long history. The Highlander Folk Schools began in Tennessee in the 1930's playing a key role in the Civil Rights Movement in the 1950's. They were one of the few institutions to accept blacks and improve opportunities for involvement in coming elections through literacy and democratic involvement. Rosa Parks and other civil rights leaders participated in these adult education programs prior to her historic role in the Montgomery bus boycott. https://en.wikipedia.org/wiki/Highlander_Research_and_Education_Center

I also recently became aware of how in 1881 Thomas Shadrach James used a similar approach at Maloga and Cummeragunja Aboriginal missions, on Yorta Yorta country in New South Wales, Australia. In the day time he taught children in the schoolhouse. At night, he ran an activist night school for adults. His students included William Cooper, Sir Doug Nicholls, Margaret Tucker, Jack Patten and Bill Onus who changed Australian history. https://www.abc.net.au › programs › the-scholars-hut

In the 1990's an approach that offered an affordable, open ended way to locate learning within communities appealed. *Building Rural Futures through Co-operation* (Sheil, 1999) was developed as an experiential resource to involve rural communities in determining their futures. The kit introduced community members to democratic facilitation skills establishing a foundation of trust and respect. Groups operate on the adult education principles of creating safe places for people to speak and be heard. Diversity of opinion is valued not silenced. From this basis groups were invited to envision the futures of their communities and take steps towards implementing a project. No timelines, agendas or targets were set.

Diversity of opinion is valued not silenced.

Study circles begin with the hope of being able to work together, despite many groups having past experience of not having achieved a great deal. A strong sense of despair can be evident in initial comments especially following disasters when energy levels are low.

It is important to listen as people speak publicly of situations, to affirm that their presence in the discussion is valued. The facilitator creates this space to begin a developmental process through dialogue. It is also important not to limit discussion as can happen when communities are directed to focus on strength based situations. Concerns over energy and time being limited are common and people speak of the small number of people involved in the many community committees. In many communities voluntary involvement has reached burdensome proportions. These concerns are common: fewer people, nobody listening, community becoming a sleeper suburb, people working away and for longer hours. It is the reality of policies that have redirected resources into larger regional and urban centres.

Groups begin by discussing how they want their group to operate. To be respectful and welcoming, to facilitate dialogue between people with very different life experiences in a safe environment. People frequently come tentatively to the initial session and finding the inclusive approach return to future sessions.

Study circles are a cost-effective, timely resource that does not determine or limit outcomes.

Study circles are a cost-effective, timely resource that does not determine or limit outcomes. The approach has the flexibility to resource and expand capacity across our diverse landscape and populations. Running for 10–12 sessions they are manageable with a definite time commitment overcoming identified barriers to participation of distance, access, cost, and culture within institutions (Clarke, 1984).

A key aspect of the project was that rural communities be supported to organise and resource study groups locally. A key difficulty was that funding was not available to provide the degree of support communities required. The demand on rural communities to voluntarily manage and financially resource the diverse social and economic structures of their communities has turned voluntary participation into a necessity for survival and a weighty burden rather than an enjoyable community activity.

lack of skilled facilitators as a limiting factor

While the response from communities, industry groups, agencies and government departments was unexpectedly high only four communities had skilled facilitators. In those communities outcomes exceeded expectations, validating the approach. (20 years later ventures begun at this time continue). Research of impact of study circles in salinity, algae and other land use programs also identified lack of skilled facilitators as a limiting factor.

To meet this need Monash University accredited a professional development program in 2000. A post-graduate Certificate in Regional Community Development in the Faculty of Education based on the collaborative engagement strategies identified in my research. Regional workers from diverse sectors enrolled in the course and were introduced to the theory and practice of the nine strategies. In communities using the *Building Rural Futures through Co-operation* (Sheil, 1999) study circle kit as a resource facilitated by a worker enrolled in the Graduate Certificate of Regional Community Development (Monash University) participation was consistently high, and outcomes, surprising.

FACILITATOR'S PROFESSIONAL DEVELOPMENT MANUAL

Just as the key to a species survival in the natural world is its ability to adapt to local habits, so the key to human survival will probably be the local community.
(Suzuki 1997:8).

To facilitate is to make life easier – in the current world crises of continuing disasters – the skills, knowledge and wisdom of facilitators who can create dialogue across divisions and feedback loops to decision makers from the local to the global are in increasing demand.

This professional development manual is an introduction to the theory and practice of community development, enabling workers with regional responsibilities to support people to plan and work together for the long term. These democratic skills are a basic building block of community life that has the capacity to build trust and collaboration and delegate responsibility. Funded regional development programs benefits from an inclusive community organization capable of incorporating the diversity of views yet respected as strengthening community involvement in a regional setting.

WHY A REGIONAL APPROACH?

A regional approach enables communities to work collaboratively on shared issues and raise awareness within policy frameworks far more effectively than in isolation. Shared experiences between communities are a valuable and trusted source of information. Networking is a key strategy to share relevant information by choice.

Regional training of community development skills would ensure:

- access to further skill development,
- recognition of the role,
- linkage to regional resources and networks,
- facilitating a co-operative approach to regional development,
- increasing visibility and access to policy,
- linking of rural communities with regional centres.

The strategies provide the initial step in 'endogenous development' that originates from within communities capable of working with the diverse people and landscapes within Australia. This local knowledge provides a foundation for programs such as City Deals, Smart Specialisation or other regional development initiatives that facilitate dialogue across multiple levels of decision making.

At the time of writing I am in lockdown due to the spread of the DELTA variant of the COVID virus: impacting on business as usual for the majority of industries, services, community organisations and life in general. The national response has initially been messy and underwhelming, leaving many without access to vaccines, safe quarantine options or income. For some, the pandemic gives thinking time, the air is clean as traffic and industry slows and we can see mountains and horizons, some for the first time. For writers and thinkers it is a time of reflection, to rethink the theory and practice of community engagement.

Our geographic communities are where policies designed in isolation have a combined impact.

There is increasing understanding of and attention to relationship to place. Our geographic communities are where policies designed in isolation have a combined impact. Investing in ways to engage with this constantly evolving experience offers knowledge that has an intergenerational interest and an integrated awareness of flow on factors that extend beyond individual institutions. To some extent positions such as 'Place Managers' and community plans have been introduced but rarely impact at levels that determine resource allocation or major planning issues.

Professional pathways in the sector often exist as individual units within graduate and post-graduate programs. This lack of recognition of the skills, knowledge and relevance of the sector is evident in institutions and industries that have limited experience of community engagement beginning with dialogue. Instead communication remains at arm's length by using surveys, consultancies and one off meetings with limited capacity to transfer ownership, develop skills or change attitudes.

we are professional, equal to other disciplines.

I recall offering to hold classes on site at a local government office rather than the University Campus. A response from a community worker was insightful. *'Oh no'*, she said. *'When we walk in the door at the Council, there is this big chart and community groups are at the bottom. When we walk in the door here, we are professional, equal to other disciplines'*.

FOR A TIME THE STARS ALIGNED

The independent status of the Centre for Rural Communities enabled funding partnerships to be established with community organisations and local governments in East Gippsland and Latrobe City. Regional development funds paid the fees of local workers enrolling in the professional development program.

To move from theory to practice workers established study circles in their work place and communities, introducing facilitation skills to schools, sporting groups and land management groups. Stories of this process are in the manual while others are available in journals and publications (See bibliography). Negotiations with TAFE colleges recognised participation in the study circles as equivalent value to Communication Units at Certificate III level. Many community members went on to enroll in further TAFE programs and facilitators went on to Higher Learning. Research of this approach was published in peer reviewed journals and book chapters earning research quantum for the University and I was invited to showcase the approach interstate and internationally.

The boundaries of ownership and responsibility merged

Community initiatives not dependent on government alone but in partnership with educational resources, community groups and private industry began and many continue. The boundaries of ownership and responsibility merged enabling new relationships to develop. The Churchill campus gained enthusiastic students and agencies, qualified and competent workers with access to skills, knowledge and resources of an internationally recognised University. Communities had locally based workers who introduced them to facilitation skills. It was a scenario with multiple winners.

By 2006, increasing pressure on regional universities to deliver on-line only and changing heads of school resulted in the practice component being removed from the course. Monash University's Churchill Campus became a campus of Federation University and academic and institutional staff dramatically reduced. I withdrew from the University partnership. The Centre for Rural Communities continued to initiate and support projects.

OPPORTUNITY FOR INVOLVEMENT BY TERTIARY PARTNERS

In 2015 following 45 days of wild fire in East Gippsland, the Centre for Rural Communities in partnership with the East Gippsland Network of Neighbourhood Houses initiated *East Gippsland Building Community Resilience.* A second study circle kit *Building Community Futures through Co-operation* (Sheil, 2015). The kit was designed as a resource to enable communities and responsible agencies to better prepare, manage and recovery from future disasters. The Collaborative Engagement strategies are designed into the resource.

Despite the lack of access to accredited programs for facilitators and one year funding to produce the resource and co-ordinate the program in six rural communities limiting potential impact, the project gave visibility to this sector and won regional awards.
https://ruralcommunities.com.au/community-engagement.

lack of clear pathways for facilitators

The model of Collaborative Engagement proved transferable across diverse programs. The contribution of an investment in ways of working to establish a democratic foundation flag an inclusive approach frequently missing in well intentioned projects that fail to change understanding, attitudes or practice. The demand and lack of clear pathways for facilitators in the face of catastrophic disasters in the Eastern States of Australia highlight the urgency of attention to this deficit and an invitation to tertiary partners to meet this demand.

CHANGE INITIATED FROM WITHIN COMMUNITIES

One of the things we do know, however, is that the communities that are best able to recover from disaster are those that are strong before the disaster occurred.
National strategy for Disaster Resilience 2013 [Australian]

While rural and regional Australians have a history of resourcefulness, implementing community led change following disasters is challenging, if this is a new approach for agencies and communities. It will take time and support for roles and relationships to shift from regulating activities to being a resource and responsive to personal and community demands following traumatic experiences. Collaboration between responsible agencies is a key foundation of recovery. This shift is dependent on changed policies at all levels as well as an investment in establishing trusted relationships between organisations and community groups.

community led change following disasters is challenging, if this is a new approach for agencies and communities

At the beginning of the COVID 19 pandemic emergency measures were put in place to enable this cultural shift in organisational management. However, a return to business as usual saw a return to competitive practices. Rather than endure the stress of continued rejection or being passed on to another agency many people impacted by disasters withdrew from requesting assistance.

Resourced local community hubs accessible when needed and able to respond or refer people to relevant organisations played a critical role in recovery. There is a time for listening and resourcing and networking and a tender blind approach to organisational engagement.

From communities there is a movement to rethink agendas towards regional reinvestment and healing of country. It is no coincidence that those of us who are settlers in this country are hearing conversations of working together, of healing country and each other from those who have been most harmed. It is from local people who have suffered under destructive policies of exclusion and division that I have witnessed both the destructive nature of hate and the recuperative capacity of forgiveness.

Collaborative engagement requires access to skills, knowledge and resources

Collaborative engagement requires access to skills, knowledge and resources in the same way as any other sector. The underpinning theory is drawn from adult education, community development and endogenous regional development. This systematic approach nurtures and invests in local people and their communities enabling each to evolve, to deal constructively with challenges in partnership with relevant organisations. Lacking this investment in local knowledge and in the absence of policies acknowledging rural and urban interdependency projects will continue to be fragmented and thrive or decline dependent on overburdened individuals. All too often facilitators are employed without access to introductory professional development. In this most challenging of times this comes at a cost to their own health, disappointment of community groups hopeful of constructive outcomes and at a cost to their employer and the sector as anticipated outcomes fail to be achieved.

Collaborative engagement is a transferable approach that enables knowledge and experiences often isolated within one sector to be visible in wider forums, reconnecting understanding of cause and effect. The process affirms the assumptions of some groups while others will be challenged in their understanding of how and why situations evolve. This dialogue will change understanding and opportunities for action beginning within ourselves, nurtured by our communities.

Investing in these points of connection not the divisions

It is in our geographic communities of place that there is knowledge of beauty, of the histories, of the relationships that nurture. It is a place where people can unite on some issues of common interest/concern while holding different views on other areas of their lives. Investing in these points of connection not the divisions is the task of the facilitators and the journey of Collaborative Engagement. Finding connection across difference is possible and originates from within Gippsland communities where historically divisions have been long and destructive over forest management, yet where that same community has united to save and restore health to a once mighty waterway. I share this story in Chapter 1.

The challenge for facilitators is to initiate processes that enable the impact of current policies and practices to be visible (Ife 2019). To remain hopeful and strategic while acknowledging anger, distress and pain around us. It is a discipline requiring clear foundations, ethical practice and an ability to continually assess and affirm involvement.

If each of us takes a look at activity in our region and calculates costs and benefits we begin to grasp the reality of the impact of current global crisis. From this point we can initiate changes or protect what we value.

In my region following three years of drought that dried up river systems, decimated agriculture and fishing and dried out forests the predictable 2019/2020 fires in South Eastern Australia generated smoke measured by European Space Agency's Corpernicus *Atmospheric Monitoring Service program as covering 20 million square kilometers (enough to blanket all of Russia with some over to cover a third of Europe) with an atmospheric impact as releasing approximately 400 megatonnes of carbon dioxide* (Shortis and Ward, 2021). A factor excluded from national accounting of Australia's contribution to carbon emissions (National Greenhouse and Energy Reporting, 2018) or evident in changed policies. While European countries responded by moving away from fossil fueled power to renewables the Australian federal government under Scott Morrison announced expansionist contracts on oil, gas and mineral exploration. Public funding went to private corporations to cover expenses of infrastructure and expansion of seismic testing for oil, gas and minerals in the Gippsland Basin
https://www.ga.gov.au/__data/assets/image/0008/109790/SRF111428-9_Gippsland.jpg

From this point we can initiate changes or protect what we value.

Yet an estimated 80% of individual Australians are taking steps to set up solar panels (30% currently have them) to reduce dependency on oil and gas, organisations are setting zero – sum emission targets, communities are investing in whole of community battery storage and distribution systems powered by solar and state governments are working with Indigenous Communities to ensure ownership of renewable energy options. At a community level people are joining environmental projects and socially beneficial programs that enrich our quality of life without damaging the earth, cultivating an ethic of care for each other and future generations (Hollo, 2019).

This is a time for regional policy and partnerships that will benefit from skilled facilitators. Adverse regional scenarios benefits from a pooling of resources, knowledge and skills from within rural communities with flexibility to adapt and rethink situations. The speed, scale and extent of overlapping disasters requires collaborative approaches that includes dialogue between governments, agencies, communities, community and

time for regional policy and partnerships

private sector organisations. Communities can lead with local knowledge and a high level of motivation, but *c*annot achieve the required transformation alone.

cannot achieve the required transformation alone.

WHO IS THE MANUAL FOR?

The professional development manual is written for the many organisations, industries and community groups with an interest in assisting communities lead change from despair or division towards optimism and action in the long term.

This includes:
- Landcare,
- Disaster planning, management and recovery
- Church groups,
- First nation communities, co-operatives and corporations,
- Community health organisations,
- Regional development,
- Industry groups,
- Recreational committees,
- Community Associations
- Local financial services,
- Community enterprises,
- Front line health and recovery workers in disasters.
- Local government,
- State government
- Federal government departments with an interest in rural communities,
- Adult education centres,
- Neighbourhood centres,
- TAFE colleges and those working with technology,
- Service clubs,
- Art and cultural organisations,
- Water management,
- Environment groups,
- Tourism,

- Universities,
- Youth Services,
- Aged Care.

For anyone interested in generating a more inclusive culture and investing in the energy, knowledge and motivation of community life.

IMPORTANT ROLE FOR REGIONAL INSTITUTIONS

In times of transition education becomes a highly important task.
(Freire, 1974:7)

The need to relearn the interdependence of all life

Tertiary educational institutions are societies think tanks: the home of existing and evolving knowledge and wisdom. A lesson of the 21st Century is the need to relearn the interdependence of all life. In this respect regions are of a size where the impact of policy decisions in regard to social, economic and environmental management can be observed and responded to. It is timely to consider new roles and responsibilities for community, government, and corporations and community organisations. Skilled facilitators are critical in this process.

PARTNERSHIP WITH REGIONAL UNIVERSITIES

Changing agendas

The way forward requires changed agendas and indicators that reflect the state of community life. If the environmental and social life valued in communities is not visible in planning and policy then only the views of corporations and institutions will be heard. While industry is a critical factor in regional life people also require clean air and water, power and food, good education and a rich cultural life. Finding common ground across different interests requires interaction between those in planning and policy and those experiencing the impact. Dialogue and feedback loops are critical and engender trust. This work is offered as a way to facilitate this discussion.

Dialogue and feedback loops are critical and engender trust.

The transition is targeted at personal and community change, which involves changing attitudes and establishing reciprocal ways of working together. Partnerships will require allocation of resources. Examples demonstrating industry partnerships benefiting from local knowledge, ownership and expertise with rural communities are discussed in the text. Government programs such as Landcare and Coastcare work in partnership with rural and regional communities providing a known framework that mainstream organisations could adopt. Such partnerships require an investment of knowledge, skills and facilities for local people within community associations, church groups, chamber of commerce, sporting organisations, service clubs, environment groups, community enterprises, community banks, First Nation co-operatives, women's organisations and increasingly those welcoming refugees.

WHY COMMUNITY KNOWLEDGE INFORMS REGIONAL DEVELOPMENT

[Market] forces are global, but the social and environmental fallout that policy makers have to manage are local.
(Legislative Assembly, 1999: xvii
Senate Select Committee Review, 2000:15).

Community knowledge has the capacity to inform decision makers in ways that take account of local populations and landscapes. This is the underpinning of endogenous regional development leading to an integrated planning approach, bringing together the rich wealth of experience and life style within communities.

Community life is not static

Community life is not static and will flourish or decline depending on the structures and institutions that foster dialogue and local ownership in a co-operative culture. To transition from past decades of exclusion from decision making to an active and accepted place at the decision making table requires an investment of skills, time and resources.

The work is about change

The work is about change. Creating change and responding to change, about making connections to reintegrate knowledge that has become siloed and dysfunctional. It is reframing communities, of involving those who have been marginalized, or reclaiming damaged landscapes and habitat. It is clear that more of the same will not lead to vibrant and resilient communities: urban or rural. Globally people are initiating responsive political systems capable of prioritising environmental and social wellbeing. The outcomes will not be known in advance, but new partnerships will emerge that could never have been envisaged. It will be a continuous journey of learning.

FURTHER REFERENCES

Brennan, M., & Brophy, M., (2010, July) 'Study circles and the Dialogue to Change Program', *Journal of Adult Learning*, Volume 50, Number 2, Australian Study Circles Network Australian, https://files.eric.ed.gov/fulltext/EJ952241.pdf

Clarke, Vivian., (1984) *Potential of Rural Women in Gippsland: Educational Opportunities: needs and Employment. Victorian* College of Horticulture, McMillian Campus, Sale.

Freire, P., (1974) *Education for critical consciousness*, Sheed and Ward, London.

Harrison, M., (Dulumunmun) https://www.youtube.com/watch?v=aiqQUrLgniQ

Hitch, Georgia., (2020) *Bushfire Royal Commission looks to past to show troubling future*, ABC News, June. https://www.abc.net.au/news/2020-06-07/coronavirus-derailed-bushfire-attention-royal-commission-so-far/12326360

Larsson, S., and Nordvall, H., (2010) *Study Circles in Sweden an overview with a Bibliography of International Literature* https://www.researchgate.net/publication/265092861_Study_Circles_in_Sweden_An_Overview_with_a_Bibliography_of_International_Literature.

Lesser, David, (2021) 'Loved to death', *Good Weekend*, Saturday Age, July 17th, pp 14-19. Podcast. Good weekend talks.

Oodgeroo Noonuccal, (2020) *My People*, Wiley, Queensland https://www.nma.gov.au/explore/features/indigenous-rights/people/kath-walker

Pearce, M., https://www.aboriginalvictoria.vic.gov.au/marion-pearce

Ritter, David, (2021) 'Empire of the Dead: the fossil fuel order and the clean energy rebellion', *Arena Quarterly*, No. 6, June 2021 pp 8-15 www.arena.org.au

Sheil, H., (2015) *Building community futures through co-operation*, Centre for Rural Communities Inc, and East Gippsland Network of Neighbourhood Houses, Nowa Nowa. https://ruralcommunities.com.au/publications

Sheil, H., (2019) 'The local informing the global. From Bung Yarnda (Lake Tyers) to Edinburgh', New Community Journal, Borderlands. Footscray. ncq@borderlands.org.au

Sher, J., & Sher, K., (1994) 'Beyond the conventional wisdom: rural development as if rural people and communities really mattered', Journal of Research in Rural Education, Vol. 10. No. 1: 2-43.

Smith, N., & Pearce, J., (1995) *Centre for Rural Communities Consultancy Report*, Monash University, Churchill.

Struggle for Landrights. Lake Tyers 1962-197 https://www.nma.gov.au/explore/features/indigenous-rights/land-rights/lake-tyers, National Museum Australia, 2021.

· CHAPTER 1 ·

• CHAPTER 1 •
PERSONAL AND COMMUNITY DEVELOPMENT

Can we relearn what humanity has known since our beginnings that we live in a complex web of relationships in which our very survival and well-being depend on clean air, water and soil and biological diversity? Or will we celebrate the passing of the pandemic with an orgy of consumption and a drive to get back to the way things were before?
June 30, 2020
https://davidsuzuki.org/story/reflections-from-an-elder-in-isolation/

FOCUS OF THIS CHAPTER

1. Introduction to community development:
   1.1 Clarifying language: community and development
   1.2 Why regional community development
   1.3 Goals of community development
   1.4 Practice of community development
2. Role of community development worker:
   2.1 Facilitation
3. State of our communities
4. Locating learning within communities
5. Changing roles: government/communitymarket place
   Further references

There is not a static 'right answer'.

In this chapter you are invited to clarify your understanding of the key concepts of personal and community development. Be aware this is an ongoing process that gives insight into our assumptions shaped by the words we use, their impact on relationships and landscapes that are constantly changing. There is not a static 'right answer'. The manual introduces the contribution of each of nine strategies in a model of Collaborative Engagement for Transformation raising awareness that communities are at different points of environmental, economic, political, cultural, social, personal and spiritual development. Your regional knowledge and experiences will inform understanding of each of these strategies.

A partner resource for facilitators to implement these strategies is the study circle kit *Building community future through co-operation* (Sheil, 2015). The kit is an experiential community resource, introducing facilitation skills and democratic processes in the context of disaster preparedness, engagement and recovery. The model is transferable to community development projects universally as a tool to incorporate complex local knowledge into public planning https://ruralcommunities.com.au/publications. As discussed the Study Circle Guidelines introduce facilitators and community members to inclusive ways of working.

The model is transferable to community development projects universally

USEFUL PRACTICES

- **Journals**

Regional workers frequently work alone. It can be beneficial to develop a reflective practice of keeping a journal to 'make sense' of events. Journals differ from the daily 'events' focused diary. They are your personal thoughts of events, insights, challenges, questions and celebrations. Not a report, but jottings, poems, notes, sketches, newspaper articles that record how you are feeling and thinking.

Regional workers frequently work alone.

Recording responses to the questions in your journal will provide an excellent guide to changes as well as affirmation of your knowledge and understanding.

QUESTIONING

Following the introduction of each subject, there are examples, then questions that invite connection and reflection on your experiences in a regional context. The sequencing models inclusive practice that facilitates existing knowledge being shared, expanded and new awareness evolving. Responses will be diverse, as each area will have different histories of challenges and resourcefulness. Documenting these experiences involves the development of language to describe the impact of change on communities and identification of patterns of cause and effect.

questions that invite connection and reflection

1. INTRODUCTION TO COMMUNITY DEVELOPMENT

In their book *Developing Communities for the Future* (2016) 5th edition, Susan Kenny and Phil Connors explain the purpose of community development as:

> *Community development is an area of study and a set of approaches and methods to assist ordinary people to work together to take control of their futures. It proposes the development of structures, resources and processes by which communities can collectively identify and address their own development and the identification of the needs and assets and the resolution of issues and problems.*
> (Kenny and Connors, 2016: xiv).

assist ordinary people to work together

While Jim Ife in '*Community Development. Creating community alternatives – vision, analysis and practice*' (2016) 2nd edition, states that:

> *The purpose of the 'development of community' is to re-establish 'community' as one location of significant human experience and realisation of human need… It is mainly used as a more meaningful alternative to remaining reliant on the larger, more inhuman and less accessible structures of the welfare state, the global economy, bureaucracy, professional elites.*
> (Ife, 2016:160).

is to re-establish 'community' as one location of significant human experience

These definitions of community development capture the key element of change. Of movement from a fragmented and reactionary status experienced by many groups, towards a balanced and participatory society taking responsibility for the environment.

Susan Kenny and Jim Ife are two Australian community development theorists and practitioners whose continuing analysis informs the integrity of this discipline. Both acknowledge the scale of the global social, economic and environmental crisis and the unwillingness of many national and global governments to address the causes. Their work pays attention to the signs of hope in the increasing interest and recognition of initiatives originating at a community level, not in isolation but assisted by skilled practitioners. Their work provides foundational references.

Questions

Have you been involved in projects with groups excluded from decision making? If so, please list (3) three.

What barriers did they/you experience in relation to policy and planning?

In what ways did this limit opportunities?

1.1 Language clarifying meaning

Neil Postman cautions that *Word weavers become world weavers* (Postman, 1996:172). He encourages people to be aware of how languages shapes our view of the world to the point we internalise values and status. Collaborative engagement invites you to 'unlearn' of language that divides and find connections across difference that heal, enrich and celebrate life.

Word weavers become world weavers

Defining Community

In this text the scope of community is geographic: the people who live, love and work in a place and those whose decisions impact on the health of that region. The perspective that the wellbeing of people and the land are intrinsicly linked is central to Indigenous cultures and social planning of a scale determined by ecological balance adopted by the 1992 United Nations Local Agenda 21 in Rio De Janeiro. https://en.wikipedia.org/wiki/Think_globally,_act_locally. This Local to Global movement was inspired by Patrick Geddes 'Cities in evolution' (1915).

community is geographic:

In European planning terms this scale of planning relates to catchments or bio-regions and in Indigenous cultures to 'country'. Both acknowledge that communities thrive or decline according to the impact of policies or actions by individuals, organisations, industries and governments on the people and landscapes they inhabit.

Our 'sense of community' emerges from the daily experiences of educating children, visiting friends and relatives, transacting business, negotiating domestic and work challenges, enjoying recreation and leisure activities that results in a sense of belonging and identity. In our increasing mobile world, where people have moved to a new country or community through choice or adverse circumstances there is often a sadness at what is left behind, as well as a hope of a new belonging. Each shift is a displacement and it will takes time for new relationships to be established.

The ability of a community to meet the needs of those who live in that locality is enhanced or damaged by the culture, knowledge and expertise of the structures that exist in a community. Community groups that are able to work openly and inclusively are able to include diverse views and lifestyles, compared to narrow fundamentalist groups that remain elite and exclusive. Other factors such as a diverse economic base add to the resilience of a community. Consequently, communities will be at different stages of their capacity to support life.

Interest groups

Chilean Economist, Manfred Max-Neef (2010) regards a sense of identity as a basic human need that has been increasingly weakened as large bureaucratic structures replace the personalised interaction of local networks and social organisations. With an increasingly mobile society, the use of technology for communication and transport, it is possible to live in one locality and transact business, social networks and recreation in other places. One's sense of community may be enhanced or diminished by groups of people with whom we have interests in common such as women's organisation or networks, spiritual association, a student organisation, commodity groups, and many others if there is a capacity to be involved. Such groups can add strength to a community, or result in further fragmentation depending on their responsiveness to local needs. Be aware of who benefits and at what cost to others.

a sense of identity as a basic human need

Reclaiming identity: one community's experience

A whale story
It's said that when the sea level rose and people were horrified to find their country disappearing the whale urged them to follow her to dry land, but she cautioned them that they would need to employ diplomacy and peace because they would be asking their cousins to share their land. It is a story the world needs to know.
(Pascoe and Shukuroglou, 2020:301)

Communities are the place where we make sense of the world and our place in it. Our ability to grow and develop will vary according to the state of relationships in our community. When members of the Meerlieu community began using the study circle kit *Building Rural Communities through Co-operation* (Sheil, 1998) they had difficulty answering the question. 'What's at Meerlieu?' (1998).

Communities are the place where we make sense of the world

The physical presence of buildings in this community are located near each other on a juncture of roads, signatured by pine trees. The hall, the cricket ground and the school, further along a Church, with similar public facilities for the neighbouring community of Bengworden further down the road. Most group members had a strong sense of community that extended beyond these public meeting places.

They faced the challenge of how to convey this quality. At a following meeting they listed on cards all the groups in the community, the families, the activities within the locality, the ways people interact. They named areas of the landscape significant to their area: the red gum plains, the river, the land with salinity, planting areas undertaken by the landcare groups, sights of local flora and fauna. Who drove children to school, or collected goods from Bairnsdale. Who plays and coaches cricket? The jig-saw that makes up Meerlieu.

The cards were spread out on the floor and people discussed the activities that different groups undertook. The playgroup, the Country Women's Association, the cricket clubs, the skydiving club, the Landcare groups, the church group, the Country Fire Authority, the quilters group and more. One of the members produced a wonderful '*Meerlieu* Map' (Michele Shugg, 1999) featuring all these aspects of community life.

This process introduced new residents to range of activities. Other member's awareness of the importance of 'community' in the locality was affirmed, but with recognition that newcomers didn't know when event were on or who to contact to find out. This hospitable group were embarrassed that they hadn't made newcomers welcome and took steps to publicise events and welcome newcomers.

In 2018 I was invited to a 20 year anniversary of the Meerlieu and District Rural Community Group. Despite the closure of the school, the hall was packed with families who continue to care for each other. Invited to sit with a group of women, one spoke quietly to me of a suicide of their child. Of how friends assisted in the creation of a garden at a respite mental health centre in Bairnsdale, a place of comfort. The garden is being used.

In a world with finite natural resources

In your journal record responses to the following questions.

In your experience how are community relationships fostered, neglected or damaged?

In describing the community in which you live what characteristics would you discuss? Give an example. (Graphics, diagrams or articles from local press can be included.)

How is this different from a statistical report?

Defining Development

Development not growth

In clarifying the difference between growth and development in regard to economic policies Manfred Max Neef, (2021) used the analogy of human development that has intense periods of physical development in childhood and adolescence accompanied by rapid intellectual and emotional development. By adult hood the rate of physical development slows down, but we continue to mature intellectually, emotionally and socially. We continue to develop but we do not continue to grow. To do so would lead to bizarre and unhealthy situations https://en.wikipedia.org/wiki/Manfred_Max-Neef%27s_Fundamental_human_needs (2021)

In a world with finite natural resources the economic rationalist view of development dependent on continually increasing the number and scale of market place transactions recorded by Gross Domestic Product (GDP) and Gross National Product (GNP) is problematic. Attention limited to nationally based market place indicators leads to situations where people read in the mainstream press of how well they are doing, when the regional reality is vastly different. The source of the sale, the environmental and social costs, or where profits are located, are absent in this accounting process.

The Latrobe Valley, the heart of Victoria's coal fired power industry, is a classic case. In the 1990's, privatisation of the industry resulted in 6,000 workers losing their jobs.

While electricity production is more efficient than ever, the impact of job losses can be seen in the progressive increase in households with relatively lower incomes. Moe, Morwell and Traralgon all had incomes higher than the State average in 1981. By 1996, Moe and Morwell had more than 66 per cent of households below the average... Unemployment has also risen dramatically from under 5% in all towns in 1981 to more than 15% throughout the Latrobe Valley, and more than 20% in Churchill and Moe. Regional Victoria as a whole has followed this general trend toward more low-income households and higher unemployment, but it has been to a lesser degree than in the Latrobe Valley.
(Infrastructure, 1999:23)

The loss of income security, of future employment for young people, closure of local business, sale of property and a mass exodus from the region was the reality. Increase in mental health issues, gambling addiction, violence and loss of hope were outcomes of the speed and extent of this imposed change.

The Morwell Experiment

If you want to know the effects of privatisation on a community, twenty years on from when you do it, and if you want to know how to epically screw it up: look at Morwell. The whole community has been disregarded, systematically. I tell people, 'If you want an idea of where you don't want to be as a community, have a good look at Morwell – then aim the other way.
(Tracy Lund in Doig, 2019)

The whole community has been disregarded, systematically

The production of power is a volatile industry and knowledgeable workers were dismayed at the lack of reinvestment in maintenance, safety and training by GDF Suez (later Engie Group). In the dry summer of 2014 the Hazelwood mine, a void that creates its own micro-climate caught fire and burnt for 45 days, releasing carbon monoxide and other toxic ash into the atmosphere. Pregnant women, families with young children, people over 65, and those with heart or lung conditions were urged to leave Morwell South to escape the smoke (Feb 28, 2014).

In the heart of the community, Tracey Lund, the Morwell Neighbourhood House Co-ordinator kept a record of health issues residents reported to her during the fire. Later research attributes 11 premature deaths to this disaster. Increased incidents of poor respiratory function is currently a focus of concern for women who were pregnant during the Hazelwood Mine Fires. In December 2016, four months before Hazelwood closed, Morwell's unemployment rate was 21%. By December 2017 it had shrunk to 15.6% as people moved away or began other employment.

The time for policies that hide the human and environmental costs of polluting industries has exceeded its 'use by date'. New Zealand economist Marilyn Waring demystifies how this occurs by looking at what is and isn't valued in Gross Domestic Product or Gross National Product. The film *'Who's counting? Marilyn Waring on Sex, Lies and Global Economics is an insightful production'.*
https://www.youtube.com/watch?v=WS2nkr9q0VU

In 2018, Marilyn Waring notes *that growing pollution has been one result of this pathological race to record growth in GDP. ….air, water and workplace pollution kills at least nine million people a year. Air pollution has a direct link to low birth rate which also predicts lifelong risks of diabetes, cardiovascular disease and other conditions* (Waring, 2018:22).

Max-Neef, like Waring advocate new economics that *'under no circumstance can be above the reverence of life, pointing out that no economy is possible in the absence of ecosystems and that the economy is a subsystem of a larger finite system, the biosphere hence permanent growth is impossible'.* Manfred Max-Neef. en.wikipedia.org › wiki › Manfred_Max-Neef's_Funda...

Indicators such as Australian National Development Index (ANDI) enable the impact of policies on children and youth wellbeing, communities and regions, culture, recreation and leisure, democracy and governance, economic life and prosperity, education and creativity, environment and sustainability, health, indigenous wellbeing, justice and fairness, subjective wellbeing, and work and life to be visible.
http://www.andi.org.au/

At this time of catastrophic environmental and health disasters many are aware a new direction is urgently needed. David Gameau's 2040 film *pursues people and identifies projects around*

the world to show that there are other ways of delivering electricity, getting around, growing crops and living with animals that don't cost the Earth and, crucially, aren't just good ideas: everything in 2040 is already working somewhere in the world. https://www.smh.com.au/entertainment/movies/damon-gameau-gives-us-a-real-glimpse-of-a-greener-future-in-2040-20190515-p51ngp.html

'It's a game changer for businesses, it's a game changer for residents, and it's a game changer for the network'

In Victoria, Yakandandah (population 1,800) has built on its co-operative skills and knowledge to take steps towards zero emission of carbon by purchasing and installing a 'community battery'. Totally Renewable Yakandandah's purchase of the 274 Kilowatthours battery not only 'turns the lights on for locals, but offers the community a backup system if the main power goes down. 'It's a game changer for businesses, it's a game changer for residents, and it's a game changer for the network' (Juliette Milbank president of Yak01, 2021).

The networking and distribution of linking homes and industries with solar panels introduces smaller scale production of electricity into a highly centralised market. The current interest is generating new thinking and network distribution industries and the manufacture of micro-grid batteries are emerging.
https://totallyrenewableyack.org.au/
https://www.facebook.com/totallyrenewableyack/

Questions

What are your experiences of large-scale development proposed or implemented in your region?

Give an example?

What was the response of local people?

How was this conveyed, and to whom?

What changes resulted?

1.2 Why regional community development

A regional planning perspective is of a scale and size that enables the reality of complex situations to be understood and action taken to benefit from opportunities and prevent harm. With a regional perspective the unique qualities of communities can become evident and attention paid to opportunities for partnerships with institutions that reinvest in rural and regional communities.

Reports in both Scotland and Australia indicate a higher level of life satisfaction in rural areas (Wilkins, 2015 in Australian Institute Health and Welfare 2018, Rural Scotland Key Facts, 2021). Despite this, rural areas continue to be labelled as disadvantaged and funding targeted for schools, health services, transport and other services to 'catch up' entrenching the view that urban lifestyle is the benchmark. Termed by researchers Jonathan and Katrina Sher a *'defacto urban policy'* (Sher & Sher, 1994) this approach perpetuates the myth of rural communities being disadvantaged and problematic.

rural areas continue to be labelled as disadvantage

People no longer have faith in the ability of large bureaucracies to meet the needs of people for whom they were designed. There are multiple examples of hierarchical institutions screening out feedback of the reality of complex local situations. Regional communities benefit from dynamic and responsive processes capable of providing information, support and resourcing across portfolios. Implementing strategies for interaction, flexibility and feedback from those who are impacted is a primary consideration that benefits from collaborative structures and partnerships. While competitive tendering policies and intergovernmental expenditure tied to this framework limit options, there are regional structures with foundations that contribute to good decision making for the long term benefit of communities. Many originate from Victoria such as Landcare, Coast Action, Rural Enterprise Victoria, Rural Women's Network and Country Education Program which all acted as forums for local knowledge to be incorporated into public planning.

regional structures with foundations that contribute to good decision making

Policies introduced in the 1990's that centralised and privatised services and infrastructure, by default relocated rural and regional wealth to urban Australia and internationally. The shift became known as 'terminal decline', as corporations took over ownership of community resources such as water,

fish, forests, fuel and the production of food. https://www.ruralcommunities/stories fishing. Prior to COVID 19 Australia was one of the most urbanized nations with over 70% of people living in large urban cities. Urban dwellers dependent on natural resources of water, food, fibre, timber, source of power and recreation from regional areas experienced a flow on effect in rising costs and declining quality.

It is timely to rethink regional development

It is timely to rethink regional development beyond the extraction of natural resources until the point of depletion of resources and damaged landscapes. A rural policy that requires a reciprocal investment in the source of natural resources and the communities who act as custodians for waterways and landscapes would transform this relationship, benefiting both urban and rural lifestyles.

Absence of rural policy

In the European Union, Canada and Japan rural policies recognise the importance of reciprocal relationships by a tax or reduced service cost to communities at the source of water catchments or natural resources. EU Rural_Development_Policy

https://enrd.ec.europa.eu/publications/smart-villages-reciprocity-contracts_en

'everything starts and finishes with country'

Investment in existing structures that foster inclusion of local knowledge across portfolios would mitigate financial and human costs incurred following crisis and disaster when people and community groups are exhausted.

Regional forums and planning frameworks

There is a growing interest in bio-regional forums, treaties and planning towards a scale that is determined by ecological balance. Geddes writing in 'Cities in evolution' (1915) led to the Local to Global concept inspiring the 1992 United Nations Local Agenda 21 in Rio De Janeiro.

In Indigenous cultures knowledge of 'country' is a constant guide and reference point for life. Aboriginal archivist Margo Neale explains that 'everything starts and finishes with country'. Historian Bill Gammage, in *The Biggest Estate on Earth, how Aborigines made Australia* (2011) and Aboriginal writer Bruce

Pascoe in *Dark Emu Black Seeds: Aboriginal agriculture or accident* (2014) along with other writers convincingly *show that Aboriginal people did farm the land, but in a different way to colonisers. Using sophisticated, sustainable methods....working with nature and harnessing its rhythms. Using a deep understanding of Country.* (Neale and Kelly, 2020).

Questions

List programs you are aware of, and rank their ability to assist community in the long term. (low 1 - 10 high)

Note if they were they initiated from within the community and if they have a partnership with a funding organisation that responded to locally identified issues?

If centrally funded and administered, what impact did this have?

Country is - a nourishing terrain that gives and receives life.

1.3 Goals of community development

Country is - a nourishing terrain that gives and receives life. A fundamental proposition in Indigenous law and society is that a country and its living things take care of each other.
(Rose, 1997: 3-4).

In *Community Development in an uncertain world: vision, analysis and practice* (1995) Jim Ife wrote that '*despite the formidable achievements of modern, Western, industrialised society, it has become increasingly clear that the current social, economic and political order has been unable to meet two of the most basic prerequisites for human civilisation: the need for people to be able to live in harmony with their environment (ecological sustainability) and the need for them to be able to live in harmony with each other (social justice).*

In the introduction to the 2nd edition published 21 years later both the environment and social relationships are in a critical state (Ife, 2016). Tim Hollo points out that the economic changes made during the pandemic give evidence that destructive past policies can be changed, that people can collaborate for the common good. That *the rules of neoliberal economics [were]*

sacrifice the environment for the sake of jobs.

broken by every government the world over, the massive policy shift interventions, shifting the entire structure of global economy are possible (Hollo. 2020).

Seemingly diverse activities have common links. The goals of social justice and ecological sustainability guide community development practice raising awareness of connection to other species, lifestyles and environments. Regional communities have all too often been told to sacrifice the environment for the sake of jobs. Sadly 'wealth' has come at the expense of quality of life as we have experienced with the COVID 19 pandemic. If people are to live in harmony with each other and care for the environment they depend upon, feminist practices, adult education and Indigenous yarning that appreciates the complexity of issues locally and globally are all of value.

In the updated book Jim Ife pays attention to ways of working that value local knowledge: Chapters 6 and 7 are of particular relevance.

Questions

What is your knowledge of local people being involved in issues within their communities/workplace?

Can you give three examples that include:

- the reason for people's involvement in the issue?
- who was effected by the work?
- what change resulted? (in the short term, in the long term)

1.4 Practice of community development

Investing in local decision making will re-build confidence in democratic systems as well as educate decision makers that local knowledge is a key resource. (Hollo, 2020)

How we work determines the culture and capacity of outcomes

Community development involves changes in attitudes and understanding. Feminist principles of involving those impacted by decisions guides a workers practice. Beginning with achievable tasks while skills and confidence increase is critical in not overburdening those involved. The process creates opportunities to relearn our individual and collective value, to unlearn the labels of disadvantage and be open to consider lives different to our own. The experience establishes sound foundations for future ventures.

A regional perspective pays attention to human activity and its impact on the natural world at a scale that provides a critical link to understanding global phenomena such as pollution, rising temperatures, dramatic weather patterns, rising oceans etc. At this regional level the interconnected nature of social, economic, environmental, cultural, political, personal and spiritual development becomes evident and ways to implement changed practices emerge.

Participation, ownership and respect are key aspects of this work

Indigenous researcher and educator Linda Tuhiwai Smith points out that awareness of this *[C]onnectedness positions individuals in sets of relationships with other people and with the environment* (Tuhiwai Smith 1999:148) transforming relationships from previous practices that regarded the natural world as resources to be plundered and a dumping ground for waste. When re-visiting her work 20 years on from her original publication of *Decolonizing methodologies: research and indigenous people* (1988) she incorporates poetry, passion and stories of the importance of unlearning how we work with 'others' of whom there are multiple and overlapping categories. Participation, ownership and respect are key aspects of this work https://www.youtube.com/watch?v=YSX_4FnqXwQ.

Motivation for people to work together will vary across communities. Sit with parents of young children and you will be aware of their motivation to create a safe world for their children. Working in response to an identified need and engaging people in envisioning a vibrant future is a critical step. With local ownership and a co-operative culture communities will be increasingly capable of setting long term agendas that invite partnerships with public and private sector organisations.

This is a different process to communities accessing funds from a statewide or national program that has defined targets and outcomes. While some have the capacity to match local needs, in many cases they are short-term projects. All too often communities have experiences of programs that raised hopes but failed to deliver the expected outcomes.

Skilled and resourced facilitators are critical

Later chapters pay attention to constructive strategies to enable people within rural, regional and urban communities to work and plan together. These inclusive ways of working require skills that resource and invest in local knowledge and structures enabling communities to actively participate in determining long term agendas. This missing link into regional decision making enables complex local knowledge to be at planning tables rather than the financially and emotionally exhausting, distressing practice of community consultation after decisions have been made.

Skilled and resourced facilitators contribute a foundation for respectful relations between community interests and responsible agencies and industries. Australia's response to waves of disasters impacting on regional communities the National Recovery Resiliency Agency states *we must be consistent in the way we respond and operate regardless of which government agency is involved; and the approach to recovery must be locally led, locally understood and locally implemented* (Stone, S., May 2021). At a policy level the critical role of community knowledge at all stages of planning, engagement and recovery is acknowledged, yet funding, structures and resourcing and integration of this within regions remains elusive https://recoveryresilienceagency.cmail20.com/ .

For bureaucrats within centralised policy and planning areas a change in attitude enabling partnerships built on respect for local knowledge of community life is critical. The containment and prevention of the spread of the COVID virus worked best where there was co-operation across departments and agencies to resource regions. Establishing collaborative ways of working between groups of people is a pre-requisite to foster more equal and supportive relationships. This is slowly being recognised in relation to Indigenous communities and knowledge.

Questions

Within your experience of community action for change can you identify groups that worked openly and inclusively?

What outcomes did these groups achieve? For people and for the environment?

In what ways do these contrast with organisations that controlled information and resources?

Who benefits from these organisations?

2. ROLE OF THE COMMUNITY DEVELOPMENT WORKER

Leadership is best when the people say, 'We have done this ourselves'.
(Lao Tzu in Shields, 1994:91)

Collaborative engagement brings together people with different interests and experiences in a democratic and participatory environment. It moves away from welfare and counselling towards initiatives that have a co-operative culture and local ownership. The workers role is to provide an experiential learning environment for inclusive practice, enabling a continuing growth of skills and knowledge within the community, preferably with the support of a regional network and access to tertiary education.

The workers task is to support this process, not direct outcomes

When people come together and experience ways of working that develops trust and respect for their difference, then the foundational blocks of social development are in place. Without this step many well-intended projects cause division within their community, rather than the celebration and strengthening originally intended. The workers task is to support this process, not direct outcomes in terms of chosen projects as a primary goal.

In rural and regional communities there are multiple demands on people with legal, financial and human relations expertise in group work. Traditionally responsibilities have included recreational activities of sporting clubs for all ages, local branches of political parties, the churches, school councils, service clubs, play groups, care of older residents, the young and the many environmental issues of great concern to rural people.

Trusted relationships reduce personal trauma in disasters

More recently, there are additional demands to provide infrastructure for management of kindergartens, schools, campaigns to create employment or protect natural assets add extra pressures. This can be exacerbated where negotiations are with distant private and corporate organisations. As increasing natural disasters impact the overlaying myriad of new responsibilities can be overwhelming if these are not resourced and integrated into relevant agencies.

The study circle kit: *Building Communities through Co-operation* (Sheil, 2015) is focused on local involvement in disaster preparation, management and recovery. Foundational principles introduced at the beginning of the kit invest in skills enabling people to work constructively together. As people move from individual concerns to an awareness of what can be achieved by a group, trusted relationships between community members and relevant agencies emerge.

Establishing good processes, prior to critical projects being undertaken, mitigates destructive practices that frequently occur in enthusiastic but uninformed groups. Trusted relationships reduce personal trauma in disasters and enable recovery efforts to be informed by local knowledge.

The facilitation of community involvement from fragmentation to a sound and inclusive foundation involves as many different stages as parenting. For those who are familiar with these strategies, this will affirm their experience of the value of investing time in establishing respectful ways of working together. For others, they may appear very simple, or even roundabout in achieving a particular understanding. You are encouraged to make journal entries on your experience of implementing these steps.

2.1 Facilitation

The overlapping crisis of dramatic weather events and global contamination of viral diseases has raised awareness of the critical contribution of collaboration within and between organisations and nations. We are all in this together.

In the beginning

Facilitation: making something easier or making something happen.
<https://www.yourdictionary.com/facilitation> 2021.

Facilitating engagement in community organisations has parallels to parenting. For those of you who are parents, reflect back to that time of informed ignorance when you thought 'the birth' was it. The birth, like the project, is of enormous significance – that magical life-giving moment that transforms your life, but it is a beginning, not an end point. For those of you who are not parents, the experience of being parented will provide a common reference point. Your expectations and frustrations are equally instructive.

From that moment of birth you begin to think differently, your focus is required to extend and take on new responsibilities. Attitudes towards you will also change as you have new responsibilities. The experience can be either nurturing or soul destroying depending on the support and experience you have to draw on. It will challenge and educate you.

Understanding is often in the telling of the stories

There are copious sources of advice in regard to preferred action in your role, but you as the responsible person have to make the choices and learn from them. Reflect on who you trusted most in this process: members of the family, the neighbour, other parents, books, the local doctor, the infant welfare sister; the personalised approach, the expert, Dr. Google or a combination of these?

Rewards and challenges

This intense and monopolising involvement has rewards in the everyday things, often things nobody else will notice. The first signs of knowing they are important, of independence, of trust. The joys of someone to share these moments with, the photo's the notes and stories shared. Understanding is often in the telling of the stories, creating identity and history, memories and hopes for the future. Remember to take photos, write to the paper, use social media thoughtfully and compassionately to record events.

Support not control

I recall my son once wrote in response to a question asked of students at his school, 'What is the role of the parent?' His response: *Parents should provide comfort and support (only sometimes they get these mixed up) and lunch money, and sometimes more money!* (Bennett).

Within the support and comfort were probably food, driving, back-rubs, listening, asking, the domestic stuff, the reliability and responsibility, the nurturing and spending time. Then there is the progression of supporting development into new responsibilities: the driving lessons. Providing opportunities for supported learning with low risks, before embarking on more hazardous and life-threatening situations.

There will be a time to let go

Letting go

There will be a time to let go, supporting people to make the transition to independence. Especially if you're a country parent this happens quite early and they need to have their own sense of morality to guide them through. A life that encourages celebration of how they are, of caring for others, for the neighbourhood, and how to call home when they need to know something, want picking up, or life just gets too hard.

Reflecting

And then they are gone – there's just you again, but very different from before having children.

This process of learning together, is about change.

You've been through a transformative change. There is a past and future, not only the present. It is now time to recharge, to write and reflect on what you've learnt, to keep in touch, but to let them find their own direction. There are parallels in being the facilitator in all these stages. You will be able to make comparisons in relation to the different stages. Community development workers go through this process repeatedly.

Like raising children, each project is different. Where you live, what institutions and networks exist at the time, will determine opportunities and challenges. This process of learning together, is about change. Just as with parenting, there is no one recipe. Each community will be at a different stage of development, depending on the skills, knowledge, resources and attitudes that welcome or limit the inclusion of local knowledge at that time.

Change brings challenges and new relationships

There are reference points, past experience and knowledge to support you through the tough and complex times. You are both a worker and educator.

Change brings challenges and new relationships. Just as with parenting, there can be a time of aloneness, as children confidently leave home to work, study or travel, there are also times of return with new friends, new partners and in time another generation. A continued growth and development.

Questions

What previous experiences have you had in this role?

What led to significant challenges in your role?

Identify times of new awareness that changed how people behaved/related?

Describe a defining time of constructive growth?

A continued growth and development.

3. STATE OF OUR COMMUNITIES: CONCEPTUAL TOOLS

There are a growing number of universal indicators that give visibility to the complexity and state of community life. Raising awareness of the impact of current situations on different groups of people. What benefits some people, may limit the quality of life for others as well as the environment.

In Sydney, Deputy Lord Mayor, Jess Scully, discusses insights resulting from introducing Community Wellbeing indicators to be more informed about the impact of policies and ways to improve community health and life style Community Wellbeing Indicators 2019 - City of Sydney - NSW ...www.cityofsydney.nsw.gov.au › assets › pdf_file › Co...

In New Zealand, Jacinta Ardern unveiled the first 'well-being' budget derived from Marilyn Waring's work that gives visibility to culture as well as considers experiences of current and future generations with an international awareness. *Ngā Tūtohu Aotearoa* – Indicators Aotearoa New Zealand engenders a very different conversation. https://www.stats.govt.nz/indicators-and-snapshots/indicators-aotearoa-new-zealand-nga-tutohu-aotearoa

Begin with issues close to people's hearts.

Jim Ife's goal of a strong and resilient community is one that has a good balance of social development, political development, personal and spiritual development, economic development, cultural development and for all these we depend upon our environmental development (Ife, 1995, 2016). In 2011 Ife added 'survival development' aware that some communities were struggling across all aspects of community life.

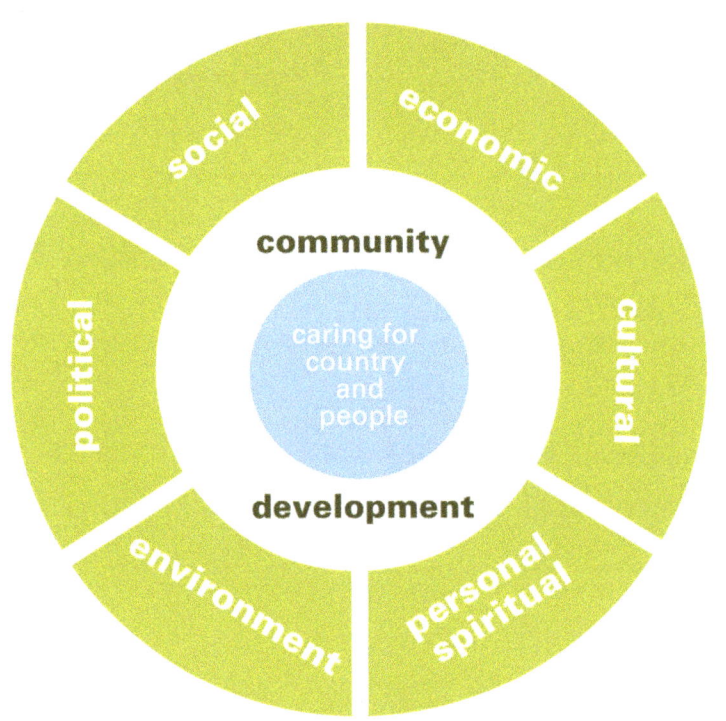

acknowledgement to Jim Ife, 1995

Begin with issues close to people's hearts. The goal is to work towards balanced development that reintegrates awareness of the connectedness of all aspects of our lives.

Regional experiences of drought, flood, fires and the pandemic highlight the interconnected and inter-generational nature of community life. Unlike in organizations, relationships are not insulated by portfolios, departments or hierarchical layers of governance. The following story is one of co-operation across difference from a shared concern for the river.

Connections across difference:
In 1989 communities on the Snowy River in Far East Gippsland, Victoria, learned of the proposed siting of a pulp and paper mill on the river flats near Orbost.

*Orbost is renowned for its public support of the timber industry...
Greenies are generally looked upon with scorn and condemnation.
Environmental concerns aren't a terribly important issue. But on
21st April, 1989 Orbost saw the 2nd largest meeting ever held. The
topic 'Pulp, Profits and People' organised by Green Labour. Speakers
included Dr. Helen Caldicott (nuclear and environmental campaigner)
Janet Rice, (East Gippsland Coalition) Gill Richardson (4th generation
farmer) Brian Bolding (Lakes Entrance Fisherman).*
(Snowy River Mail, Richardson, 1989:40).

Local farmer, Heather Richardson lived on the Snowy River. Her family were aware of the declining flow and health of the river due to diversion of water to the Murray River without consultation with Snowy River catchment communities. Concerned for the impact of a Pulp Mill on the Snowy River, Heather convened a meeting resulting in the formation of the Pulp Mill Women's Awareness Group. Researchers Gamble and Weil (1997, 2010) note that concern for their families was a common motivation for women to initiate environmental action.

Farmers, conservationists and community members worked together to find out the reality of employment potential and impact on river health. The culture was one of 'give and take' of ideas as people found out about other pulp mills, or past decisions impacting on their lives, not an out sourced research project.

The women are concerned that there has been widespread confusion over the issues, information and facts received by the public of Orbost and that there has not been sufficient objective and factually based information made easily accessible. The women formed into small research and working groups to gather information and obtain funding.
(Carol Crowe, 1989:41)

While successful in preventing the Pulp and Paper Mill being located on the flats, raised awareness of the degraded state of the river resulted in the continuation of the group as the *Orbost Women's Awareness Group* (OWAG). In 2008 OWAG's submission to the Draft Environmental Impact Statement documented the impact of past water allocation away from the Snowy River and the communities living along the river. *We ...view with great anger, the ecological degradation which has been visited on the Snowy River below the Jindabyne Dam...since 1967* (The Jindabyne Dam removed 99% of the water from the river).

The women argued that the social cohesion, the socio-economic necessities of this region depended on the Snowy River being able to maintain its ecology by having sufficient of its own water to do so. *The communities situated in the Snowy Valley and beyond had the right to use their river in the same ways as the people of the Murray River expect to do, and to use their river. This is important to us in exactly the same ways as it is for them but is not acknowledged by Government or the Bureaucracy – and is not contained in the Draft Environmental Impact Statement* (Richardson, 2008).

This is important to us in exactly the same ways as it is for them

The financial and environmental cost to the Snowy communities, of the granting for free to the Murray area and the subsequent environmental problems of salinity and erosion continue (Miller, Snowy River Story, 2005: Chapters 1-4).

The OWAG met for 20 years making time to enjoy walks in the bush and exploring the region together. With the establishment of the Snowy Scientific Committee there was hope of an increased flow of water to the Snowy River. Acacia Rose, a member of the Snowy River Alliance writes graphically of what was possible up until 2014 in restoring some health to this once mighty life supporting river system. With rising temperatures the impact of this political decision remains a grief to those who remember. *Is there a similar story in your region?*

Task

the impact of this political decision remains a grief

As personal experiences give insight into the impact of policies on a landscape as well as the complexity of community life, the following questions invite people to speak of the social, political, environmental, economic, cultural, personal and spiritual change from their perspectives. Continuing crisis experienced by individuals, societies and nations has led to the inclusion of the question of survival development.

Rate the state of each of these aspects of community life using Low / Medium / High / Excellent

Date this work, to provide a future reference.

The indicators of balanced development are familiar to Australians as they indicate fire danger ratings for the Country Fire Authority, and swing depending on local circumstances and influences. Being able to track highs and lows provides good information on how to act. At some times we can relax, at others local people need to become involved, active and strategic.

Questions

Political development. How would you rate your current political involvement? That is your ability, to participate in decisions that impact on your life that may originate within community or locally, or a state, national or international level.

Social Development. How would you rate your current capacity for social involvement that facilitates interaction within communities? Consider current opportunities or burdensome situations that impact on your energy and time to participate productively.

Economic development. How would you rate the current state of economic development in your community? In responding you may consider issues of employment, circulation of money locally and reinvestment into the area. Re-investment or depletion can be thought about in regard to a balance between use of current resources and skills in the area and options for the long term.

Environmental development. How would you rate the current state of policy and planning in regard to environmental issues impacting on your community? Are processes open and accessible? Is there an ability to share knowledge and be involved in decisions and actions for care of the environment?

Personally and Spiritually. How would you rate your ability to 'have a life' that has personal expressions of creativity and spirituality? To what extent are there opportunities to reflect on what guides your daily journey, you interaction with others and your sense of place in the world?

Cultural Development. How would you rate the state of cultural activities in your community? The private or public celebrations of creative life in song, dance, festivals, art, artisans, food and recreation in all its dimensions.

Survival development. How would you rate your capacity to meet universal human needs of subsistence, protection, affection, understanding, participation, idleness, creation, identity and freedom (Max-neef 1191). While relating to previous questions an ability to thrive adds the dimension of crisis within a region/population

As words have different meanings to different

COMMUNITY INDICATORS

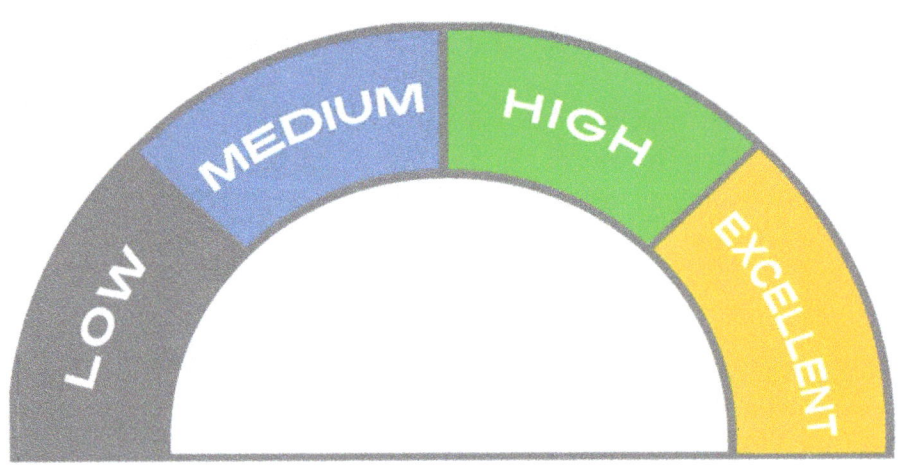

As words have different meanings to different people you may choose to adapt them for your own use.

The exercise is designed to assist by:

- introducing a first step in making situations people care about visible and enabling understanding of the complexity of issues that can be lost when general statements are made from one perspective that everything is good, or everything is bad. (For whom? For how long? What environmental impact?)

- identifying specific situations of concern or interest in the community people are able to speak publicly about issues, and reclaim legitimacy for their value,

- directing attention to consideration of why some aspects of community life are vibrant and others vulnerable provides valuable information for further research on ways to change a given situation.

Remember 'community' is not a static concept. At times communities will be strong and resilient, capable of caring for the wonderful mix of people who live there. At other times their capacity to do this is reduced and divisions become apparent. There may be some people whose needs are met at the expense of other groups and the environment. This is the constant tension in a world experiencing the stress of a finite natural system.

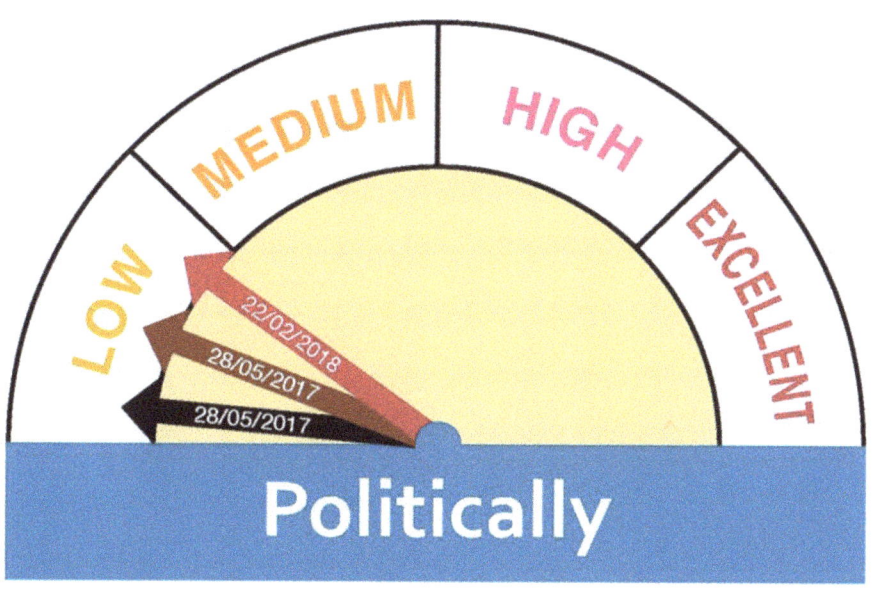

'community' is not a static concept.

4. LOCATING LEARNING WITHIN COMMUNITIES

Study circles enable people to overcome the isolation of individuals and the lack of interest in what is common, equality is at the heart of the matter in democracy.
(Larsson, 2001:210)

By 2021 policies introduced in the 1990's underpinned by the belief that 'bigger is better' and private more effective than public impacted severely on Victoria's scattered populations.

The withdrawal of services and the transfer of ownership and profits to large regional and urban organisations continues.

Regional educational institutions are not exempt. Primary schools, the heart of many communities have closed. The amalgamation of tertiary educational institutions central to regionally relevant and outreach programs are limited or have ceased. Curriculums have become increasingly determined by industries. The quality, scope and integrity of many courses has diminished. Well-designed facilities are underutilised and dedicated and skilled staff unemployed.

consistently began by meeting with and resourcing communities.

At a time when there is an urgent need to contribute to regional planning at all levels access to knowledge, skills and resources are either absent or slowly being re-invented. In East Gippsland, programs in art, conservation and value adding in timber industry, design and production that individuals and organisations had worked hard to establish to world class standards ceased. People are turning to Indigenous land management groups for responsible leadership. While recognition of value of First Nation's thinking is a welcome shift, it will take time to step into a guiding role and unrealistic in the short term.

Past programs that successfully enabled marginalised groups to be active in planning consistently began by meeting with and resourcing communities. Study circles offer an affordable, open ended way to locate learning within communities. *Building Rural Futures through Co-operation* (Sheil, 1999) designed to enable rural communities to determine their own future provided an experiential resource. Jane Vella's text, *Learning to Listen, Learning to Teach (2002)* provides foundational principles to guide this interaction. Groups operate on the adult education principles of creating safe places for people to speak and be heard. Diversity of opinion is valued not silenced. From this basis groups were invited to envision the futures of their communities and take steps towards implementing a project. No timelines, agendas or targets were set.

In the academic language of adult education and regional community development study circles focus on dialogue, time, networking, local ownership and co-operative culture. To enable rural communities to move beyond discussion towards envisioning more vibrant futures steps the extra strategies of visioning, action, reflection and transformation were designed into the kit. Outcomes affirmed the validity of the process while highlighting the critical contribution of skilled facilitators (Sheil and Smith, 2006:70-76). Projects begun at this time continue some 20 years later. https://www.ruralcommunities.com.au/publications

It is a foundation for appreciating the complexity of issues and finding a way forward setting a very different agenda to that of 'the greed merchants' whose primary agenda is profit without acknowledgement of costs to place and people (Neil Murray: Hindsight, 2017).

Accredited facilitators

A post-graduate professional development program in Regional Community Development was designed and accredited by Monash University to meet the demand for skilled facilitators (2002–2007). The course introduced regional workers to theory and practice of Collaborative Engagement prior to them implementing the strategies in their workplace or community, then evaluating the approach.

Community resourcing and planning

Located within communities study circles provided a forum for people to bring community interests to the table as central, not peripheral issues. With a networked approach they had access to greater resources, skills, knowledge and links to research within tertiary institutions and libraries. Communities were no longer dealing with complex issues on their own, but were tackling manageable projects with good outcomes. The approach engaged with the social, economic and environmental issues of our time with access to resources and knowledge that led to changing attitudes and understanding.

With a networked approach they had access to greater resources, skills, knowledge

Locating learning within communities provides a forum that links into local motivation, resources local knowledge and energy. Outcomes and results are consistently in excess of anticipated targets or benchmarks.

Latrobe City Council's Strengthening seven small towns, (2003) employed facilitators from within each of seven small towns and established a reference group of community members, township association representatives, shire staff, Centre staff and community based agencies (Sheil, Pugliese, Gay, 2004). Facilitators lived in the communities and were enrolled in the Graduate Certificate of Regional Development (Monash University) providing an on-going sounding board for their community engagement. This activity put the small communities on the map with a range of services and agencies previously absent. Collaborative approaches between the communities was an unanticipated development as community groups gained insight into council budgeting processes. Rather than compete for limited funds, they sequenced applications for recreational facilities first in one community, then the following year in another. They collaborated instead of competing. Skills, knowledge of processes and contacts and resources remain in these communities and proved valuable in recovery efforts following fires (Smith and Sheil, 2006:79-81).

They collaborated instead of competing.

Aboriginal elders affirmed this democratic way of working

The trusted way of working led to community members initiating small projects. As people gained confidence, contacts and resources expanded into ventures that continue to contribute to social, economic and environmental sustainability of those communities. In Victoria, the amalgamation of local government areas had left many communities without an identity or presence to profile issues of importance. Taking ownership of local newspapers and newsletters filled this gap, featuring local events, activities and people. Stories of local children, of older people, of environmental work, or cultural events, increasing opportunities for public involvement, sharing of concerns, celebrations and affirming the importance of community life. Ventures begun to meet social needs also led to economic development. Landcare projects that linked to rail-trail access and environmental reclamation continue as do child-friendly facilities. Development with a social/moral conscience originating from within communities termed 'endogenous development' (Huggonier, 1999).

Aboriginal elders attending the study groups affirmed this democratic way of working that began with people sitting round a table sharing a cup of tea. In his book *Sand Talk: How indigenous thinking can save the world* (2019) Tyson Yunkaporta explains that *'Yarning moves beyond monologue and is vibrant, dynamic and deeply stimulating, ..it has protocols of active listening, mutual respect and building on what others have said rather than openly contradicting or debating ideas'* (Yunkaporta, 2019:131).

reclaim legitimacy in democratic practices

This inclusive approach underpinned the process for drafting the *Uluru Statement from the Heart* meeting with groups across the nation to have dialogue about past, present and future policies and representation (2017) https://ulurustatement.org/

At a state level Jess Scully, Deputy Lord Mayor of Sydney and author of *Glimpses of Utopia* (2020) is researching ways of working that bring people together in forums that have ongoing presence in decision making (Dumbo Feather, Jess Scully is a leader with vision, August 2020: 64: https://www.scribd.com/article/475248475/Jess-Scully-Is-A-Leader-With-Vision

All steps reclaim legitimacy in democratic practices and rebuild trust that those in power will engage with issues of community importance rather than be dominated by corporate lobbyists.

Questions

Are you aware of projects/ventures within your community that have:

- provided skill development in group work prior to undertaking a project?
- supported local people to determine the area of interest?
- What changes are you aware of from resourcing people within their communities?

5. CHANGING ROLES OF GOVERNMENT/COMMUNITY/ MARKET PLACE

We're at an inflection point in history.

We're at an inflection point in history. The current world is over, burnt to cinders on a pyre of its own making. In order to both turn around ecological, economic and social collapse, and generate the resilience we need to survive and thrive in the decades ahead, we urgently need to cultivate from the ashes new, regenerative democratic norms and institutions.
(Hollo, 2019:3).

The above statement was written in the midst of the 2019/2020 bush fires in central and southern Australia, prior to closing of borders, industries, cafe's hotels, tourism due to the global COVID pandemic that changed the way people could interact. This timely acknowledgement of the urgency of moving away from policies that located wealth in the hands of very few and increasingly stripped natural resources from communities and the environment resonated with many. With the global pandemic, relationships and allocation of resources were thrown into constant flux with all players contributing (or detracting) from a healthy outcome. Weaknesses in stretched health and aged care services were a major concern.

It is an opportunity to rethink goals away from extraction or resources and centralisation of power towards goals that acknowledge the depletion or investment in water, soil, clean oceans, air, forests and knowledge of First Nation people. The message is not a new one. Despite barriers to change, some nations are taking steps to implement long overdue changes, to be compassionate and wise.

Role of government

The role of government is to develop structures inclusive of local knowledge and expertise at all levels: subsidiarity in action. Examples of structures to implement communication and involvement in decision making from the local to central level have existed at a state and federal level through the Landcare, Credit Care, Rural Enterprise Victoria, and the Rural Women's Network. These organisations linked into a Rural Affairs Committee of Cabinet that toured regularly to meet and talk with local people. While currently weakened by policies of economic rationalism, the knowledge and experiences still exist in rural Australia. These organisations provide a means for local people to work together and achieve outcomes far greater than could be achieved in isolation. Regional policy across all departments could include structures and strategies to establish partnerships. Partnerships that are resourced across portfolios and support work at the local level. Managed locally and resourced centrally by state/federal government departments.

Currently in the United Kingdom a movement to re-engage with decision making has seen a social movement of Independents re-entering local councils. Peter Macfadyn, frustrated with local council processes set about making politics relevant, efficient and fun and called it Flatpack Democracy. '*After four years in power the Independents for Frome group took all 17 seats on Frome's town council in 2015 with vote shares as high as 70%. They had won the election with a complete takeover of the town council based on their simple but appealing promise: future policies will be made as joint efforts with the entire community.*' https://www.flatpackdemocracy.co.uk

Despite policies advocating good working relations within and between communities, the capacity of organisations to implement these policies is minimal. Emergency management organisations have been slow to invest in disaster prevention or preparation despite policies advocating this as a high priority. The Australian White Paper 'The Challenge' (2013) called for a refocusing of investment from response and recovery to investing in community and organisational resilience to improve protection and capacity for recovery'. However, the reality was only 3% of funds allocated prior to disasters (White Paper, 2013).

The current state of resourcefulness within rural and regional communities is fragile and in need of well-targeted resources. How best to allocate resources will require strategies for listening to and resourcing the capacity of local people and agencies to work and plan together. It is estimated that for every $1.00 spent in disaster preparation $10 are saved in recovery and minimisation of trauma (ibid).

Role of market place

The idea that it always costs money to do something for the environment should be considered extinct….Hales 2020.
https://news.griffith.edu.au/2020/11/10/eco-efficiencies-save-smes-money-and-boosts-economy/

A change in approach from commodity driven agendas to include consideration of environmental and community costs provides opportunities for sustainable partnerships.

A sustainable business, is an enterprise that has minimal negative impact or potentially a positive effect on the global or local environment, community, society, or economy—a business that strives to meet the triple bottom line.

1. It incorporates principles of sustainability into each of its business decisions.

2. It supplies environmentally friendly products or services that replaces demand for nongreen products and/or services.

3. It is greener than traditional competition.

4. It has made an enduring commitment to environmental principles in its business operations. https://en.wikipedia.org/wiki/Sustainable_business

The Bendigo Community Bank returns profits to the community organisation for local projects, employment or knowledge development. https://www.bendigobank.com.au/community/community-bank/

Other organisations such as Griffith University's Centre for Sustainable Enterprise works with a range of businesses and organisations to implement sustainable practices for people and the environment. This includes working with small to medium businesses on reducing environmental impact. The EcoBiz

program is estimated to save costs, increase productivity and reduce carbon emissions (Hayles 2020). Research into Urban Food Agriculture benefits rural producers and urban consumers. Awareness of personal ways to contribute to the political vision of reduced carbon emissions is addressed in practical terms in *Your Life Your Planet* (Ebbs 2021). The Centre has inspiring examples of healing land following fires, high cost of habitat reduction to increasing emissions, cost of increased demands on health services due to stressful circumstances, power of culture to increase quality of life and move away from welfare. In all these steps access for community to resources and partnerships is a key ingredient.

The language of Corporate Social Responsibility https://solutions.yourcause.com/think-globally-act-locally/ and Ethical Investment is playing a constructive role in some organisations www.australianethical.com.au/

Role of community
Community enterprises, organisations and associations can take on increasing responsibility for the provision and management of services at a local level if they have access to relevant training, support and expertise. Collaborative ventures between communities and private and public sector orgainsations are returning social and economic capital to communities.

Community enterprises originate to meet a need in a community or region. It may be a meeting place such as purchase of a hotel, establishment of a FM radio station, general store or recreational facilities. It is a model that reinvests into the community. https://www.coopdevelopment.org.au community enterprises.html

Community organisations that have a fundamental commitment to the community are distinct from the Community Sector that frequently operates on managerial principles and generation of profit. While they may have branches and agencies within communities such as Red Cross, Salvation Army etc. they are not directly accountable to community members but a board of management.

Community associations can exist to establish and maintain recreational facilities, environmental programs, hall committees, children's services, art groups, animal welfare, and men's sheds for example. They are the foundation of community life and each will have a distinct history and culture. Again support for these organisations to operate inclusively, have sound environmental policies and to be resourced to do so benefits all levels of government. Investing in the sound functioning of community organisations is a sound preventative strategy in disaster planning.

At the beginning of the 21st Century, resourceful communities responded to the withdrawal of services by taking ownership of valued infrastructure and establishing partnerships with public and private sector organisations. Partnerships such as Bendigo Community Banks or community owned hotels, supermarkets or arts centres create services, employment and circulate money regionally. These communities had greater independence in investing in local environmental rehabilitation projects or infrastructure. Such stories of collective ownership and the flow on to greater independence in initiating caring health services, child-care, schools, recreational facilities and good employment opportunities offer a glimmer of hope.

They reclaimed involvement and strengthened community relationships and generated opportunities to invest in the local economy and environment.

This approach provides a critical step in skill development within communities and with professional staff recognising the valuable knowledge and care-taking role taken on by those living and working in rural communities.

It is a time of unlearning

It is a time of unlearning of the superiority of practices and lifestyles introduced from other nations. To take steps in becoming aware of the complexity and integrity of lore of First Nations people in relation to identity, culture, enduring lifestyle embedded in governance systems that cared for the land.

Questions

Are you aware of ventures initiated by local people in your community?

Have these established partnerships with other groups/organisations/government departments?

What skills local people managing these ventures has required?

How have people learnt these skills?

Which organisations have they been able to access for skill development, information and other resources?

This first chapter provides an overview of concepts and understanding for more focused work in later chapters. The aim is to clarify your own level of knowledge and experience, while adding to the growing awareness of events in rural, regional and urban communities. .

FURTHER REFERENCES

https://www.researchgate.net/publication/265092861_Study_Circles_in_Sweden_An_Overview_with_a_Bibliography_of_International_Literature.

Curtis, Jane (2020) *The Scholar's Hut*, James, Daniel https://www.abc.net.au/radionational/programs/the-history-listen/the-scholars-hut/12736892 Radio National 28th September,

Fussell. W. (1996) *The value of local knowledge and importance of shifting beliefs in the process of social change.* Community Development Journal Vol. 31. No. 1

Hollo, T., (2020) *The climate crisis and coronavirus bearing down on us the age of disconnection is over,* The Guardian, March 28, https://www.theguardian.com/commentsisfree/2020/mar/28/with-the-climate-ciris-and-coronavirus-bearing-down-on-us-the-age-of-disconnection-is-over

Ife, J., (2016) (*2nd Edition*) *Community development in an uncertain world. Vision, analysis and practice.* Cambridge University Press, Port Melbourne.
(Chps. 3 Foundations of social, economic and Chp. 4 Post-enlightenment and indigenous understanding, Chps. 10 and 11: Social, Economic, political, environmental, cultural, personal and spiritual development. Chp. 12. Roles and Practice

Ife, J., (2015) Community Development Conference, *Transitions/ Solutions* https://www.youtube.com/watch?v=IahIyqAH134

Kenny. S. and Connor P., (2016) *Developing communities for the Future: Community Development in Australia (5th edition)* Cengage Learning Australia Pty Ltd. Australia. Cengage.com.au

Thompson, H, Dahlhaus, P., Graymore, M., Courvisanos, Miner, A., Ollerenshaw, A., Sheil H., McDonald, K., and Corbett J., (2014)
Understanding the 2011 Grampians Natural Disaster Research, addressing the risk and resilience, Centre for eCommerce and Communications, Federation University. Ballarat.
http://www.gndr.org.au/

Max-Neef, Manfred, (2010) outlines basic shift urgently needed…and systematic outlining of Universal Human Need
https://www.democracynow.org/2010/9/22/chilean_economist_manfred_max_neef_us

Miller, C., (2005) *Snowy River Story: the grassroots campaign to save a national icon*, ABC Books, Sydney.

Pascoe, B., and Shukuroglou V., (2020) *Loving Country: a guide to sacred Australia,* Hardie Grant Travel, Melbourne.

Sheil, H., Pugliesie,T., and Gay, L. (2004) Local values and Local Knowledge shaping community involvement. Role of regional university, New Community Quarterly, 2 (No 4 Summer) 13-20

Sher. J. & Sher. K. 1994 *'Beyond the Conventional Wisdom: Rural Development as if Australia's Rural People and Communities Really Mattered'.* Journal of Research in Rural Education. Volume 10. No. 1. 2-43 USA.

Suzuki. D. with McConnell. A., and Mason, Adrienne (2008) (3rd edition). *The Sacred Balance: Rediscovering our place in Nature.* Allen & Unwin. St. Leonards. N.S.W. (Introduction)

Suzuki David, (2016) Seven things Australia could learn from Indigenous people, https://www.sbs.com.au/nitv/article/2016/03/09/dr-david-suzuki-reveals-seven-things-australia-could-learn-its-indigenous-peoples NTIV News.

Tuhiwai Smith, Linda (2020) Decolonising methodologies 20 years on, Sociological Review https://www.youtube.com/watch?v=YSX_4FnqXwQ

Vella, J., (2002) *Learning to Listen, Learning to teach. The power of dialogue in educating adults*, Jossey Bass, San Francisco.

Who's counting? Marilyn Waring on Sex, Lies and Global Economics https://www.youtube.com/watch?v=WS2nkr9q0VU

Waring, M, (2018) *Still Counting. Wellbeing, Women's Work and Policy-making*, Bridget Williams Books Ltd. Wellington, New Zealand. www.bwb.co.nz,

Williams, Portia Adade, Sikutshw Likho, Shackleton Shona, (2020) *Acknowledging Indigenous and Local Knowledge to facilitate collaboration in landscape Approaches* file:///C:/Users/toshi/Downloads/land-09-00331.pdf

CHAPTER 2

• CHAPTER 2 •
STRENGTH IN DIVERSITY

Visionary thinking, moving into the twenty-first century, has to be inclusive, and it has to allow people to create common ground.
(Josè Ramos, 2023:156)

FOCUS OF THIS CHAPTER

1. Challenges of change
2. Beginning: the important first step
3. Role of community development worker
4. Same but different
5. Opportunities to learn together: unpacking the myths
6. Resilient communities: a dynamic quality
7. Why and how people change
8. Reframing through legislation and policy

   Further references

INTRODUCTION

For facilitators the initial challenge is to bring people with different life experiences to a shared table. Change involves inviting new people to participate in public decision making, as well as those traditionally regarded as leaders. Moving from a generation of corporate management to establish community partnerships following disasters takes time and an investment in participatory ways of working by organisations as well as within communities. The following conversation with Wairewa community members in East Gippsland gives this process a context of drought, fire, the COVID pandemic and a community led recovery committee (2020).

Extract with Matt Zagami, Francine Gilfedder and John Appleby, Elizabeth Bakewell and Brian Blakeman
https://ruralcommunities.com.au/reflections-blacksummer-bushfires/

STRATEGIES: BEGINNING THE PRACTICE

As you work through the material, discuss the concepts with friends, families and colleagues. Clarifying what these ideas mean for you and other community members will assist in the development of language, as well as your ability to articulate why they are important.

Ask don't tell

Each section includes questions inviting you to reflect on your experiences. A practical exercise invites consideration of situations you may encounter and strategies to bring about long term change. The focus is centered on how this occurs: the process. Again, this is modelling ways of working within communities. Ask don't tell is an important tenet in adult education and enables people to speak of issues important to them rather than the assumed priorities. (Peavey https://www.context.org/iclib/ic40/peavey/

Use your journal to record responses to questions on the different ways people respond to change. You may find this informative in later work.

1. CHALLENGES OF CHANGE

Creating time to take stock of values and priorities, then initiate achievable changes

For rural and regional communities imposed changes have been rapid and extensive. Many people are so busy surviving, that there is little energy to engage in different ways of working. The Collaborative Engagement strategies designed into study circles or other projects that invite people to explore their current situation and learn (re-learn) skills of working and planning together. Creating time to take stock of values and priorities, then initiate achievable changes involves a transition from being the recipient of imposed change, to leading change.

Collaborative engagement is not about a return to the past. People may initially come to gatherings angry, frustrated and in despair as what they value has been dismissed or not valued. Making the time to listen to people speak of experiences and acknowledging and respecting their situation is important.

The difficult task of acknowledging the grief of current situations requires that sufficient time is given to include people needing to be 'held' before they can face a changed future. The sequenced approach provides this opportunity, and as a regional community development worker it is important to be aware of the impact and opportunities such change can bring. This is not counseling, indulgence or negativity. It is an opportunity for the harm of past practices to be acknowledged. In colonized Australia's short history there is a growing list of shameful situations for which the next generations have taken responsibility to say sorry and begin works of repair. These steps offer hope and changed practices.

Change, whether positive or negative requires people to adopt a different approach and is often initially stressful. The speed with which change occurs adds a further layer of shock and trauma as people have little time to adapt, or make other arrangements. If conditions deteriorate people often revert to what they know.

Inviting people to reflect on good processes of community engagement reminds people of what can be achieved working together. Involvement in projects such as Landcare, Men's Sheds, Neighbourhood Houses, Bush Nursing Centres, Rural Women's Network projects all offer experiences where local people participated in planning and were resourced to do so. When the COVID pandemic restricted travel there was increasing recognition of the value of Citizen Scientists (local observors) enabling local knowledge to influence planning decisions and resource allocations in environmental management.

These relationships are very different to closure of regional broadcasting, hospitals and regional government offices or continued logging, mining or diversion of water imposed externally by agendas with little consideration of the local social, economic and environmental implications.

Inviting people to reflect on good processes of community engagement reminds people of what can be achieved working together.

Questions

What does change mean for you?

Describe recent experiences of change?

Describe recent experiences of change in the community?

Are you able to identify the cause of the change?

How do you feel about this situation?

What was the response to this situation? (This may involve a sequence of responses: some short term, some for the long haul.)

Are there distinctions about change, which you chose, and were able to plan for, and change, in which you had little or no say?

Change ourselves and others can work with us differently.

2. BEGINNING: THE IMPORTANT FIRST STEP

This system of development gives people a platform for community organizing and democratic decision making to empower people to take part in the planning process to ensure it meets their needs.
https://ctb.ku.edu/en/table-of-contents/advocacy/advocacy-research/study-circles/main

People come together because they are aware of the need to work differently. Each person is part of the change, this also includes you, the worker. Working with other people is the beginning of change.

Establishing the group is the first step. As skills of working together become familiar, people begin to appreciate what can be achieved collectively, and more ambitious ventures can be planned. In every step of this work be aware of finding a balance of involvement of people having the time and energy and being safe enough to participate, while slowing down those who feel they have 'the answer'. In this respect there is often a period of personal change, of gaining the skills and confidence to enter a more public arena. This investment needs to be recognised as important, but not an end stage. Change ourselves and others can work with us differently.

While the initial group may not include a great diversity of people, it is still a beginning. Once skills are learned locally, the original group can include new people in particular those whose views are often excluded from public decision-making. The first group is encouraged to work through the strategies of Collaborative Engagement in the kit, to experience these ways of working and become confident in the outcomes prior to involving a new circle of people.

3. COMMUNITY DEVELOPMENT WORKERS ROLE

The role of the community development worker is to encourage and support people with an interest in the future of their community come together. The worker will need to explore means of communication that work for people and be flexible in this regard. You cannot predetermine the direction the group will take, but divisions within communities have a chance of being overcome if people begin to talk and hear each other.

The difficult task is to find a balance between support and direction. Adult learning educator, Jane Vella (2002) reminds us 'that we cannot learn for someone else' but we can design educational processes that respect the learner and their situation. Vella speaks of this as the dynamic tension of being decision maker and a dynamic listener (Vella: 2002:34) based in processes that factor in what the learner needs to know, informed by conversation and research. Think back to the analogy with parenting. The goal is to provide a space within the community for people to speak and listen to each other, to learn the skills of working and planning together. This will take practice and will go through some rough spots because it is about change.

It is a leap into the unknown as you begin this journey with each new group. You are privileged to be part of the process and to assist those involved stay on track, to learn skills they can use in diverse situations. The guidelines in the study circle offer a shared reference point that moves away from personalizing communication styles. Vella's 12 points of adult learning also provide a reflective tool.

In talking with people, listen to what they are talking about. It may concern their children, their lifestyle, the lack of work, the cricket club amalgamation, their concern over the river, the coast eroding, and fear of climate change. It may be profound grief or a general unease with how isolated they feel. The important response here is to assure the person that their concern is legitimate to bring to the gathering, that their involvement is valued. The work of Fran Peavey (1993) in *Strategic Questioning* and Jane Vella, (2002) in *Learning to Listen, Learning to Teach* are foundational to this process.

Some people will be tentative. They will need to speak of situations they have found difficult to deal with, there may be anger, frustration and sadness. It is a time of listening, of

In talking with people, listen to what they are talking about.

acknowledging the pain of hurtful or stupid decisions impacting on people's lives, or the pleasure when positive action has been taken. This is about acknowledging the reality of people's lives in a safe public forum.

Beginning with small manageable decisions invites the creation of relationships around low risk situations. At the first gathering people are invited to agree on a suitable time and location.

Asking what suits people affirms that involvement by a particular person is welcomed and valued. This step also provides an experience of decision making where all people are included in the process.

In our communities we generally tend to go to meetings with only one sector: the business association, the environment group, the church community, the school community, the sporting community, the senior citizens, the new mothers. This is an opportunity to interact between different interests and groups. Remember there may be some anxiety about this arrangement if there have been past divisions in the geographic community.

The ideal of involving many different groups is important to keep in mind. It is the goal of social justice (a guiding flag). In reality old hurts and lack of confidence will not be overcome overnight. As the community development worker you can invite, and encourage while respecting the choice of people to participate, and to allocate time according to their priorities.

Think about how you would provide an environment similar to in your home to ensure people felt relaxed and welcome. As organiser of the first gathering you may provide food and drink, and discuss how this might be continued at future meetings if this helps people juggle their time and commitments. The study circle kit recommends some points to consider when deciding on a venue and time, you may like to refer to these.

The environment facilitates dialogue: talking and listening between people with different worldviews and different life experiences. For anyone who has been involved with the reconciliation study circle you will have experienced the powerful changes that can occur in your thinking when new ways of understanding the world are shared. New experiences and new values become apparent, as we start to expand our understanding.

In your journal keep a record of the beginning of each group and you will become more aware of the importance of this first encounter. Important indicators of the safety of the group are laughter and people returning to the next session.

Questions

Consider how the group will be publicised?

What networks will be used? How could this be extended?

Are you aware of barriers that may limit participation?

How could you take steps to overcome this situation?

Important indicators of the safety of the group are laughter and people returning to the next session.

4. SAME BUT DIFFERENT

We all start as strangers and in uncertain times, kindness connects us all.
(Deborah Bird Rose, 1997).

'Same but Different' sounds a contradiction, however those who work through the kit will find that despite having different life experiences, and different ways of dealing with issues, they may also have a great deal in common. Each person can contribute a different 'piece' towards a more informed understanding of a given situation. From this wider pool of skills, resources and knowledge opportunities for change begin to become evident. As they work together, discussing, sharing ideas, information and experiences, connections become evident.

Each person can contribute a different 'piece'

In chapter 1 the power of language to create connections or divisions was introduced in regard to rural and urban relationships. In this chapter you are invited to consider ways the impact of labels that define someone as 'different' translates into categories of inferior and superior and how this is internalised publically and personally. The reality for many people is an overlapping multiplicity of barriers created by divisions Deborah Bird Rose refers to as 'a matrix of multiple hierarchical oppositions or absences (them and us) that provide powerful tools for oppression' (1997:2). Dualities of man/woman, culture/nature, mind/body, active/passive, civilization/wilderness [urban/rural, young/old, private/public, black/white] creates a pervasive and destructive framework.

Explore the history of any sector categorized as 'other'

The outcome is a pyramid, with at its peak an elite with life experiences limited to those of white, male, privileged, Western educated and wealthy with an expanding base of people with diverse life experiences excluded from decision making that impacts on their lives. Explore the history of any sector categorized as 'other' to find out if this status extends to legislation that ensures benefits flow to the powerful group at the expense of the 'other'. The lack of ability to participate removes the rich diverse knowledge and life experiences of many groups from the public arena. Aboriginal singer songwriter Kev Carmody encouraged people to find connection across the divisions of black, green and red (https://www.kevcarmody.com.au/) to be many voices together. This wisdom would greatly enhance our society's ability to work in inclusive and realistic ways in the implementation of planning and policy towards vibrant and sustainable communities.

Matrix of multiple absence

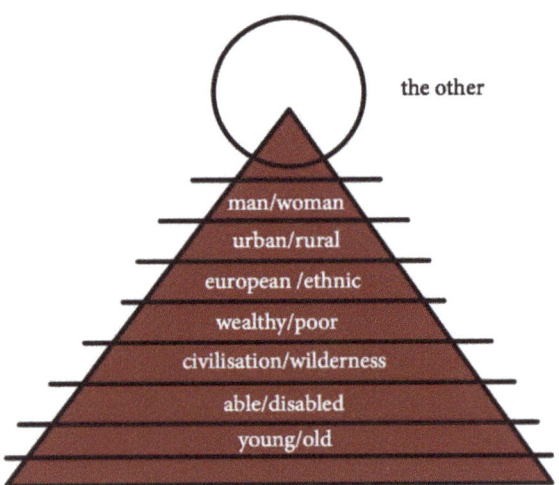

© Deborah Bird Rose 1997

This manual introduces the theory and practice of strategies that facilitate potential connections and minimises divisions. The process breaks down barriers of hierarchy that are destructive of new relationships being established and greater understanding of the importance of diversity and interdependence.

This extract is a story of one women making connections across nations when she attended the 2nd International Women and Agriculture Conference in Washington in 1998.

No longer involved with cropping, I was only slightly aware of the debate about the gene manipulation of grain seeds. The anger and frustration aimed at western chemical and/or seed companies by Iranian (and other emerging nations) women surprised me. These women felt that the seed gene manipulation was endangering their role as producers and providers of food for their families. Since the new seed are hybrids, the women were no longer able to save the seed from one harvest to the next. As well, modern intensive farming practices were depriving them of their role in the traditional family circle. If we find it difficult to keep up with today's technologies, how must these women feel? In this new global economy, the concerns of all the nations need to be understood and taken into account. Unexpected findings like these are probably the most important part of international conferences for the people attending.
(Walcott, 1998:32)

Through the use of technology and networking women made alliances between nations. Despite being from different countries, as rural women they shared the same concerns and sense of responsibility; to family, to community and to sustainable industry.

Questions

When we use the word 'different' what do we mean?

Think about this for a moment.

If you are asked, Why is this project for rural communities and how are they different?

Consider how you respond to this question, and what happens in the process?

How do you feel when this happens?

Are you aware of any long term implications?

5. OPPORTUNITIES TO LEARN TOGETHER – UNPACKING THE MYTHS (LIES)

The facilitator's role is to initiate opportunities for people in different community groups to meet. This section encourages recognition of the importance of providing 'a space' for people with different experiences and backgrounds to meet and explore experiences as equals.

Each group is important, but there will be little opportunity for change if they remain separate.

Each group is important, but there will be little opportunity for change if they remain separate. Many rural communities have become smaller, kindergartens, schools and churches closed. In some even the hotel. The result can be that resources and interaction between groups and families becomes minimal. Communities fail to thrive if there are not occasions to interact. Sadly the COVID pandemic further limited interaction.

Some communities stepped up and maintained connections via zoom or other social platforms, other communities initiated local newsletters such as Wairewa Grapevine https://www.facebook.com/ABCGippsland/posts/10158121837829825?comment_id=10158123923524825 and Lake Tyers Beach newsletter. https://drive.google.com/.../1xcXGQFmxpiMQYealD3S/view

What opportunities are we missing when we only talk with likeminded people?

Talking to, and about oneself is termed a monologue and is not the source of change

Our politicians are frequently accused of only talking within their own circles, or as some writers have described it 'talking to their own reflections in the mirror' (Brady 1994 and Rose 1997). Talking to, and about oneself is termed a monologue and is not the source of change. When we provide opportunity for people with different backgrounds to come together there is a chance for discussion between people, an opportunity to broaden or reaffirm our thoughts on an issue, to change. Just as rural people know they have important knowledge and contributions to make, there will be other groups with equally valuable wisdom. This is the purpose of dialogue: discussion between groups of people.

Projects designed with Collaborative Engagement strategies provide a forum for dialogue with people participating by choice. This experiential process raises awareness of conditions that facilitate people working constructively together.

Questions

In your community list the groups you normally interact with.

Are these people who think like you?

Who have life experiences similar to yours?

Are you aware of events that supported your involvement with a wider group of people?

How did this change your understanding of their lifestyle?

Are you aware of other situations where constructive connections across difference have been made?

6. RESILIENT COMMUNITIES: A DYNAMIC QUALITY

In Building Community futures through Co-operation (Sheil, 2015) Section 4, attention is focused on democratic group processes that welcome difference and clear communication. Shared roles increase the resilience of a group. Dependency on one individual can become burdensome for that person and in time limiting. Issues such as determining the agenda, sufficient consensus decision making, taking care of business and stories of partnerships can be shared clear processes lead to trust. Trust is an essential foundation of resilient communities, particularly leading up to, during and recovering from disasters. Partnerships established prior to disasters establish this trusted foundation.

Dependency on one individual can become burdensome for that person and in time limiting.

The following stories are of community initiated change resulting in new partnerships. While adversity often triggers new ways of working, operating from such stressful situations comes at a huge personal cost that is minimized when there is an investment in incorporates local knowledge and ownership prior to disasters.

The Bendigo Community Bank model was conceived in the late 1990s in response to a series of bank branch closures in rural Australia. Between 1993 and 2000 over 2,000 bank branches had closed across the country as government services and

utilities were consolidated and/or privatized, and businesses in turn abandoned these increasingly economically challenged communities. Alarmed by the closure of their banks and the impact on local economies people began to explore options to have financial services that reinvested in their communities rather than stripping assets.

The model is giving local leaders the skills the business acumen, and the confidence

Bendigo Bank also viewed this centralization of government and business with alarm, as it lowered the resilience of both the local and national economy and arguably the banking industry as well http://fieldguide.capitalinstitute.org/bendigo-community-bank-model-part-one.html Bendigo Bank sensed this was an opportunity to establish a viable partnership were both profits and losses were shared.

To address the economic decline many communities were experiencing, it was agreed a percentage of each Community Bank Branches profits, would be allocated on a permanent basis to community directed grant-making. Initially a challenging concept, Mike Hirst the CEO of Bendigo Bank soon realised that *sharing the revenue with the community was the very thing that was driving the engagement.*

Follow the development of this initiative and the potential of this model that involves 2000 directors, 1600 staff, 60,000 shareholders, and a couple of hundred thousand customers networked, 'The model is giving local leaders the skills the business acumen, and the confidence they will need to support their communities transition to a regenerative economy'. (Sam Moore: head of Bendigo Bank's Community Branch 2015).

Partnerships and hope from unexpected sources

The Black Summer fires of 19/20 will forever be remembered as a choking inferno that decimated wildlife, homes and lives.
'Fired up' pays homage to the spirit of resilient nation and celebrates those times where help arrives when you least expect it from a mate you've never met.
https://en.wikipedia.org/wiki/2019%E2%80%9320_Australian_bushfire_season

In 2019-2020 in south east Australia communities were severely impacted by 3 year drought leading to devastatingly hot fires that burned long and hot. These 'unprecedentedly hot fires' enveloped communities in smoke for months, 5,900 buildings (including 2,779 homes), 34 humans and habitat of an estimated

3 billion reptiles, marsupials and birds. 80% of Australians were impacted and an estimated 306 million tons of carbon emitted, that has global implications (Wikipedia 2020). The pandemic restrictions associated with COVID that began in early 2020 and subsequent lockdown (if you had a home) added another layer of complexity and isolation. Grief for the massive loss of life human and other species continues. https://en.wikipedia.org/wiki/2019%E2%80%9320_Australian_bushfire_season

The Islamic community from Melbourne responded by coming to East Gippsland with food and cooked for fire fighters and community members in many small communities. In Bairnsdale a local Indian restaurant and the Bairnsdale Neighbourhood House opened their kitchens and worked with the Sikhs providing food to families who had evacuated.

In just seven days since the New Year's Eve, 35-year-old Sukhwinder Kaur has cooked thousands of meals for bushfire victims of East Gippsland.

Initially, we had up to a hundred people coming to our food van but in the last three-four days, there are many more people who have been evacuated from their homes are coming to have a meal. So, these days, we are preparing up to a thousand meals every day," Ms Kaur told SBS Punjabi. "The day starts at about 5 am and I am cooking until 11 in night. There's a lot of work that is done between a small team of four people in the kitchen. And I have my room right next to the kitchen where I sleep, (spoken in Punjabi but with insightful photos and English text).
https://www.sbs.com.au/language/english/audio/we-are-a-big-family-meet-the-woman-cooking-thousands-of-meals-for-bushfire-victims?

Communities became stronger, as people worked together with a common goal.

In the process friendships are renewed or made, alliances established, old prejudices diminished. Communities became stronger, as people worked together with a common goal. While not advocating a crisis, for this never comes without a high cost, the opportunities for change that emerge when local people are motivated to work together is evident.

In New South Wales and Victorian community's relationships continue with the Sikh communities returning with Christmas gifts and to share food again for the screening of 'Fired Up' https://www.crisconsortium.org/new-events/fired-up-short-film-and-photographic-exhibition

Sarsfield Lucas Mill Partnership builds hope for landholders

The idea of local farmer, Ingrid Biram, with the guidance and suggestion of farmer and friend, Bill Higgins, set in motion a positive project taken on by local Lions and Rotary clubs, working together to deliver a new and practical on-farm timber milling business for farmers who have fallen timber on their properties and no fences due to the 2020 bushfires.

The Lucas Mill demonstration on launch day last Friday at the Biram family farm at Sarsfield. The mill operators were Mark Biram and his son, Jarrod.
https://www.youtube.com/watch?v=3g_B-ckY5aw

Sarsfield is an East Gippsland community severely impacted by the fires. Homes, farms and businesses were burnt and landscapes, domestic animals and wildlife devastated. Families worked hard to protect houses, but fences and sheds burnt.

Partnerships came from urban and rural service clubs, government departments and local businesses. The community owned Lucas Timber Mill Project not only created partnerships between local Rotary and Lions Clubs for the first time, but urban and rural Lions and Rotary Clubs. A home recorded video East Gippsland Timber Mill Project gives insight into the myriad of partnerships that brought this project to life and ensure its continuation https://www.facebook.com/watch/live/?v=243190260871592&ref=watch_permalink

The community initiative enabled local service clubs, urban service clubs, TAFE, local government Department of Environment, Land, Water and Planning, Bushfire Recovery Victoria, National Recovery and Resilience agency, the creators of the Lucas Mill, local businesses to create a functional practical and emotional resource. The teams cutting timber on the farms are hearing the difficult stories of the impact of the drought, fires and the isolation of COVID. Stories that may lead to insights on how to live on this land.

By 2021 the project has grown to 2 mills, 2 trailers, 2, 4 wheel drives and 2 teams. There is a need for ongoing support for the management team, the Lucas Mill operators and the farmers. It may lead to new partnerships.
https://www.communitybushfireconnection.com.au/sarsfield-portable-lucas-mill-partnership-rebuilds-farms-post-bushfire/

A challenge in this work is to support collaboration in planning community futures prior to the trauma of flood, fire, drought, and closure of services, loss of employment and de-regulation of industry or any one of the other many changes impacting on remote, rural and regional communities. Community involvement in preparation saves human and financial costs of appeals, campaigns as well as in recovery, human trauma and landscape devastation.

Community involvement in preparation saves human and financial costs of appeals, campaigns as well as in recovery, human trauma and landscape devastation.

Questions

Are you aware of a crisis within your own community that motivated people to work together?

How did people respond to this loss/change?

Are you aware of changed relationships and language in this process?

7. WHY AND HOW PEOPLE CHANGE

While it is not possible to impose motivation, workers can be alert to interest in bringing about change. The nature of the change is often initially undefined, rather a general unease between what local people value and what public policies advocate. As people speak of these issues and seek further information the process of owning change rather than being a silent recipient has begun.

There is a myth that if sufficient information is targeted at a group, people will change their behavior. In reality, there may be an information overload. As far back as 1993 Neil Postman named the era as *'The Age of Information'*, (Postman, 1993) predicting that the amount of information available would double every five years. With current access to multiple media platforms, some conveying 'fake news' the need to retreat from a barrage of information has increased. This excess of information brings its own problems, and people will require new skills. To find their way through conflicting reports and documentation produced by groups with very different agendas.

Information is an important ingredient of change, but consideration of how and when people are motivated to access information, and ways to strengthen these processes are key areas of learning. Involving people is a critical factor to engage with their circumstances. Beginning within our communities and providing opportunity for respectful

There is a myth that if sufficient information is targeted at a group, people will change their behavior.

Exercise on Water Use and Access

The issue of water use, access, cost, quality and quantity has become increasingly important as demand for water increases at the same time as contamination through toxic algae blooms, salinity, sediment, or drought and floods is increasing along with the sale of water not associated to land.

For many people access to good quality water has been a given, a right not a responsibility and bringing about change in this attitude is a major challenge.

Questions

When do we pay attention to our use of water for domestic, commercial, or recreational activities?

Who is responsible for water access, cost, quality and quantity?

Are you aware of criteria on which policies for use of water are determined?

What are the ways the authorities with responsibility for managing water bring our attention to the need to use water wisely?

How effective are these strategies, and do they bring about long term change?

Who are these strategies targeted at?

Can you think of strategies that may result in a different approach to the way we think about our use of water?

Ideas for how change occurs will build on the earlier section of our experiences of change. Are you aware of common themes developing in relation to positive change and the ability to initiate change for the long term?

8. REFRAMING THROUGH LEGISLATION AND POLICY

> Bhutan's green strategy? Trees. It has broken world records for tree planting. Its constitution also protects 60% of land as forest. The result: 7m tons of CO_2 absorbed every year versus 2m tons generated. It also exports most of its hydro-electric power, slashing net emissions further. A country-sized carbon sink!

In these critical times of climate change and growing awareness of the ongoing trauma from colonization groups seeking change are using legislative frameworks to shift entrenched and powerful attitudes and practices.

Legal frameworks challenging assumed right include:

The Mabo Case

The Mabo Case was a significant legal case in Australia that recognized the land rights of the Meriam people, traditional owners of the Murray Islands in the Torres Strait. Lodged in 1982 the legal proceedings gives insight into the threats perceived by some groups and their manipulation of the law to block change.

The five Meriam people who mounted the case were Eddie Koiki Mabo, Reverend David Passi, Sam Passi, James Rice and one Meriam women, Celuia Mapo Sale. Eddie Koiki Mabo was the first named plaintiff and the case became known as the Mabo Case. It was was successful in overturning the myth that at the time of colonisation Australia was 'terra nullius' or land belonging to no one. The High Court recognised the fact that Indigenous peoples had lived in Australia for thousands of years and enjoyed rights to their land according to their own laws and customs. Twelve months later the Native Title Act 1993 was passed.

This opened the way for claims by Aboriginal and Torres Strait Islander peoples to their traditional rights to land and compensation. https://aiatsis.gov.au/explore/mabo-case

Rights of Nature

Rights of nature would bring Australian law more into line with Indigenous lore in regards to our relationship with the natural world. https://www.abc.net.au/news/science/2019-03-16/rights-of-nature-science/10899778

Within communities you will encounter a great diversity of situations. This is the complexity of inter-connecting human life, just as in nature, resilience comes from dynamic and diverse interaction rather than static qualities dominated by a single interest or attribute.

The Rights of Nature movement is a legislative approach that recognizes the health of a regional catchment as a legal entity, existing for itself

The Rights of Nature movement is a legislative approach that recognizes the health of a regional catchment as a legal entity, existing for itself https://www.earthlaws.rg.au/what-is-earth-jurispudence/rights-of-nature.

From a rights of nature perspective, most environmental laws of the twentieth century are based on a framework that considers nature to be composed of separate and independent parts, rather than components of a larger whole. A more significant criticism is that those laws tend to be subordinate to economic interests, and aim at reacting to and just partially mitigating economics-driven degradation, rather than placing nature's right to thrive as the primary goal of those laws.

This critique of existing environmental laws is an important component of tactics such as climate change litigation that seeks to force societal action to mitigate climate change Wikipedia

There is a growing interest in forums and treaties to reframe thinking towards a scale of social development guided by ecological balance. In Indigenous cultures knowledge of 'country' is a constant guide and reference point for life.

New Zealand is amongst a growing list of countries that have recognised the rights of rivers. A regional chapter of International Rights of Nature Tribunal is working with concerned people on the Great Barrier Reef. The International

Association of Earth Laws Alliance has an active Australian presence in Australian Earth Laws Alliance (AELA) since 2016 www.earthlaws.org.au

The Australian Earth Laws Alliance and global initiatives such as New Zealand's parliament passed a bill declaring the Whanganui River system a legal person with 'all the rights, powers, duties and responsibilities of a legal person'. In 2017, 'Te Awa Tupua is an indivisible and living whole, comprising the Whanganui River from the mountains to the sea, incorporating all its physical and metaphysical elements,' a parliamentary statement said at the time. As part of that ruling, a $NZ30 million dollar contestable fund was set up that could be used to advance the restoration and health of the river. A Bolivian law from 2012 recognised the 'rights of Mother Earth to life, diversity, water, clear air and restoration'. High Courts in India, Colombia and Bangladesh have all recognised natural assets as legal entities in cases in the last 12 months, according to Michelle Maloney, a lawyer and co-founder of the Australian Earth Laws Alliance (op.cit abc 2019).

Failure of Duty of care – from young people

A landmark class action launched by school students advocating for government responsibility on climate change has resulted in a federal court judgment that the federal environment minister has a duty of care not to cause them harm from climate change.

It's a unique case that claimed that the government would be in breach of its duty of care to protect young people from the impacts of climate change if it approved more coal mining. The proposal for the Vickery Mine, owned by Whitehaven Coal, would see a 25% expansion in the amount of coal extracted from its site if it's approved. That extension alone would result in 100 million tonnes of carbon emissions over the next 25 years, equivalent to about 20% of Australia's total domestic emissions from 2019.

In his judgment, Bromberg said the evidence presented to the court showed the potential harm the children could face due to global heating 'may fairly be described as catastrophic, particularly should global average surface temperatures rise to and exceed 3C beyond the pre-industrial level'.

'rights of Mother Earth to life, diversity, water, clear air and restoration'.

'Perhaps the most startling of the potential harms demonstrated by the evidence before the court, is that one million of today's Australian children are expected to suffer at least one heat-stress episode serious enough to require acute care in a hospital,' he said.

'Many thousands will suffer premature death from heat stress or bushfire smoke. Substantial economic loss and property damage will be experienced. The Great Barrier Reef and most of Australia's eastern eucalypt forests will no longer exist due to repeated, severe bushfires.'

Bromberg found that the minister had a common law duty to take reasonable care not to cause the children personal injury when using her powers under the Environment Protection and Biodiversity Conservation (EPBC) Act. {Currently under review 2021}

https://junkee.com/teens-government-climate-change/296232

Questions

Have you encountered the repeal of legislation that previously limited participation in workforce, political systems, land ownership, careers or relationships?

What changes occurred in language and understanding and opportunities and for whom?

In regard to policy – these legal frameworks provide a guide for local and state governments to implement policy frameworks in accordance with the legislation.

Give examples of policy frameworks that provide levers for change in relation to your sector.

FURTHER REFERENCES

Eversole, R., (2015) *Knowledge partnering for community development*, Routledge, London and New York.

Foley, G., (1999) *Learning in Social Action: A contribution to Understanding Informal Education*. London. Zed Books.

Foley, G., (May 2021) *Information on Black Australia's 240 year struggle for justice*, Koorie History Website http://www.kooriweb.org/foley/vids/history_clips.html (Koorie.web.org)

Harper, H., (May 2021) *Life Matters: Putting women on the map – interview* You might be hard pressed to think of a street or a place named after a woman.

Mallacoota and District Recovery Association Inc. Community Led Recovery: Webinars on Fuel Management (May 2021) https://madrecovery.com

Peavey, F. & Hutchinson, V. 1993 *'Strategic Questioning for Personal and Social Change'*. San Francisco, C.A.

Ramos, J., (2023) 'How could one bring futures to life?' in *Futures bought to life. We are no futurists*, Times Up, University of Applied Arts, Vienna. https:timesup.org/publications

Sheilds, K., (2000) *In the Tiger's Mouth. An empowerment guide for social action.'* Maleny, Qld. (Chapter 5. Listening for Change)

Vella, J. (2002) *Learning to Listen, Learning to Teach: the power of dialogue in educating adults*, Jossey-Bass, San Francisco.

CHAPTER 3

• CHAPTER 3 •
SAFETY AND RESPECT

SAFETY AND RESPECT

Human scale development…focuses on development by the people and for the people and is founded upon three pillars: fundamental human needs, increasing self-reliance and a balanced interdependence of people with their environment.
(Manfred Maz Neef – Wikipedia accessed May, 2021)

FOCUS OF THIS CHAPTER

1. Principles of regional development as if communities really mattered
2. Involvement and participation
3. Safety
4. Practice and reflection
5. Healing divisions and damage

   Further references

INTRODUCTION

A community development approach invests in re-integrating local knowledge into public planning. It is multi-layered, inviting involvement from people with diverse life experiences raising awareness of opportunities for partnerships with relevant organisations. Within communities this begins with facilitating processes for mature discussion and tolerance of different views. It is a shift *towards human scale organisations that invite involvement rather than gigantic systems hierarchically organised where decisions flow from the top to the bottom and screen out feedback is a critical requirement* (MaxNeef, 1991:8).

A transition from our current culture of competitiveness and hierarchical decision making towards partnerships requires an openness to consider mutual benefits. Providing an environment for these changes to occur, and for those involved to experience the opportunities for personal and community growth contributes to this change. It can be an emotional liberating journey. Anticipate challenges along the way, both for those new

to public involvement as well as those in power positions moving into new situations that reduce dependency on a few individuals.

1. PRINCIPLES FOR REGIONAL COMMUNITY DEVELOPMENT

Principles underpinning this work are that:

- the learning of rural and regional people should be affirmed, acknowledged and legitimised,
- rural and regional people have a knowledge and relationship to the places in which they live,
- shared learning is empowering,
- shared learning within communities has the capacity to reintegrate knowledge,
- the reintegration of this knowledge is critical in the healthy development of resilient regions.
- rural and regional people should have support for, and control over their learning.

(Beth Randell's framework for working with rural women 1995).

The content, direction and speed of learning are determined within each group

These principles frame the content and design of the *'Building Community Futures through Co-operation'* study circle kit (2015), and this professional development manual. The kit and manual provide basic resources to foster access to learning located in communities. The content, direction and speed of learning are determined within each group ensuring immediate relevance and local ownership of decisions. Facilitation of community engagement creates a democratic foundation enabling people to plan for the long term. From this basis, relationships with central organisations begin to transition from directing and regulating community life to resourcing relevant partnerships.

People in rural communities understand that they will not be rescued by government, or by industry or corporations, but rather through their own efforts in partnerships with relevant organisations. These changing boundaries require access to learning, resources, skills and knowledge.

Facilitating community forums that enable the reality of rural and regional situations to be understood, rather than through an urban lens changes conversations. In relation to disaster preparation, engagement and recovery, stories in 'the kit' share examples of the value of investment at a local level.

The experience of the *East Gippsland Building Community Resilience* project was that collaborative approaches led to improved communication and increased trust. Agency workers welcomed participating in forums that were not adversarial, where they could actively share knowledge and resources. Everyone learnt of local landscapes, resources and changing conditions. The skills, knowledge and experience to become involved in this process may not previously have been experienced. They require time and practice for confidence with this way of working to respect community led change to evolve.

The examples indicate the potential for rural and regional development if organised communities are involved in decision-making. Mallacoota Community Led Recovery gives insight into this journey https://madrecovery.com/ People's republic of Mallacoota (ABC TV and IVIEW)

Rural communities are as diverse as their geographic base. Collaborative engagement does not prescribe solutions. It {Collaborative engagement} facilitates a process and access to skill development for community members motivated to work towards a sustainable future. The starting point is to establish a local forum where attention is paid to practice of working and making decisions together – not to isolate and divide but to find points of connection. Decisions can be made that include considerations for social, cultural, environmental and long term economic decisions, rather than those motivated by distant share-holders profits that have collectively impacted so harshly on rural and remote populations and landscapes.

It {Collaborative engagement} facilitates a process and access to skill development for community members

Task

You may find it useful to refer to these principles as you begin the practical work of engaging with community members. In your journal record the indicators of changing confidence evident by increasing ownership of agendas from within community. This could include the following discussion points.

What occurred when community members were affirmed and acknowledged as important when they spoke of issues and concerns of local significance?

What occurred when community members were able to determine the content and direction of their learning?

How did study circle members include local knowledge of environment and social culture into their long-term decisions?

What opportunities for action and increased understanding became evident through shared learning?

Are you aware of instances where community members gained information and skills from a variety of sources/disciplines to tackle a local issue?

Are you able to identify new opportunities or actions that resulted from this process?

2. INVOLVEMENT AND PARTICIPATION

Collaborative engagement strategies create opportunities for community members to experience a forum which respects their right to speak of issues and concerns. A key underpinning is that this requires a reciprocal recognition that other people's experiences may be different. Especially following trauma this can be emotional and take time for people to hear each other in a thoughtful way. The critical element is the provision of a safe environment for people to begin to speak publicly, to be acknowledged and valued. Grief is ongoing and it can take time before people are able to function beyond their daily survival activities. Small projects that offer comfort and involvement can give people space to heal.

Everyday Democracy points out the importance of establishing ground rules based on small group democracy to ensure that all viewpoints are taken seriously, and each participant has an equal opportunity to participate. *(Everyday democracy – the toolkit and public dialogue sections)* https://www.pgexchange.org/index_option_com_content_view_article_id_149_Itemid_143.html

For some, the attention to process appears slow and tedious, as the potential outcomes have not been experienced. It is important to encourage community members to stay with the process and support skill development in order for changed understanding to occur. Taking turns to facilitate the group expands understanding, capacity and responsibility to act respectfully. This is a very different way of working that remains open ended, allowing the content to tap the motivation, energy and inspiration from within communities.

As they began to experience the benefits of respectful forums community member's attitudes shifted from despair and frustration to optimism and action. The transition takes time and continued attention to processes for involvement and participation in decision making.

> An example from *Building Community Futures through Co-operation* (2015). *The existence of community hubs meeting and planning for fire preparedness and recovery was new to many agencies and they initially attended public meetings apprehensively. In all situations staff consistently reported relief at a welcoming environment where they can share expertise on conditions, resources and developments while hearing community concerns.*
>
> *Community members welcomed the opportunity to raise concerns and receive prompt follow up and action. There is a growing awareness that similar concerns are experienced across the communities and the willingness to share information and ideas is well received. Discussion extended beyond questions of whether to burn, or not burn and agencies learned that many community members were unaware of meeting places, preparedness information or other information that was routine for those in the know. Embarrassingly, in some communities there was disagreement in where relief centres were and who was to trigger their opening and resourcing.*
>
> *It was not uncommon for the facilitators to be initially met with aggression at even being asked to the gathering turning into an apology, even a hug or tears at the end of a session. More people and agencies involved led to access to better resources such as maps and information, contacts and more informed preparation.* (EGBCR – notes and report 2015).

Questions

Can you list (3) three groups where your opinions have been overlooked or not asked for?

Could you list (3) three groups where you have felt valued and able to speak openly?

Are you aware of protocols that existed for the groups?

3. SAFETY

It is critical that all members experience a feeling of safety and respect within the group.

The emphasis on promoting discussion with equal involvement by all members of the group is a key strategy. Each group is invited to establish procedures, and agree to the way it will operate, the location, time and frequency of meeting. This begins the process of including everyone in decision making without high stakes being involved. At this stage the work is based on skill development and establishing respect and involvement.

The requirement to listen and respect those with different experiences establishes a safe environment for people to speak publicly of issues previously only thought about privately. Personal development is facilitated through language. As each person speaks and is affirmed, they are on an intellectual and emotional pathway that encourages tolerance and capacity to understand difference without diminishing individuals. It is personal development within a nurturing community.

Continued attention to include and listen to all members of the group provides a forum to hear from people whose life experience originate from vastly different circumstances. For larger gatherings of people this can be achieved by breaking into smaller groups. It is not required that people agree with each other, but that they will listen and attempt to understand how this view came about. Respect will lead to relationships developing on many different levels.

Each group is invited to establish procedures, and agree to the way it will operate, the location, time and frequency of meeting.

Personal development is facilitated through language.

Not only will people's life experiences be different, but their experience of being able to influence public decision-making will also vary. Action is not the intended outcome at this stage, but the creation of inclusive and respectful ways of working. The provision of a forum and the process of inclusion for interaction between groups breaks down isolation within and between communities.

The approach require a series of meetings, recognising that it takes time to change attitudes, and to develop new understanding of how to work collaboratively. Opportunities for change from on-going dialogue is very different to the one-off consultations; surveys, submissions or public-meetings where information may be sought but relationships rarely alter. Public meetings may provide good networking opportunities, but rarely involve hearing equally from those traditionally outside the decision making process. The ownership, outcomes and opportunities for change are limited in such arrangements. Frequently it is still the people with the loudest voice, the ability to speak convincingly, to present 'research' rather than share experiences that has space at such an event. Involvement by those traditionally marginalised holds a significant stress and risk factor within many communities.

Many of you will have either personally experienced, or witnessed such processes

Many of you will have either personally experienced, or witnessed such processes, entered into with hope and commitment, only to once again be ignored or be regarded as outside the legitimate terms of reference. The process offered here has the potential for positive and liberating outcomes.

Questions

Have you been involved in groups that established ground rules for involvement?

How were the rules established?

What were the guide lines and how where they negotiated?

How useful did you find these guide lines in the functioning and operation of the group?

Are you aware of divisions within your own community in regard to those who are regarded as legitimate public-decision makers, and those who are overlooked?

How have people responded to this situation?

What change occurred?

Group members become aware of the need to include others and not dominate.

4. PRACTICE AND REFLECTION

The word praxis is the Greek word for theory and practice. The study circle approach encourages community members to rotate positions of responsibility. Sharing roles puts the theory of working democratically into practice, in a safe and supported environment. As each person has responsibility for chairing meetings, they become more familiar with the skills required to encourage and respect involvement by all members. The rotation of responsibilities reinforces the understanding of the group being strong because of the involvement of all members, rather than one leader with particular expertise.

The experience raises awareness of the skills and processes of constructive and satisfying meetings: such as being prepared for meetings, speaking publicly, organising the time available. Group members become aware of the need to include others and not dominate. These are all skills that require practice and a supportive environment to enable people to venture into this activity, some for the first time. Regular sessions provide opportunity for reflection on positive strategies, as well as times of disorganisation and frustration. All are opportunities to reflect and learn.

Following the Delburn Fires that impacted on the Boolarra community in 2009 study circle participants from 4 study circles facilitated by community members applied their knowledge of democratic decision making to local and regional events, openly, confidently, and with the support of their communities. They had developed respected relationships with local and state government departments and agencies enabling recovery to be targeted at existing or agreed upon ventures. Frustration was minimal and trauma reduced (Smith and Sheil, 2006).

Following the traumatically hot dry summer and multiple fires begun by arson destroying 29 homes the Boolarra community voted to hold the Boolarra Folk Festival on March 2009. Photos from this event show people sitting together listening to music in the small strip of land in the centre of the town (old railway land) that is unburnt. It was a chance to sit, to take care of children and each other – to be together. Singing, massage, food and compassion were evident. People held each other, taking time out from the tasks that faced them. For up to date information on Boolarra go to Boolarra Link http://www.boolarralink.org.au/http://www.boolarrafolkfestival.com.au/gallery-2/nggallery/thumbnails

Questions

In your role as community development worker what strategies would you engage in to contribute to a safe and respectful environment in which meaningful learning can occur?

List (5) five strategies, with examples.

5. HEALING DIVISIONS AND DAMAGE (BETWEEN PEOPLE, COMMUNITIES AND NATURE)

This is a gaping, festering wound at the heart of our democracy, and we will never succeed in building a democracy for the common good until we heal it. What's more, the more we learn about Aboriginal society, about their relationships with the land and with each other, their commons-based society, the more we find it has hugely important lessons for us today.
(Hollo, March 2018)

The imposition of competitive tendering by local, state and federal government and the sale of state infrastructure to corporations resulted in divisions among groups that traditionally co-operated and shared resources. Sub-regions and communities have competed with each other for public or private funding and facilities. The approach has damaged rather than strengthened community and regional relationships. Service providers in health and education have tendered against each other for scant resources causing ill will and lack

Sub-regions and communities have competed with each other for public or private funding and facilities.

of trust. Allocation of funding frequently favoured urban based providers with little knowledge or commitment to working with communities for which they received funding. The result has been distrust, isolation, and the loss of networks and reciprocal arrangements that facilitated access in rural communities.

In the context of current traumas from environmental, health and cultural disasters opportunities for people to meet together are critical. Gatherings begin the work of reuniting group**s** within the community that have become fractured through divisive practices embedded in political and social systems.

Past harm of individuals and the damage to communities needs to be acknowledged before constructive work can be entered into. The levels of stress and worker burnout are high. Work will need to progress at a pace, which recognising the internalisation of devaluing the involvement of rural people.

The solutions are not known in advance.

The solutions are not known in advance. Populations and landscapes are changing, requiring different approaches and partnerships to inform future actions. Safety in sharing is an important step in the process, the continued involvement and development of relationships.

A great lesson in the need for learning of the reality of people's lives comes through the memorable events of the reconciliation process. Aboriginal reconciliation involved 20 years of faith in the ability of ordinary people to learn of the history inflicted on indigenous people, of people sitting down together and talking as a means to implement change. https://issuu.com/reconciliationaustralia/docs/ra_newsletter_2021_issue_45_small/22

This was the approach taken in the consultative process that informs Uluru the statement from the heart. https://ulurustatement.org/our-story

While there is increasing access to the stories of harm and on-going impact through stories, songs and documentaries told by First Nation people, legislation to recognise the status of First Nation people remains in limbo.

The Uluru Statement from the Heart

There is a more encompassing life story emerging into the public arena in Australia at this time. A story many have dedicated their lives to listening to and documenting, to sharing publicly again and again. At the time of writing seven years after First Nations people met at the National Constitutional Convention in 2017, the incoming Prime Minister, Anthony Albanese endorsed the Uluru Statement from the Heart. In this conversation begun by First Nations people 'we are invited to walk with (us) in a movement of the Australian people for a better future'. https://ulurustatement.org/
https://ulurustatement.org/the-statement/view-the-statement

A voice to parliament is nothing new: it was first sought 89 years ago'

The response to this long and extensive engagement through the 2023 Referendum termed the Yes campaign and the Voice to Parliament was a divisive No from diverse sectors of the community. While there was a growing swell of support from non-indigenous people there were factors and factions that resulted in a defeat of the campaign. Analysis is valuable as ways forward are explored. Essayist Tony Wright, in an article titled, *A voice to parliament is nothing new: it was first sought 89 years ago* gives background and context to the campaign along with historical and political limitations in the public responses from those in positions of influence at the time https://www.caac.org.au/news/statement-on-the-result-of-the-referendum/

The Central Australian Aboriginal Congress released a statement expressing their disappointment stating, *Nevertheless, one thing remains certain: sooner or later the nation state must deal with the enduring fact of Aboriginal sovereignty.*

In the meantime, our struggle for equality, justice and self-determination will continue. https://www.caac.org.au/news/statement-on-the-result-of-the-referendum/

You are encouraged to find out more of the on-going discussion and actions on future actions for political recognition through Treaty or legislation that will bring Acknowledgement of Country and Welcome to Country into greater clarity and influence.

The following stories give insight into the consistent generosity evident from some most harmed. Change comes with acknowledgement and the growing wealth of songs and stories from those who were kept silenced changes our awareness.

Each educates.

The following stories give insight into the consistent generosity evident from some most harmed.

Mother Earth births everything for us. Father Sky carries the water and oxygen for us to breathe. Grandfather Sun warms the planet, warms our body, gives us light so we can see, raises the food that the Mother births and raises most of our relations, all our plants and trees. Grandmother Moon moves the water and gives us the woman-time and our birthing' Uncle Max Dulumunmun Harrison, Aboriginal elder of the Yuin people. 'My People's Dreaming' (2012)

Uncle Max also speaks of forgiveness in his approach to drawing attention to massacres and the need to heal the land. Smoking and healing ceremonies. https://reclaimkosci.org.au/2019/02/25/traditional-healing-ceremony-at-birth-place-of-the-murrumbidgee/

Alice Ann Pepper interview with Rachael Lucas ABC on FLOAT residency. https://ruralcommunities.com.au/listen-to-alice-ann-peppers-interview-with-abc-radio-gippsland/

Eileen Harrison and Carolyn Landon (2011) *Black Swan: a Koorie woman's life*, Allen and Unwin, NSW.

Archie Roach, https://www.youtube.com watch?v=UhSBHSuFNtU

Ziggy Ramo, Seizing his moment, Ziggy committed himself to educating through music, reworking the original with a new First Nations perspective on invasion, intergenerational trauma, lost history, and Indigenous deaths in custody. Channelling power, passion, and pain, by the end of the song, Ziggy was brought to tears. As Paulo Freire was aware the oppressor is also oppressed (Friere 2017). https://www.abc.net.au/triplej/news/musicnews/ziggy-ramo-paul-kelly-little-things-every-australian-should-hear/13366924

Kev Carmody and Paul Kelly wrote the legendary *From Little Things Big Things Grow* song to tell the Wave Hill story. https://www.youtube.com/watch?v=tbHR-apIHLU

The impact of imposed change in which those affected have no part, and takes no account of local culture and circumstances have common elements. The processes for change within this manual have been learnt from positive experiences of ordinary people who have reclaimed their right to be an active partner in determining their own futures.

Questions

Have you experienced the opportunity to speak publicly of issues about which you feel strongly? If so, what forum were you able to use?

Did this result in change?

For yourself?

For others?

FURTHER REFERENCES

Everyday Democracy: Toolkit
https://www.ala.org/tools/librariestransform/libraries-transforming-communities/everyday-democracy

Freire, P., and Bergman Ramos, M., (translator Donaldo Macedo) (2018) Pedagogy of the oppressed, 50th Anniversary edition, (audio book) or Penguin Modern Classics, UK (2017).

Hollo T., (2020) With the climate crisis and coronavirus bearing down on us, the age of disconnection is over, Guardian https://www.theguardian.com/commentisfree/2020/mar/28/with-the-climate-crisis-and-coronavirus-bearing-down-on-us-the-age-of-disconnection-is-over

Hollo, T., (2018) Tim Hollo on an ecological democracy where 'everything is connected' and embedded in nature. Fifth Estate. March 2018. https://thefifthestate.com.au/columns/spinifex/tim-hollo-on-an-ecological-democracy-where-everything-is-connected-and-embedded-in-nature/

Henningham Nikki et al. (2017) Update: *The Invisible Farmer: securing Australian farm women's history,* Australian Feminist Studies. Published online: 30 Aug.

Max-Neef, M., https://www.rightlivelihoodaward.org/laureates/manfred-max-neef/

Randell, Beth., *The Invisible Farmer* https://www.pressreader.com/australia/benalla-ensign/20170726/281479276480969 https://invisiblefarmer.net.au/

Vella, Jane (1997) *Learning to listen, Learning to Teach.* Jossey-Bass Publishers. San Francisco. California. Part one.

Wright, T., (2023, October 14,) *A voice to parliament is nothing new: it was first sought 86 years ago.* Sydney Morning Herald. smh.com.au/politics/federal/a-voice-to-parliament-is-nothing-new-it-was-first-sought-86-years-ago-20231010-p5eb68.html

Yulendj group - Bunjilaka - Museums Victoria https://museumsvictoria.com.au/bunjilaka/about-us/first-peoples/yulendj-group/

CHAPTER 4

• CHAPTER 4 •
(The Model)
COLLABORATIVE ENGAGEMENT FOR TRANSFORMATION
Goals and Implementation

The old answers will not do, because the old questions will not do. What new questions can we ask about being human, about human and non-human flourishing? Resilience, relinquishment and recovery (Bendall 2018). Resilience is about staying strong in facing our reality, relinquishment is about what we need to let go, and recovery is about what we need to draw from past experience (Ife: 2019:66).

FOCUS OF THIS CHAPTER

Strategies in Collaborative Engagement for Transformation

1. Dialogue
2   Time
3. Local Community Ownership
4. Visioning
5. Co-operative Culture
6. Networking
7. Action
8. Transformation
9. Reflection
    Further references

Paying attention to:

- what each strategy offers,
- how to implement each strategy,
- examples of outcomes,
- creating opportunities to invite involvement,
- contribution to personal and community change,
- your experiences.

The 'model' is a map,

The 'model' is a map, naming strategies on the journey of engagement. Each step introduces experiences that inform understanding of ourselves and the environments on which we depend. The loop of infinity represents the continuous nature of this journey, see graphic. In the current global environmental and humanitarian crisis community development theorist, Jim Ife notes the urgency of paying attention to the two biggest challenges of our time: assisting people to live and work together (social justice), so we can care for the places in which we live (ecological sustainability) (Ife 1995/2020).

These guiding goals are depicted as flags that keep thinking and practice on track. Ife acknowledges the scale of challenges and the increasing emphasis on community knowledge informing survival. The issues are urgent, complex and frequently involve difficult conversations.

assisting people to live and work together (social justice), so we can care for the places in which we live (ecological sustainability)

Within regions, communities will benefit from regional networks to share stories, resources and knowledge. Each episode of community engagement will expand understanding, contacts and resources. Collaborative engagement involves continuous dynamic relationships that evolve as we talk, building knowledge, initiating agreed upon action and reflecting on our individual and community experiences.

The following graphic *Collaborative engagement for transformation* provides a way to reflect on what we collectively know, to create processes that work for both people and the environment, not one at the expense of the other.

to create processes that work for both people and the environment,

The theoretical and practice elements of the model draw on skills and knowledge from adult education, community development and sustainable regional development. A brief rationale for each strategy is followed by ways to implement practice, then examples of outcomes.

Nine Steps of Transformative Engagement

© Sheil/Lorraine 2020
https://www.ruralcommunities.com.au

Checklist

Dialogue
Ask and Listen. Respect differences.
Support language development.
Find common ground.

Time
Invest time to: establish trusted relationships, facilitate personal and community development.

Local Community Ownership
Offer support not direction.
Nurture ownership of ideas relevant to place.

Co-operative Culture
Be open and generous.
Practice group participation skills.
Communicate clearly. Clarify roles.
The goal is mutual development.

Visioning
Create a safe environment.
Invite people to share their hopes and dreams. Visioning shapes future community planning.

Networking
Meet with other communities.
Use newsletters, internet and radio.
Invite decision makers to visit.

Action
Change requires action. Begin in small achievable ways. Celebrate milestones.
Take a break. Begin again.

Reflection
Evaluate constructively. Design before and after records (photos, stories, financial records, capital indicators).
Celebrate achievements. Tackle areas to improve. Evaluate both processes and outcomes.

Transformation
Is there new confidence and involvement? New language and stories? Both reshape future partnerships and opportunities.
What next? A rest, a new venture/partnership?

COLLABORATIVE ENGAGEMENT FOR TRANSFORMATION

1. DIALOGUE

Dia-means 'between' logos means 'word'.
(Vella. 1994 p3)

1.1 Rationale (Why)

Power lies in the ability not to hear what is being said, not to experience the consequences of one's actions, but rather to go one's own self-centric and insulated way.
(Rose-Bird, 2004:20)

Deborah Bird Rose writes of the damaging impact of only hearing and speaking with those who share a similar world view, of silencing all others. In order to know what is in the minds of people with whom you are meeting, engagement is carried on in conversations: dialogue. This is the opposite of monologue - one person usually the expert, bureaucrat or teacher passing on information from their perspective.

Despite good will, without dialogue opportunities for meaningful engagement that can lead to inclusion of local knowledge in regional development will be missed, often at significant cost to organisations and community members. In his work with Brazilian farm workers, adult educator, Paulo Freire (1972), came to understand the arrogance of imposing knowledge while failing to comprehend the lives of local people. Malcolm Knowles (1975, 2016) and Jane Vella both recognized that dialogue viewed 'learners as subjects in their own learning and honoured central principles such as mutual respect and open communication' (Vella, 2002, 2019).

learners as subjects in their own learning

The focus on dialogue provides opportunity for each person to speak, to craft words about their experiences, to place their own emphasis on events. Sharing as much, or as little, as they are currently able. In the process the realization that there are whole bodies of knowledge about which we know little, and that open our minds and hearts to a more expansive, connected understanding of balanced development may be triggered. When we listen to local conversations these expand beyond short term economics to include social, environmental, cultural, political, economic, personal and spiritual development (Ife 1995). Respectful dialogue can lead to local actions influencing global understanding and practice.

In this exchange:

- personal development is nurtured as people speak of the reality of their situations in public, facilitating personal growth and greater understanding,

- dialogue initiates a process of moving from marginalized silence to public involvement in decision making that impacts on our lives,

- the 'gift of listening' is given, as each person speaks the value of their involvement is affirmed,

- each person's contribution creates opportunitites for connections,

- a more informed understanding of a situation and the complexity of community life becomes evident,

- the process is rather like a jig-saw, with no two pieces being the same, yet each adding to a more complete picture of community life,

- diverse involvement reclaims legitimacy of all aspects of development,

- when there is awareness of issues, motivation to take action towards a long-term change is frequently established.

dialogue facilitated personal development

Research by Belenkey et al., (1986, 1997) came to an awareness that dialogue facilitated personal development as well as being essential to gain insight into the complexity of changing situations. In this time of constant crises, when agencies and communities are both struggling, respectful dialogue establishes a foundation that enables the limits and capacity of current situations to become evident. From this awareness informed action can be taken.

be mindful that not everyone enjoys reading

Indigenous writers on de-colonisation regard dialogue as a critical component of transforming relationships between Indigenous people and those who came to their countries (Tuhiwai Smith, 1999).

1.2 Implementation of dialogue (how)

*In both popular education and democracy, equality is fundamental.
Equality is at the heart of the matter of democracy.*
(Larson 2001:201).

The facilitator's role is to invite conversation and listen.

The principle underpinning this approach requires the facilitator to respect the knowledge and learning of local people. Jane Vella invites facilitators to be mindful of their own values, but to keep these tucked away in their pocket. The facilitator's role is to invite conversation and listen.

1.2.1 Establishing guiding principles takes practice. To create a lasting foundation, participants are invited to discuss the Study Circle Guidelines and from their experience nominate those they regard as important for their group (Sheil, 1998, 2015 https://ruralcommunities.com.au/publications/ Sec: 1.1-1.7). This introduces the experience of respectful participation within a safe environment. The study circle guidelines can be adapted for any group, putting into practice the adult learning principles of learning through involvement, action and reflection where all experiences are valued. Beginning by welcoming involvement conveys a sense of meaningful engagement and is different to lobby or action groups. Taking the time to engage contributes to moving from assumptions of how groups operate as well as establishing ways of dealing with people who become overly dominant or stuck. Invite people to keep a record of agreed upon steps for future reference.

As the facilitator, be mindful that not everyone enjoys reading, or has a common first language. If there is reluctance to read, give people time to speak and be heard then move on to the next person. Community members may question the relevance of investing (wasting) time in discussing how the group will work before knowing what the group will do. Invite them to be involved and at the close of the session ask for feedback on their experience. Remember, how we work will determine the outcomes. Valuing each person 'at the table' establishes the group culture.

The area of interest is agreed to by the group,

Study circles invite people with different life experiences to a shared table. By agreeing to listen to each other relationships can be radically altered as partnerships of interest are established. The area of interest is agreed to by the group, respecting that while people may disagree on some issues, they may also share common concerns. Study circles offer a foundation compatible with the goals of community development to take care of people (social justice) and the places (ecological sustainability) they live. The introduction gives a glimpse of the challenging and diverse situations that adopted this approach to transform difficult situations and to enhance the quality of life for all.

I was introduced to this inclusive approach through Aboriginal Reconciliation, and graduates of Graduate Certificate of Regional Community Development implemented the approach in their communities and workplaces to plan their futures in rural Victoria (Sheil 2000). People came together to protect waterways and to implement programs for young people, while they held very different views on forest and land management. It is an evolving process. In Sweden the Study Circle Association is extensive and study circles are used for cultural activities as well as integrating refugees into Swedish communities. In America, citizen movements challenged the status of African Americans. In the Basque region of Spain, the cycle of study, practice and reflection continues to inform worker-led co-operatives in Mondragon.

All are welcome at the table and will be listened to.

1.2.2 Affirming diversity. Sharing experiences gives insight into why a group member holds a particular view. Discussion may challenge the views held by some members, and affirm others. The consistent message is that all are welcome at the table and will be listened to.

In the study circle kit, stories provide examples of how different viewpoints were considered legitimate, reinforcing awareness that diversity is not only acceptable, but adds to the richness of community life.

1.2.3 Open-ended questions. Neil Postman recognizes the powerful contribution of questions to unpacking complexity of local situations *[Q]uestions we might say: are the principal intellectual instruments available to human beings* (Postman, 1995:173). By designing open-ended questions the facilitator is creating the opportunity for people to speak of the reality of their situation. Creating a safe space for people to speak of issues that have been unspoken or publicly silenced creates opportunities to broaden understanding and transform relationships.

1.2.4 Strategic Questioning

Strategic Questioning is a way of talking with people with whom you have differences without abandoning your own beliefs and yet looking for common ground which may enable both parties to co-create a new path from the present situation. In every heart there is ambiguity; in every ideology there are parts that don't fit.

(Peavey 2012)

http://www.cruxcatalyst.com/2012/05/21/strategic-questioning/

Fran Peavey (1986, 2012) recognized the transformative nature of strategic questioning as a catalyst for positive, locally owned change in her community work.

Strategic questioning facilitates movement.

Strategic questioning is a sequence of open-ended questions that facilitate and honour people speaking about their current situation and then invite consideration of ways to expand understanding and opportunities to transform distressing or dysfunctional situations. Strategic questioning facilitates movement. The questions do not have predetermined answers or limitations such as by requiring that it be strength or asset focused.

The following sequence of questions can be designed to explore any given situation. They begin with questions about people's current experiences inviting people to share either positive or negative experiences.

How do you feel about…. the current situation?

As people comment on how they feel, as well as what they know, different types of knowledge and ideas emerge. This exchange gives insight into circumstances that led up to a particular event for example drought, new licensing agreements, expanded knowledge etc. Following trauma this can take time, and a willingness to revisit situations.

A second layer of questioning explores the source of knowledge and attitudes.

What do you know for sure? Who could help us find out more?

What personal experiences shaped attitudes? What circumstances may have led to this understanding? Did information come through the media? Which media and how reliable? What influences may have shaped this view? What other sources of information might be useful? How can the group find out more?

Once trust has been established a third layer of questioning invites people to imagine and share their dreams and hopes for the future.

How would you like it to be?

At this stage people are asked to identify knowledge, skills and resources that can assist them in moving from the current to the desired situation. As each person contributes what they know, or by identifying where they can seek further information an expanded awareness of new opportunities evolves.

ideas rarely emerge fully formed

1.2.5 Development from silence to mature involvement. Be aware that ideas rarely emerge fully formed. They may initially be shared tentatively or expressed in anger and frustration. If you provide a respectful listening environment, this will change as people continue to put words (or create art/craft) around their situations. Chapter 6 gives insight into the contribution of narratives to personal and community development, and looks more closely at the contribution of language to liberating outcomes for those involved. This process takes time and a safe environment for personal thoughts to be publicly shared.

Belenkey et. al. is an excellent reference that identifies the stages of development from silent, received, subjective (inner voice), subjective (quest for self) procedural (voice of reason) procedural (separate and connected) to constructed knowledge, a maturity of integrated understanding (Belenkey, 1986, 1997). Be aware that this sequence is rarely linear and when critical incidents occur people can revert to less mature stages. Fear is a common trigger. The role of the facilitator is to establish accepted ways of working together that will continue to resource the process, rather than create dependency on one individual.

Fear is a common trigger.

1.3 Outcomes: (what for)

The following extracts are from facilitators of *Building Rural Futures through Co-operation* study circle kit (Sheil, 1999).

- *Dialogue was the most important strategy during the establishment phase of The Bruthen and District Study Circle. Communicating with participants was important in commencing the process of developing respect and sound relationships between participants and the facilitator. Prospective participants needed to feel safe coming along to the first meeting, feel valued and not be afraid they would be placed in an uncomfortable situation. This was not only an intense period but also a stage of significant personal growth for me. Becoming active among the community, becoming a public figure and advertising the Study Circle program created a degree of community responsibility that I did not have previously* (Caling, New Community Quarterly: Vol. 3 No 4 – Summer 2005:31-38).

- *A shared interest emerged to investigate volunteering and community options for people with a disability. The facilitator adapted the steps as people found the existing format daunting. People spoke of little experience in making decisions as it was often their carer or a worker who had this role. They spoke of their experiences in groups 'as being put down', 'not given an opportunity to speak', 'dominating personalities' and 'information not being provided in a way that they could understand' they began to see that these were common issues, plus people not knowing how best to include someone with a disability. They welcomed the opportunity to practice working with each other respectfully and would speak up in support of each other if enough time was not given to listening or if someone was left out* (Bruce, New Community Quarterly Vol. 3 No 4 – Summer 2005:26).

The East Gippsland Building Community Resilience project (2015) invested in community and agency preparation for future emergencies. The sequenced approach led to greater awareness of different levels of preparedness in neighboring communities and ways they could support each other. People realized changes had occurred in the way responsible agencies and residents 'found out' about each other.

An example from Nowa Nowa:

- At the time of the 2013/14 fires the Nowa Nowa Community Health Centre was in transition from being independently managed to becoming an outreach service of Gippsland Lakes Community Health. The community health centre had been a focus for Wairewa, Nowa Nowa and Lake Tyers Aboriginal Trust since it was established in 1974. Despite a reduction in opening hours and operating on policies of closure during days of high fire danger it remained listed as the contact for emergency services with the Country Fire Authority and East Gippsland Shire. The result was confusion for the community and emergency services. Community members sought information at the General store, the hotel, camp parks or with people they knew, none of whom were linked to accurate information. The demolition of houses due to VicRoads road changes and new intersection with subsequent road changes were not on Emergency Services maps.

- Local people invited East Gippsland Shire Emergency Management staff, Department of Environment, Land, Water and Planning, and Country Fire Authority members to meet with them to share their concerns and find ways to engage with a community that lacked a recognised community hub.

- The Nowa Nowa community became aware that updating changes to emergency services managed by East Gippsland Shire and Country Fire Authority was a community responsibility and implemented through the Local Incident Management Plan (LIMP).

- Ideas also came from Bruthen who had a TV screen in the General Store linked to East Gippsland Shire Emergency Services and from Buchan Neighbourhood House who had a well-established phone tree. Following the project Department of Environment Land Water and Planning (DELWP) held Fire Scenarios in these high-risk communities bringing all agencies, organisations and community members together. Nowa Nowa drew on this experience in the 2019/2020 fires.

unlearning the internalised destructiveness of being insignificant,

Questions

What are your experiences of living and working with local communities?

Have you been involved in programs that significantly influenced your understanding of your own potential and ability?

What was significant about this learning?

What opportunities for personal and community development did this program provide?

What new contacts and support did you gain from a regional project?

2. TIME

It takes time for roles to change and for safety to work its magic towards honest dialogue.
(Vella 1984:184)

2.1 Rationale (why)

People coming into groups have different experiences of participating in public forums. Some will have had few opportunities to participate in public decision-making, while others may have valuable experience to share. Establishing a new group benefits from investing time in discussing the way they would like this group to function. It may begin with unlearning the internalised destructiveness of being insignificant, of being outside of decision-making that impacts on their life. For others it may be a stepping back to give space for others to speak and be heard. A process of growth and learning begins as participants gain confidence in their skills, reinforced by respect for their competence by group members as the group takes on tasks and projects. With a sound foundation the group can flourish for decades.

Gloria Steinem, legendary social justice organizer known for her work in the women's and black civil rights movements throughout her lifetime finds connection with the 'talking circles' and the guidelines of the member-led chapters of the Black Lives Matter movement

(M)ove at the speed of trust...Trust is the foundation of every healthy relationship, which is why, within any social movement, each individual must be listened to, and their experiences validated. Productive, fulfilling discourse demands we move as slowly as necessary to ensure each participant feels safe enough and trusting enough to engage in the dialogue.
(Steinem: Power in progress, Fessler 2018)
https://qz.com/work/1467935/gloria-steinem-says-these-are-the-best-guidelines-for-difficult-conversations/

2.2 Implementation (how)

2.2.1 Regular Commitment. The regular commitment of time to participate in the group provides 'space' for the development of skills and knowledge in a safe environment. The study circle kit is designed for use over a manageable timeframe of 3 months with regular weekly or fortnightly meetings. The trusted foundation established in this time is apparent in coming ventures over years and mitigates the need to engage in damage control, which is rarely entirely successful.

Be aware that it will take time to develop trust.

2.2.2 Sharing the time available. Planning to utilise the time available in an inclusive manner benefits from everyone respectfully listening to people sharing their experiences, without continually dominating the space. This requires sensitivity as to who has confidence to speak publicly, and who requires encouragement. Do support people, but be wary of overwhelming them. Be aware that it will take time to develop trust. Begin to practice involving everyone in discussion. If a large group this can be broken up into smaller groups so that everyone can participate and practice the facilitation skills they have discussed. Respect is a guiding principle rather than the corporate restriction of confidentiality that can limit people sharing experiences and finding affirmation from others of their circumstances.

Respect is a guiding principle

2.2.3 Strengthening Relationships. Learning the skills of listening and speaking, of paying attention to different points of view, and being able to discuss these in relation to personal experiences takes time. Relationships entered into on common ground, and responsibilities shared for the healthy functioning of the group strengthen social relationships.

2.3 Outcomes (what for)

Insights from past study circles

- *Over time, participants began to develop a growing ownership of the process by volunteering to take on tasks and contributing constructively to the conversation. By session three, group members were showing their willingness and ability to take on the challenge of facilitating. This demonstrated that people felt safe, comfortable and able to express their views. People understood the guidelines to the Study Circle and were adhering to these.*

- *As time progressed the group functioned cohesively and demonstrated they were starting to develop the skills and knowledge to work and plan together. By week four participants were able to begin the process of deciding upon a collective vision for the group. There was a growing ownership of the issues, with less of 'them and us' language being used and more a commitment to a collaborative approach. At this stage my role moved more to support the group, rather than lead as in the initial stages. This marked a transition in both the group and myself – the group was no longer reliant on me* (Caling, 'Bruthen and District Study Circle', *New Community Quarterly*: Vol. 3 No 4 – Summer 2005:31-38).

- *During the initial stages of the study circle, people did not feel that they were in a safe environment to really share their stories and time was allowed for this to occur. As the weeks went by, people became more comfortable with each other and they learnt that there was time to listen to their stories and that they were valued for their input. ... The Study Circle provided opportunity and time to develop people's ideas, to discuss thoughts and feelings both negative and positive. As many group members had not previously experienced this opportunity, some people took more time to become comfortable than others. Very few sessions have been missed by participants with a disability, they have been extremely keen to participate and to adapt to new ways of learning and working together* (Bruce, 'Evaluation and change', *New Community Quarterly*: Vol. no 4 – Summer 2005:26).

Regular gatherings featured in the FLOAT project: a floating art studio linking art+enterprise+environment on Lake Tyers (https://www.float3909.com/) invited people to contribute to an ALMANAC to share interests, passions and concerns about Bung Yarnda (Lake Tyers). People met weekly for Tavern Tuesday – a cuppa at Waterwheel Tavern for over 2 years.

Comments from Almanacers

- *The project has provided us with opportunities to develop creatively and plan for a life beyond formal education* (Flaherty and Payne, 2019).

- *FLOAT has opened up so many opportunities to celebrate / experience cultural activities. It has brought art to the forefront. Indigenous culture was evident (showcased) by the corroboree and the whole community were inspired and emotionally affected by what they saw/felt* (Karen Murdoch, 2018).

A highlight was the exhibition at Lake Tyers House.

- *The exhibition demonstrated individual creative abilities coming together in a fantastic community setting. Overall it was empowering and I've learnt a lot about cultural processes, development of relationships and issues attached to these processes. Being able to advance myself creatively within a community arts project has been a fabulous experience and one that will stay with me. I am sure others will be inspired to continue their creative endeavours as I intend to do. It has made me realise that there is a purpose to art in more ways than one. I would never have had the opportunity to develop relationships in the community had it not been for my creative choices and achievements* (Helen Crossley, 14/2/2018).

Questions

Who is involved in the process of change?

Can you identify the changes that occur in this process?

How is this change evident and reinforced?

Who learns from this process?

Where is knowledge held for future situations in your experience?

3. VISIONING

Redescribing a world is the necessary first step in changing it.
(Rushdie in Brady 1996:79)

3.1 Rationale (why)

Endogenous development originates from within a region. The opportunity to dream, to speak of how life could be different is a critical step. Making time to speak of how you would like things to be marks a turning point and contributes to moving from surviving to thriving. All too often 'community consultation' occurs after industry or organizational decisions have been made. Community is not at the decision-making table. Reacting to an imposed development is divisive and exhausting for community members and in the long term can be more expensive for the proposer. A clearer understanding of one's own priorities and how they could bring about change marks a transition from reaction to leadership. Taking ownership of a new initiative informed by local values and knowledge can shape future plans with the opportunity to invite new mutually beneficial partnerships.

3.2 Implementation (how)

3.2.1 Providing the opportunity. Making the time and space to enable dreams to emerge is an important step. The sequencing of this strategy is important. Group members need to have developed sufficient trust in each other and group processes to tolerate listening to views that are different from their own or ideally be welcoming and delighted at new ideas. If scheduled before trust is established it can be divisive and damaging. Laughter is a good indicator that all is well.

Make different arrangements for the visioning session – a place people can relax and think expansively. Listen to all the dreams. While this may amount to more than a group can tackle in the short-term ideas can be talked about and incorporated into longer-term plans. Experiences from Girgaree using an Ideas bank. https://en.wikipedia.org/wiki/Ideas led to ideas being implemented when time and resources allowed. www.girgarre.com.au.

The opportunity to dream, to speak of how life could be different is a critical step.

Laughter is a good indicator that all is well.

3.2.2 Inspirational stories. Each community is encouraged to develop and speak of their own situation, to dream of a more vibrant, nurturing future. Networking to hear of other people's dreams becoming reality can be inspiring without being prescriptive.

3.2.3 At this point an awareness that as a group they can plan more boldly than individuals acting alone becomes evident. With a regional approach communities can collaborate on projects.

as a group they can plan more boldly than individuals acting alone

3.3 Outcomes (what)

Extract from study circles.

- *Boolarra study circle. The process was to produce an outcome not defined before the group came together. This was unique and difficult to grasp, as traditionally groups get together to respond to a problem, issue or need.*

  Our raised awareness transformed into action as members gained skills in negotiation, conflict resolution and general communication taking these skills into family, workplace and social situations. A pivotal session on visioning included shared food, some wine, candles and music, building a comforting atmosphere on what was a wild, stormy evening. A group meditation promoted the possibilities of personal dreams for the future of our town. Combined results took the form of a letter to Santa for a street party enjoyed by everyone, with music, laughter and lanterns adorning our picturesque town common. A special plea for participation in the clean-up as well as the celebration!

  Our street party eventuated in co-operation with the exhausted Christmas Carols Committee, helping organise the event, providing salad for the sausage sizzle and three costumed angels gathered Christmas wishes and a video was made to record the spiritual event.

  And like all good stories, this was not an end but truly a beginning (Sheil and Cartwright, 'Making Local Knowledge Work', *New Community Quarterly*, Vol. 3 No. 4. 2005: 14-21).

The group was motivated 'to put Bena on the map'.

- *The process undertaken by the Study Circle resulted in a decision to request and collate everyone's visions for a future Bena long term planning document. A questionnaire was designed to collect the information. A free lunch in the Hall was organized for interested*

community members to firstly socialise and secondly to indicate their priorities for preferred action. As expected, many suggestions centred on things they wanted supplied or repaired, but there were also wider visions such as a gardening group, book club, walking group, places to walk etc.

Have you been to Bena? A study circle participant suggested designing and producing a Bena promotional sticker to be sold on the day. This suggestion met with approval and the planning and decision-making process was exercised again as this idea was bought to life. One hundred stickers were produced and sold and another 200 ordered.

The day was a great success with Study Circle participants reporting many positive reactions from community members regarding all aspects of the day. Shire support in the form of maps, a display stand and financial help also boosted the attitude of many Bena community members towards the Shire and the overall positive response to the planning exercise certainly encouraged Study Circle members to continue their involvement beyond the current life-cycle. (Twite, 'The Bena Study Circle Experience', New Community Quarterly *,Vol 3. No. 4. Summer 2005:39-41).*

Questions

Can you identify significant changes occurring with this process?

Given other opportunities to hear of this group's work, what subtle differences could you imagine occurring?

What does the existence of a group offer to the process?

Are you aware of such an opportunity in your community?

4. LOCAL COMMUNITY OWNERSHIP

The COVID-19 crisis and the magnificent response of the public has proved yet again that local people know what is best for themselves. They also know the actions that need to be taken to make where they live a better, vibrant and more caring place.
(Blog – Peter Macfadyen – *Flatpack democracy*, May 2020
(https://www.flatpackdemocracy.co.uk)

4.1 Rationale (why)

Development in each community proceeds according to the skills, knowledge, energy and resources available. Each is unique and not encouraged to 'be like' another community. No service agreements, timelines or expected outcomes are imposed. The significance of respecting local people's wisdom and knowledge becomes evident as local people determine the direction of involvement originating from dialogue in a safe, respectful environment.

No service agreements, timelines or expected outcomes are imposed.

The study circle approach respects the unique life experiences of each person at the table (Larsson, 2010). The safety of this approach enables community members to express diverse viewpoints. This investment in developing trusted relationships enables an appreciation of the complexity and vibrancy of community life to become evident. Steve Garlick terms this quality *'our sense of place', the close associations between people built on ethical principles, common goals and a shared understanding,* (Garlick 1997:24) that is often missing in regional planning.

As people express their views and hopes for their community and environment, motivation for action comes from within the group. The process provides opportunities for individuals to develop personally as they strengthen their relationship with each other, along with their sense of responsibility to the locality. The opportunity to speak of local situations increases the sense of belonging, strengthening relationships and contributing to healing following traumatic experiences and exclusion. If they are listened to, collaboration begins.

The process of exploring options within a group and collaborative decision-making implements a transition from individual dreams to community-initiated action as ideas are discussed and broader involvement canvassed. The impact of beginning with projects people agree about strengthens relationships and trust in the process. The result is dynamic partnerships as energy and motivation, enabled through an investment in skill development and access to knowledge leads to a more resilient region. At a local planning level initiatives with parallel goals include the United Kingdom's Flatpack democracy (Macfadyen, 2014) and Flatpack 2.00 (Macfadyen and Andrews) 2019.

This collaborative approach facilitates a reintegration of knowledge that has become fragmented as organisations become larger, more hierarchical and screen out feedback and understanding of connection. For example, the domination of corporate and commercial frameworks led to financial deregulation and centralising of banking services that stripped communities of local banks that provided employment, circulated money locally and re-invested in local organisations. Assets were transferred from rural communities to urban centres. In response rural people sought other ways to offer financial services in their communities and partnerships with the Bendigo Community Bank evolved. The same scenario occurs in water and land management. For those living in close proximity to rivers, forests, lakes and oceans the social and environmental impacts of decisions made in distant boardrooms are immediately evident and of concern.

4.2 Implementation (how)

Constantly comes to mind – reaching decisions. I can live with 100% of the people being 70% comfortable with each decision that was made.
(Study group member 1999)

4.2.1. Group identity. Taking the time to invest in group skills and paying attention to guidelines of how the group will operate and make decisions may initially frustrate some people. However, as groups work through the collaborative engagement strategies (designed into the study circle kit/or a project), their impatience evaporates as they experience what can be achieved personally and for their community as everyone pools ideas and resources. The sense of belonging in the community becomes stronger as attention is paid to projects that the whole group agrees upon.

A 'sufficient consensus' format (Gale & Dunn 1997) is advocated

4.2.2. Decision-making. Learning to work democratically to strengthen community relationships requires adopting inclusive decision-making processes. The familiar 'majority rules' inevitably isolates and diminishes the contributions of a minority creating greater divisions of 'them and us' and battles for power. While 'consensus' decision-making is frequently promoted as an alternative it can put pressure on people to agree rather than block a decision which they may see value in but not be entirely comfortable with. A 'sufficient consensus' format (Gale & Dunn 1997) is advocated whereby the requirement that 100% of the people are 70% comfortable with each decision.

This inclusive formula encourages people to speak up about aspects of a decision they are not happy about and enables other perspectives to be considered rather than silenced.

Sufficient consensus honours the principle that participation and process are as important as the project outcome, indeed they determine the outcome. Communities found that this broke the cycle of one group implementing practices at the expense of other community members. It can be a shift away from 'old school' extractive practices towards investment in communities and the environment.

4.2.3 Change from within. Stories of community-initiated change are shared as inspirational stories that offer ideas, information and a sense of hope, rather than being prescriptive. Community projects were not inspired by external funding, imposed top-down agendas, or imported solutions. These stories offer points of contact for networking that can be facilitated through a regional approach that raises awareness of common issues and points of contact for agencies. This was the experience of *East Gippsland Building Community Resilience* as communities took steps to be better prepared for emergency situations.

4.2.4 Resourcing community involvement. While community knowledge is a trusted source of information by other communities there are personal and financial costs involved. Time away from business, community and family responsibilities as well as travel need to be considered. Agencies can contribute to travel costs, home office supplies and recognition of time, rather than an assumption that community members can be present 'for their own good'. Workers can attend local events and contribute to venue and catering costs rather than organizing additional meetings. Ideally a resourced regional approach to community engagement links communities.

Moving from visioning to implementation expands community involvement.

4.2.5 Clarifying roles and responsibilities. A matrix developed for the *East Gippsland Shire Sustainability Kit* (2013) clarifies roles and responsibilities across a spectrum that includes individual, household, community, business, community organization, local governments, state government departments, federal and international governments and alliances. A useful and flexible planning tool https://www.float3909.com/ and https:https://ruralcommunities.com.au/east-gippsland-environmental-sustainability-toolkit/

4.2.6 Realistic goals. Bigger is not always better. Begin projects with achievable short-term goals. Consider the metaphor of teaching someone to drive. If a sequence of achievable targets is planned and achieved, skills and confidence develop until the learner becomes confident and capable of independent planning and action, able to venture into new situations and journeys. The same is true for community development. Success with practical achievable projects that are low risk and have limited costs leads on to more ambitious endeavors as skills, confidence and awareness increase. Jane Vella's work continually reminds practitioners of the importance of 'knowing that you know' by the incremental changes experienced and documented (Vella, 2002:115, 243).

The opportunity to put ideas and theory into practice is a critical component of adult learning and community development. Action invites involvement and seeks recognition of the group's contribution, changing attitudes and opening up new opportunities.

4.3 Outcomes (what for)

Moving from visioning to implementation expands community involvement. Facilitators of *Building rural futures through co-operation* (1999) study circles involved wider community through public meetings and social events. Alliances with organisations increased involvement and resulted in community/ organisational support for planned activities.

- *Study Circle participants worked with the Bruthen Market Committee to hold the September, Bruthen Village Market around their theme 'Valuing the Natural Environment'. At the market, natural resources management agencies: Landcare. Parks Victoria, DSE Fire Management, DSE Flora and Fauna, Land for Wildlife, Fishcare, Coastcare, Greencorps, Trust for Nature etc. were invited to provide information stands on display for the public. On the same day information displays were provided outlining the Bruthen and District Study Circle and the Bruthen Community Plan. A presentation ceremony was held in the morning whereby a respected community leader, Joy Manley, spoke of the Bruthen and District Community Plan and the history of Bruthen. This was followed by Dr. Helen Sheil speaking of the Graduate Certificate in Regional Community Development and the Study Circle program. I discussed the Bruthen and District Study Circle and its outcomes to date, whilst East Gippsland Shire Mayor, Cr. Jane Rowe concluded by presenting Study Circle participants with their TAFE certificates. The Bruthen Hall was full with information displays and people* (Caling: (37-38) op.cit.).

A regional perspective to local ownership

The East Gippsland Building Community Resilience project worked with six existing community hubs and became an effective way for agencies such as East Gippsland Shire, Department of Environment, Land Water and Planning (DELWP), mental health workers, churches and Country Fire Authorities (CFAs) to communicate across the region. Hub coordinators were trusted local people. The coordinators presented to the *Living with Bushfires* conference at Federation University (2014) https://news.cfa.vic.gov.au/news/gipps-bushfire-community-conference, and at a statewide Neighbourhood Houses conference 2015, 2020. https://www.nhvic.org.au/annual-conference. *East Gippsland Building Community Resilience won awards for Community-led Prevention and Preparedness Awards f*rom Emergency Management Victoria https://ruralcommunities.com.au/fire-awareness-award-winner/ The project led to Bruthen working with Buchan Neighbourhood House to apply for its own funding for a Neighbourhood House that became an important resource during the 2109/2020 fires and in the recovery. The other community hubs became more informed about who to contact and shared responsibilities.

Hub coordinators were trusted local people.

Benefits of a regionally networked community hub approach included:

- giving communities a voice, strengthening connections with multiple agencies,
- employing local facilitators invested in local knowledge, economics and flexible access,
- providing interface between agencies, co-ordinators and communities,
- improving relationships between community members and agency staff,
- more informed access to resources,
- establishing open and respectful relationships,
- Neighbourhood houses/hubs providing foundational future interface with agencies,
- communities initiating action supported by agencies,

- showcasing the approach at regional and state conferences,
- updating and being involved in Local Incident Management Plan (LIMP),
- using local arts and community newspapers (print/on-line) a key link in communication,
- Study circle kit on line and available as future resource,
- networking with other regional communities,
- generation of hope and sound practice.

Questions

Are you aware of ventures initiated from within your community, supported through a networked approach?

How are these ventures able to build on local skills and knowledge?

Are you aware of other resources that invest in local community ownership?

What benefits return to the community?

In the short term?

In the long term?

5. ACTION

Even with vision, the substitution of new theories for the old, fatalistic ones is simply not enough. At the same time there must be structures at hand through which action can be undertaken – a reform movement, political party, community organisation, or a social movement or the potential for developing such structures.
(Heaney & Horton 1990:87)

Action is about change. Not a return to the past.

5.1 Rationale (why)

Steve Garlick (1997) recognized that an integral part of community life is shaped by local people's connection to place. Action is about change. Not a return to the past. Action may involve revaluing of community relationships and quality of life with an inter-generational perspective. Each activity a community group initiates reclaims the humanity and sense of identity of the members. The focus may be social, cultural, environmental, local economic ventures or spiritual projects, all of which add to the richness of community life. In these ventures economic activity is often only one component of general community wellbeing.

5.2 Implementation (how)

5.2.1 Achievable goals. Moving from planning to action is a critical step in changing attitudes and inviting involvement from those who have been 'watchers'. Groups are encouraged to begin with projects that are achievable with current time and resources. Particularly after times of trauma, initiating a new activity can be daunting. Beginning small provides safety while people are learning to combine theory and practice in an environment without high risks. While being successful is an important step in confidence building, if a culture of reflection is cultivated then awareness of changing situations enables a group to evolve.

to begin with projects that are achievable

5.2.2 Legal Structure. Moving from a learning environment into action requires groups to establish legal structures. All groups made this transition by forming an alliance with community organisations, many of which were struggling for members and direction. In this way study circles supported existing organisations. As ventures and confidence expanded, some established new organisations and alliances with regional institutions.

5.3 Outcomes (what)

- *The Boolarra Story. The economic downturn and regional centre 'sponges' resulted in local retail businesses surviving on secondary income. Closure of our service station threatened community sustainability and motivated incorporation of Boolarra and District Community Development Group (BDCD) in March 2002. Like other small towns, rural community needs were often ignored when administered by an amalgamated Regional City Council. Even the name Latrobe City denied the presence of rural towns. Our concerned residents group hoped to engage the Local Council and effect some positive change.*

  Community workers in the Streetlife Program recruited BDCD assistance in mapping the area's needs by inviting residents to

capture positive and negative aspects of the local environment with disposable cameras. The BDCD involved a cross section of people and the resulting presentation provided a good foundation to identify local appeal. This led to working partnerships with local and state government to strengthen and sustain rural towns.

Developing interest drove my completion of the Graduate Certificate in Regional Community Development at Monash University…that included my facilitation of a study circle with twelve adults in Boolarra (learning by doing). At the time the gender balance in the BDCD was reduced to one or two women out of membership of twelve – so I recruited. I contacted women asking if they would support my study. Commonality in our reasons for residing in a beautiful rural environment, the safety and health of our family as core values cemented this group of individual thoughtful women into a mutually supportive group. (See visioning insert re: beginning with letter to Santa and street party.)

Future developments include:
A folk festival has become an annual free event (3,000 people attended the first event) and it continues to evolve being a gathering place following bushfires in 2006. Proprietors of a new plant nursery in town introduced community market stalls and in 2005 inaugural Boolarra Rodeo. In response to identified poor health outcomes a study circle member introduced a walking group, a New Year's Eve dance and an exercise group to combine fun and fitness. A stroke support group is ongoing and a healing group in response to 5 untimely deaths, the list continues…

A second study circle by a graduate's daughter focused on health of the Morwell River involving West Gippsland Water Catchment Management Authority, Department of Sustainability and Environment, Landcare, a forestry company – Grandridge Plantations, farmers and local and state government along with community.

Keen to understand the approach more community members enrolled in the Graduate Certificate…and expanded the pool of skilled workers. *Boolarra was justly proud that local outcomes supported the joint application for Commonwealth funding of $239,000 for the seven small towns in the Shire to use this approach* (Cartwright and Sheil, 'Making local knowledge work', New Community Quarterly, Vol. 3. No. 4. 2005, 4-21).

Strengthening seven small communities administered by Latrobe City, employed seven local facilitators 24 hours a week over a 12-month period in 2004. The project was developed through a reference group with representatives from all of the small towns and the facilitators funded to enroll in the Graduate Certificate in Regional Community Development at Monash University. Each town indicated specific needs, but common themes were to engage young people and support disadvantaged people. Both the Commonwealth and the Local Government respected the rights of the communities to determine their own directions during the Study Circle process and did not limit the scope of activities. This was a significant factor in ensuring local ownership of activities and is evident as groups continue to initiate projects.

Strengthening Seven Small Communities outcomes included shared events between and across communities leading to an integrated network of valuable knowledge and skills. Youth activities have included bus trips to Sk8 parks and movies, youth groups and forums. Joint community activities included a vocal work shop, exercise groups, trial bus services, community directories and newsletter and the 'Other Awards'. The major outcome from this project is a pool of skilled facilitators, who can cross-pollinate ideas and link local and academic knowledge with energy to continue strengthening rural communities, organisations and the regional campus. (Sheil and Cartwright, 2005 op.cit.)

is a pool of skilled facilitators, who can cross-pollinate ideas

Involvement in the *Building Rural Futures through Co-operation* study circle introduced democratic skills and stories of co-operative ventures from other communities. Inspired by the story of Mirboo North taking ownership of the local paper the Bruthen and District Citizens Association began the production of a monthly newsletter, the *'Tambo Rambler'* in 1999. The paper profiled local people, events and issues providing a community forum for a town that was rapidly becoming a commuter town as people traveled to Bairnsdale to work. 20+ years on 'The Tambo Rambler' continues to provide a local perspective, critical during recovery from bushfires while community members were isolated due to COVID 19.

The Bruthen and District Citizens' Association (BDCA) also supported a later study circle that led to an Environmental Conservation Sub-Committee in 2005. This led to the Bruthen & District Landcare group re-forming in November 2005 encompassing Wiseleigh, Bruthen, Mossiface and Sarsfield, approximately 20 km north east of Bairnsdale. In 2006, Bruthen

 and District Landcare began the restoration of habitat on the north bank of the Tambo River at Bruthen township between the highway and the Rail Trail bridges.

The 'Bridge-to-Bridge' site was described as one of the worst weed-infested areas in East Gippsland. Despite this, considerable progress has been made in getting on top of some of the major weeds which dominated the area, especially blackberries, hemlock and honey locust trees. In addition, over 2,000 indigenous trees and shrubs have been planted and are now becoming well established, despite recent drought.

The main aim of the project was to control erosion and help the Tambo river rebuild its banks and improve local biodiversity. However, a longer-term goal was to provide an attractive site on public land along the river to be enjoyed by locals and visitors alike. In mid-2007 the Bruthen Streetscape Study recommended the creation of a River Loop Walk, starting from a planned new Visitor Information Centre along an existing unsurfaced track to the river, along the Bridge to-Bridge site and finally linking with the Rail Trail to return to the town centre.

Bruthen Landcare developed links with other stake-holders – including Bruthen & District Citizens Association, East Gippsland Shire and VicRoads - to extend the scope of the Bridge-to-Bridge Project to include completion of the River Loop Walk. The first phase of this work commenced in early 2010. *We know we'll see much enhanced habitat conditions - and the creation of a valuable community amenity* (East Gippsland Sustainability).
www.eastgippsland.vic.gov.au › files › our_environment

Questions

Are you aware of collaborative ventures in your community?

In what ways have these strengthened relationships within the community?

Are you aware of changed attitudes to your community because of these ventures?

From whom?

6. NETWORKING

Networking includes all those activities that allow for the free exchange of information, and the development of links which activate the discussion about issues of concern. It encourages people to find their own solutions and directions that are sought.
(Mitchell 1994 in Franklin et. al. 147)

6.1 Rationale (why)

Networking is a personalised way of extending knowledge

Networking is a personalised way of extending knowledge that encourages individuals to have control over their own decisions, learning and future directions. In clarifying the difference between top-down dissemination of information and networking one of the original networkers of the Rural Women's Network, Jenni Mitchell, stated that *'It is personal, it is based on trust and it is about change'* (Mitchell 1994 in Bailey et al. 14).

Networking complements the principles of supporting community members having support and control over their own learning as well as affirming and celebrating their knowledge and wisdom. Networking expands the potential of shared learning and gives insight into unique local situations as community members discuss community projects.

Networking involves community members as the subjects of their own research and interpreters of information, rather than the objects being studied by an external researcher. Locally owned knowledge has an immediacy that can be incorporated into planning. Action from commissioned reports can be delayed with changing staff or priorities of government departments.

Networking also facilitates the development of language and identification of concerns in a trusting and reciprocal environment. Relationships are entered into with the understanding that information given, or requested, will be used for the benefit of community life. It is not restricted by privacy rules or Chatham house protocols as it contributes to mutual and dynamic learning between community members, planners and policy makers. www.chathamhouse.org/about-us/chatham-house-rule

6.2 Implementation (how)

Design networking strategies into a program to facilitate community members sharing and seeking information.

6.2.1 Face to face networking. While the spread of COVID viruses have radically challenged opportunities for face-to-face networking, the principles remain relevant.

Forums, gatherings, summits and meetings with time for people to interact all provide public opportunities for networking. The opportunity to make personal contact with people from outside one's community, with peak agencies, policy makers and planners and others who may be helpful in the future begins a wider circle of interaction. In this way, networking breaks down the circular discussion when we only talk with people with similar experiences to our own. Invitations to visit other places or organisations, involvement of guest speakers with experience of community-initiated change, can add to greater awareness of opportunities and understanding of possible action as well as inspiration.

Local ownership remains a key principle

Local ownership remains a key principle to ensure the content and style of networking suits those involved. Linking with local organisations and seeking their advice on when and where to host events accommodates seasonal and other commitments.

6.2.2 Print (on-line) networking. Newsletters, newspapers and blogs incorporating personal stories of people's experiences are an important means of print and on-line networking. In the initial years of the Rural Women's Network Newsletter, the requirement of 85% of content being contributed by rural women ensured that content reflected the reality and diversity of life for rural women. Within the study circle kit, and this manual, stories are shared to provide a print networking component. Names and contact details are supplied by the authors who generously contributed to the process of developing material for the project.

85% of content being contributed by rural women

6.2.3 Using the media: Radio: community radio, such as Mallacoota and Genoa community radio https://www.3mgb.org.au/ and Omeo Shire Community Access Radio (OSCAR) and Australian Broadcasting Commission all provide extensive opportunity for networking through talk-back programs and interviews. Community radio stations are excellent forums for speaking with those involved in local issues and can counter mis-information that spreads in times of crisis through social media. Community managed and owned media usually welcome involvement from all ages.

6.2.4 Electronic and social media networking. Electronic networking through email, chat lines, facebook, zoom, teams, etc have become an important means of networking across distance. If affordable and public access is available in rural and regional areas electronic networking can provide excellent opportunities for discussing issues, accessing information, being involved in decision-making and policy formulation.

6.2.5. Telephone/facetime/group conversations. Making contact by phone with someone you have met, read or have heard about begins conversations and relationships that can be mutually beneficial.

6.2.6 Interest group networking. Networking opportunities can be built into organisational planning, providing regular opportunities for people to meet within a region, state or more broadly. Industry networks, youth networks, women's networks, the list is endless.

6.3 Outcomes (what)

6.3.1. Within projects networking breaks down stereotypes and isolation.

Study circle extract.

- *Contact was made with workers from a range of community-based organisations at Latrobe City, Latrobe Information and Support Services, Access for all Abilities, Department of Sustainability, Landcare Co-ordinator, state member for the area to find out what they did and where there were gaps in services. The group also produced a survey to find out about disability friendly groups and contributed an article to the newspaper, which happened in one of the sessions. Many had not done this before and found it a valuable experience. Five participants volunteered their time to mail 433 questionnaires to organisations listed in Latrobe City's Community Directory, using the Latrobe Shire Offices in Morwell and with the support and assistance of the staff.*

Networking will remain a main component of the project to facilitate two-way learning for community groups and people with a disability. The final step in our project is planned to be a networking expo, showcasing some organisations who are leading the way in inclusiveness and allowing opportunity for all people with a disability to see what is available in the community for them to participate in. The group identified the need for a safe environment, which prompted the decision to locate disability friendly organisations. Five members of the group will be attending the Community Engagement Conference later in the year, which will provide an opportunity for networking and a means of sharing what they are doing with other community members.
Leanne Bruce, 'Evaluation and Change' New Community Quarterly, Vol. 3 No. 4. Summer 2005, 25-30)

Within the project *East Gippsland Building Community Resilience* (2015) regional networking events provided for personal interaction that affirmed the value of the project and facilitated co-operation between groups. Department of Environment, Land, Water and Planning (DELWP) staff in Orbost commented how they initially attended the event with reservations but found those attending keen to share experiences and learn from each other.

6.3.2 Organisational networking

Both groups identified a need to tackle issues of land degradation.

Landcare originated in North East Victoria from a partnership between the Victorian Farmers Federation president Heather Mitchell and Joan Kirner, Conservation Minister in the Labour Government in 1984. Both groups identified a need to tackle issues of land degradation. This state initiative went on to be brokered at a national level by Rick Farley of the National Farmers Federation and Phillip Toyne of the Australian Conservation Foundation. The potential change that begins with such alliances is rarely understood until people develop the skills and knowledge of how to work together, and undertake joint ventures. Mutual development and mutual benefit are the key components of such ventures. https://landcareaustralia.org.au/landcare-in-focus-july-2019/

There are around 600 Landcare groups and 64 networks in Victoria that facilitate interaction within and between groups www.environment.vic.gov.au › landcare

Regional celebrations are held and a Landcare Magazine showcases work in other localities.

Neighbourhood Houses originate from within communities as a need is identified. They are diverse in their focus, design, history and operation yet share common features to provide a welcoming environment – a meeting place for community members particularly women and young children. Regional networkers are funded to support the development and functioning of the houses, to share information and to advocate on behalf of the sector. Annual conferences showcase activities across the State. Common concerns such as threats from natural disasters and strategies to respond to crisis feature at these events.

share common features to provide a welcoming environment

6.3.3 Successful state programs become national.

The Australian Neighbourhood Houses and Centres Association (ANHCA) is the national peak body for Neighbourhood Houses and Centres in Australia.

> *With a vision for strong local communities ANCHA represents nationally over 1000 Neighbourhood Houses/Centres – the generic name used for centres called Community Houses, Learning Centres, and Community Centres - which are member organisations of their state and territory peak representative bodies.*
> https://www.anhca.org

Or city programs become statewide: Melbourne City of Literature (MCOL) links literary events across the State through a Regional Presenters Network cityofliterature.com.au. While each writers festival, storytelling event originated independently across the State they now have the capacity to network with each other through an annual Roundtable and a funded network visit to another festival of their choosing. The strategies benefit both the MCOL as a dynamic organisation and individual festival presenters who collaborate on how they plan, what works for them, what they are learning, and funding sources across the state and internationally.

6.3.4. Internationally:

> *Launched in 2004, the UNESCO Creative Cities Network (UCCN) aims to strengthen cooperation with and among cities that have recognised creativity as a strategic factor of sustainable development as regards economic, social, cultural and environmental aspects.*

By joining the Network, cities acknowledge their commitment to sharing best practices, developing partnerships that promote creativity and the cultural industries, strengthening participation in cultural life and integrating culture in urban development plans. cityofliterature.com.au

collaborated to tackle problems too large to achieve in isolation.

Questions

What have been your networking experiences to raise issues of concern, or access information?

Where and when have you utilised networks to initiate change in your community?

Are you currently linked into any organised networks on a regular basis?

Take the opportunity to network with a rural community development worker from another locality. Identify 3 issues you have in common.

7. CO-OPERATIVE CULTURE

'Each for all and all for each'.
Mutualism should be understood as acting in co-operation with one another to achieve objectives, which are unachievable for us as individuals.
(Mathews 1999).

7.1 Rationale (why)

A constant theme in Collaborative Engagement is the positive nature of community initiatives where people are able to work together to identify and meet community needs. For people with different life experiences to overcome prejudices formed by stereotypical language, it requires the active creation of safe places for people to become aware of common interests and develop a co-operative culture.

Organisations such as Landcare are an example of how individuals and rural organisations have collaborated to tackle problems too large to achieve in isolation. The potential change that begins with such alliances becomes evident as people develop the skills and knowledge of how to work together and initiate joint ventures. Mutual development is a key component of such ventures.

Co-operative ventures have been a strong contributor to regional development. Agricultural and fishing co-operatives enabled individual farmers and fishing people to have sufficient volume to be viable in purchasing and marketing. The introduction of quotas on fish catches and the corporatisation of both the fishing industry and farming has stripped regional ownership and circulation of goods and finance, operating on very different principles.

Co-operative movements such as those of the Basque Region in Spain www.mondragon-corporation.com › en and the Maleny Co-operatives http://proutglobe.org/2011/05/maleny-cooperatives-examples-of-small-scale-cooperative-enterprises/ in Queensland offer a third way to long term viability for present and future generations. Both began with small ventures that introduced people to the principles of worker owned co-operatives and continued to invest in improved practice, research, development and education on co-operative practice and theory.

7.2 Implementation

Community building takes a lot of energy, so you must make the most of every chance for 'plerking' – combining play and work. They (Maleny) have a community fair where all the various groups of the community are invited to attend – it shows the community to itself, and demonstrates its diversity.
https://permaculturewest.org.au/resources/archives/rowell/jill-jordan-on-community-building/

7.2.1. Universal principles. At an organizational level the Rochdale co-operative principles are: voluntary and open membership, democratic member control, member economic participation, autonomy and independence, education, training, and information, co-operation among cooperatives and concern for community... en.wikipedia.org › wiki › Rochdale_Principles. Such principles can be incorporated into a range of legal structures.

Groups are encouraged to affirm and value the involvement of all members.

7.2.2. Skill development. Establishing a co-operative culture requires a shift away from hierarchical structures that screen out feedback and local ownership. Rather like parenting, facilitating the development of everyone within a group requires time, skill and experience. Groups are encouraged to affirm and value the involvement of all members. It takes time to unlearn attitudes that place some individuals and groups as superior to others and to nurture personal development within a supportive community. Providing time out for people to recharge following times of high stress is as important as achieving aimed-for milestones. If attention is paid to skills and processes that foster a co-operative approach, everyone benefits.

7.2.3 Establishing trust. The understanding that individuals are as important as the product or group project is grounded in an awareness of community responsibility and resourcefulness. The Study Circle movement creates a safe forum to appreciate the origins of diversity and find points of connection. Groups are encouraged to rotate positions, sharing responsibilities for facilitating gatherings. Collaborative leadership shares responsibilities moving away from dependence on a few individuals that is unhealthy for the lone leader as well as the integrity of the organization.

Collaborative leadership shares responsibilities

7.2.4 Communicate clearly and clarify roles. Taking the time to establish clear communication processes, to establish agreed upon ways of working together, with regular opportunities to reflect on how things are going, builds trust. Roles need to be clearly defined and accountable while being adaptable as situations change. Within the co-operative movement small study circles provided the space for both technical skills and discussion on progress, relationships and size (Mathews1999:162). The timing is right for such a shift to establish a foundation that cares for everyone in the community rather than prop up a system that fails to meet current needs.

7.3 Outcomes (what)

The vision to provide the people of Mondragon with the technical skills necessary to support a social vision for the region.
Catholic Priest, Don Jose Arizmendiarrieta (Mathews 1999).

Co-operative ventures evolve to meet a need. An opportunity to take ownership of a service, or producing and marketing of goods, or from a sense of loss or grief following trauma, when the motivation to get something started in a community is beyond the capacity of individuals.

The famous Mondragon Co-operative in the Basque region of Spain began in 1956 with a desire to re-establish a Basque identity and economy after the destructive trauma of Franco's policies that banned the Basque language and killed, exiled or imprisoned advocates for Basque culture and economic organisations.

Mondragon began with 12 apprentices learning technical skills for oil-fired heaters and democratic principles of worker co-operatives. The guiding principles of co-operation, participation, social responsibility and innovation continuously informed both the technical and organizational skills through research and establishing Mondragon University. This continuing opportunity to reflect on progress of manufacture and marketing led to the realization that if an organization exceeded 500 people the quality of human interaction deteriorated, 'bigger wasn't better'. Integrity was maintained if new co-operatives were established to meet new needs. *By 1995 the Mondragon co-operatives had become a massive conglomerate of over 100 industrial, retail, financial, construction, service and support co-operatives* employing over 1 million workers, the overwhelming majority remaining viable throughout economic crisis and downturn (Mathews 1999;180) theconversation.com › the-mondragon-model-how-a-b...(2012)

Alan Greig, a founding member of Mercury Co-operative Ltd., wrote an insightful assessment of this approach to the Australian situation. *Building community wealth. Are Mondragon's Co-operative ideas transferable to Australia?* https://www.smea.org.au/blog/building-community-wealth-are-mondragon%E2%80%99s-cooperative-ideas-transferable-to-australia

In 1995 The Mirboo North Times newspaper, operating for 103 years, was about to cease production. Keen to maintain a local paper the community took steps to produce the weekly paper. Community ownership meant many hours of unpaid work and financial, legal and social responsibility. The Committee worked hard to put effective polices in place with a shareholder base approaching 100. As well as learning about newspaper

production, coordinating the work of 50 volunteers a week required investment of time and clear communication processes. Policy at the pub (and pizza shop) sessions were well attended by people with diverse interests. The focus was to establish a co-operative approach that would underpin future involvement. Apart from a small initial grant from the Royal Automobile Club of Victoria (RACV) and in-kind support from South Gippsland Shire, the paper has always been financially independent. Income is from advertising and sales.

The Mirboo North Times continues to support community infrastructure and the environment. The maintenance and up-grading of the Baths Road Pool, the Lyrebird walk, the campaign to not sell off Strezlecki Ranges timber as well as 100% support for 'Lock the gate' on fracking: all locally important issues covered by the paper. Local ownership led to local investment. In 2002, the co-operative instituted a local grants program. In the first 4 years more than $36,000 was distributed.

Supporting other community papers, Neil Smith, involved in the setting up of the Mirboo North Times was instrumental in forming the Community Newspapers Association Victoria to support the establishment, operation and celebration of community newspapers across Victoria. cnav.org.au

Transferability of skills and knowledge.

Transferability of skills and knowledge. Two years after the community took ownership of the The Mirboo North Times as a co-operative the National Bank in the town closed, followed by LaTrobe Country Credit, and finally the Commonwealth Bank. A public meeting considered the proposal to return financial services to the town, and began to seek information, support and a viable structure for this operation. Twelve months later, and many, many late night meetings saw the opening of a Bendigo Bank Agency in Mirboo North in partnership with Ridgway Financial Chambers, supported by the Mirboo North Community Support Co-operative Ltd.

In less than 12 months this agency was on track. The estimated level of funds handled by the Bank, doubled, as did the estimated number of accounts open for this period and the agency was looking set to begin returning profits to the community. While the learning curve was steep, the venture marked a turning point of growth in the community, rather than decline. The step to become Mirboo North and District

Community Bank was taken in 2010. By the AGM in October, 2022 the community bank had returned $1.3m in grants, sponsorships, scholarships and donations to community organisations in Mirboo North, Boolarra, Yinnar and surrounding communities. https://www.bendigobank.com.au/branch/vic/community-bank-mirboo-north-district/

Maleny Co-operatives. A similar pattern of one co-operative venture blossoming into multiple ventures is evident in the hinterland community of Maleny in Queensland. The Maleny Food Co-operative began to source and distribute fresh and dried foods between members. The principles and benefits of this venture were then adopted more widely: the up-front club, child-care, credit union and other ventures that reinvest $millions to the community. https://www.filmsforaction.org/watch/creating-prosperous-communities-cooperatives-in-maleny/

Community co-operatives like the Yinnar Hotel, Yackandandah petrol station, hardware store, and Totally Renewable Yackandandah, building of recreation facilities, partnerships with Bendigo Community Banks are all mutual social, economic and frequently environmental developments initiated by communities. totallyrenewableyack.org.au

Questions

What is your experience of collaborative ventures with other groups?

How did the alliance come about?

Are you in contact with other similar ventures?

What structure and strategies are in place to support the arrangement?

How has the arrangement benefited the community?

8. TRANSFORMATION

It is the time for poets and prophets and speaking of our love for one another publicly, personally, politically, regularly, gratuitously, dangerously – to our neighbours, our workers, our estranged friends, our family members, the ones who voted with us and the ones who voted against us, who perhaps are just as terrified as we are and that's how we arrived at this moment.
(Ife 2019:65 New Community Quarterly Vol. 17 (2) 66 -2019)

We are all in this together.

8.1 Rationale

The continuing local and global environmental and health crisis signals an urgent need to shift beyond adversarial thinking and divisions of us and them (man/woman, culture/nature, mind/body, civilization/wilderness, rural/urban, first/second people, wealthy/poor…). (Rose Bird 1997) discussed in Chapter 3. The global COVID pandemic has a global impact. We are all in this together.

Jim Ife's concept of balanced development (1995) links with the important work on social relationships by Robert Putman (1993) and Eva Cox (1995). Social capital refers to the processes between people, which establish networks, norms and social trust and facilitate co-ordination and co-operation for mutual benefit (Cox 1995 p15). Without this base, assistance and funding have few long-term results, and limited resources are not utilised in the interests of caring for local people or the places in which they live. *The Black Lives Matter* movement co-founders, Alicia Garza, Patrisse Cullors and Opal Tometi, advocate guidelines that recognise the complexity and significance of involving those who have been marginalised https://blacklivesmatter.com/black-lives-matter-co-founders

Collaborative Engagement strategies invest in creating awareness of connections between groups of people and the environment. Frameworks that acknowledge the interdependence of people and places include bio-regional planning, that has taken on a legislative approach in Rights of Nature and in First People's lore custodians of country (Yunkaporta 2019: Maloney 2020). https://therightsofnature.org/

Transformation has a magical quality. The story of a caterpillar transforming into a beautiful butterfly captures the essence of changing from one state to another. A shift that becomes evident through new language and new stories that have an active presence and optimism.

community projects may be motivated by an awareness that life could be better.

Study circles or community projects may be motivated by an awareness that life could be better. This is not limited to times of disaster. The National Strategy for Disaster Resilience (2013) acknowledges that communities with a solid foundation of trust and processes to engage in looking at the complexity of local situations manage crises and respond to disaster with less trauma than communities where these relationships and forums are absent. This was evident in Gippsland. The Buchan community had active involvement of bush nurses, neighbourhood house coordinators, Country Fire Authority members and a well-prepared community plan, honed over years that kept everyone safe despite horrific fires. In Orbost and Cann River despite less flame impact people spoke of confusion and misinformation regarding evacuation triggers and refuge areas resulting in high levels of stress, uncertainty and divisions within the community.

The Mallacoota and District Recovery Association began by investing in local knowledge and re-establishing damaged relationships in democratic groups. People were able to share their experiences and choose ways of working together resulting in constructive initiatives. Community members led change resulting in action and optimism enabling new opportunities and partnerships to emerge. https://madrecovery.com/

Unlike the butterfly analogy, the transformation of relationships is not an end point, rather a beginning of community collaboration. There are indications of a transition towards a richer cultural life, not dependent on continual consumption of material products that deplete natural resources, outsource its waste and cause harm to the environment and ourselves.

8.2 Implementation: (how)

Subsidiarity is a principle of social organization that holds that social and political issues should be dealt with at the most immediate (or local) level that is consistent with their resolution.
https://en.wikipedia.org/wiki/Subsidiarity

as an accounting system with 'no debit' column.

Marilyn Waring points out that the universally accepted indicators Gross National Product (GNP) or Gross Domestic Product (GDP) that records the national and international financial transactions in isolation to its impact on people or the environment, is contributing to our global health and environmental crisis (Waring, 1988, 2018). Waring describes this approach as an accounting system with 'no debit' column. Language and indicators that give visibility to regional activity that reinvigorates communities and landscapes compared to those that deplete regions are urgently needed.

8.2.1. Self-evaluation. Feminism understands that the personal is political and begins by entering into conversations to hear firsthand of the reality of people's lives. Collaborative Engagement honours the premise that the learning of local people should be affirmed, acknowledged and legitimised. The first evaluation strategy is therefore self-evaluation. At the beginning of a new venture people are invited to speak of their current situation. Hearing of the reality of experiences across different ages, genders and background gives insight into the qualities that strengthen or destroy community life. From this awareness connections can be made and the degree of change implemented by new ventures appreciated.

8.2.2 Making the invisible, visible. Based on the Country Fire Authority's visual fire danger ratings that convey information on weather conditions, the State of Community indicator invites community members to rate their experience of social, political, environmental, economic, cultural, personal and spiritual aspects of community life. The State of Community data records changing conditions for individuals, organisations and community groups.

phenomena beyond the scope of one community to transform in isolation.

Used over a 12-month period this provides a framework to observe and analyse changes in the life of a project. The measure of community resilience increase or decrease makes evident a community's capacity to work towards social and ecological sustainability. In recent years Ife has included an overarching term of survival development that is relevant in current experiences of extreme weather, fires, floods, landslips and global pandemics (Ife 2000). These are phenomena beyond the scope of one community to transform in isolation.

8.2.3. Observation and correlation.
A second evaluation tool involves observation and the identification of common regional outcomes. Focus group discussions and questionnaires provide opportunities for participants to speak of individual and community change. Newspaper articles, films and stories may also provide context that can then be looked at in relation to data on health conditions, income, population and environmental changes. Issues of bureaucratic processes depleting opportunities for local involvement may prove insightful.

8.2.4 Re-investment or depletion?
The indicators reveal ways some industries create local employment while others strip an area of resources, exporting wealth to urban centres or internationally. For example, the community banks as partners between private enterprise and community organisations returned profits to community ventures such as opportunity shops, schools, health centres and sporting groups. These practices strengthen relationships within the community at the same time as expanding economic options.

8.3 Outcomes (what)

8.3.1 Self-evaluation in Communities for Children,
a Kilmany Uniting Care project noted the improvement of the health and wellbeing of families and primarily, the health, wellbeing and early development of young children in the East Gippsland local government area. https://ruralcommunities.com.au/stories-my-community-told-me/

Responses indicating the impact of the project, personally and on the community:

> *The study circles acted as a catalyst to generate interest, confidence and a pathway to positive change. A locally owned, locally directed and locally relevant program is rare but vital to positive long lasting and enjoyable community engagement* (Buchan facilitator 2007).

> *I think it's necessary to make the time to be involved in these kinds of activities. Complacency at a community level leads to isolation within a community. I don't want my children to ever think this is acceptable* (Bairnsdale study circle participants 2006).

8.3.2 Common outcomes.

The East Gippsland Building Community Resilience Project

Local facilitators established community forums that took the time to develop respect and trust and initiate manageable activities. Supported by a regional steering committee the project strengthened and formalised relationships with relevant agencies. The final report notes the following changes and learning: https://ruralcommunities.com.au/fire-awareness-award-winner

Personal change led to:

- respect and trust of group members,
- confident, skilled community members able to work together,
- positive and constructive attitudes,
- responsibility to community became the priority,
- an agreed upon long term vision for their communities,
- solutions designed locally,
- capacity to work in partnership with relevant authorities and organisations,
- active partnerships with all levels of government,
- recognition by community as well as public and private sector agencies.

What we learnt:

- We achieve more when we work together.
- Greater visibility of small communities through participation in EGBCR Advisory Committee meetings attended by agencies.
- Participation in combined Regional Recovery Project meetings with East Gippsland Shire, Regional Development Victoria, Department of Environment, Land Water and Planning.
- Invitation to represent Neighbourhood Houses and Centre for Rural Communities on Municipal Emergency Management Planning Committee (MEMP).
- Sponsorship by Country Fire Authority (CFA) to attend Living with Bushfires Conference (2014) and present at the 2015 conference.

- Presented at Association of Neighbourhood Houses and Learning Centres Conference in Geelong as a case study of Neighbourhood Houses' involvement in Bushfire Recovery with Commissioner Craig Lapsley.

- Recognition that inclusion of Neighbourhood Houses and community groups in identifying manageable levels of responsibility for catering and contracting (machinery operations) is a welcome shift for communities and organisations. The EG Shire circulated forms to update information.

- Bruthen was funded for a Neighbourhood House in 2019.

Comments reflected shared experience of improved relationships with agencies.

The Buchan community's comments and relationships with Emergency Services and Agencies has shifted since this project started, before very sceptical, feelings of exclusion, not in our hands, now feelings of value and that local knowledge and history pertaining to our district is being listened to and a further positive understanding and trust between communities and agencies has emerged (Davies 2015).

Tubbut Neighbourhood House coordinator Deb Foskey commented. *Our communication is generally through monthly meetings which have been invaluable for information sharing, networking and relationship building. I believe those relationships will endure beyond the life of the project* (2015).

Limitations:

- Less than one year funding to develop resources, introduce workers to facilitation skills and engage community and agencies compromised outcomes.

- No accredited professional development pathway for facilitators, often underprepared for complexity and stressful nature of the work.

- Part-time with multiple demands on their time.

- Challenge of dealing with changing organisational staff.

- Increased attention to policies and practice informed by local knowledge within agencies.

https://ruralcommunities.com.au/wp-content/uploads/2020/10/East_Gippsland_Building_Community-Resilience_Report2015.pdf

Increased attention to policies and practice informed by local knowledge within agencies

The Program Manager, Community Engagement and Stakeholder Relationships, Department Environment Land Water and Planning, Gippsland, (2015) Julianne Sargant attended monthly meetings and following the project, initiated a series of fire scenario forums with high fire risk communities Buchan, Bruthen and Nowa Nowa. The facilitation of all agencies meeting with communities to work through a scenario and share information on their capacity and response to an imagined fire emergency was a significant outcome. The scenarios were well attended and provided a reality check for agencies and communities. Everybody learnt and took steps to be better prepared with their own plans and improved communication.

The scenarios were well attended and provided a reality check

FLOAT Almanac (almanak)

Regional Arts Victoria funded the building of a floating arts studio on Lake Tyers in Victoria in 2017 www.float3909. As the FLOAT vessel was in planning and development, collaboration with a broader community of residents to research and document the seasonal changes of Lake Tyers catchment and create a FLOAT ALMANAC began. The Almanac commemorates the changing cycles of the area at the time creating a reference for future residents and visitors.

Interested people met weekly at *The Waterwheel Tavern* (Lake Tyers Beach) to share thoughts, observations and showcase their endeavours. Tavern Tuesday, as it became known, had no membership, no attendance records and the group numbers swelled or dwindled according to family, travel and work commitments. Numbers ranged from a dozen to 60 or more on a weekly basis that continued for 3 years. The foundation was small group democracy inspired by the protocol of study circles (Larson & Nordvall 2010). All were welcomed in this facilitated discussion, their presence affirmed and valued.

Capital indicators of people and place

Country is - a nourishing terrain that gives and receives life. A fundamental proposition in Indigenous law and society is that a country and its living things take care of each other.
(Rose 1997:3-4).
https://www.academia.edu/4539641/Nourishing_Terrains_Australian_Aboriginal_views_of_Landscape_and_Wilderness_Australian_Heritage_Commission_Canberra_1996_

As discussed in Chapter 1 the reference is geographic communities. I draw on insights from Deborah Bird Rose in explaining the relationship to place. *Country is multi-dimensional [it] consists of people, animals, plants, Dreamings, underground, earth, soils, minerals, surface water and air. There is sea country and land country, in some areas people talk about sky country. Country has origins and a future, it exists both in and through time.* (Rose op.cit.)

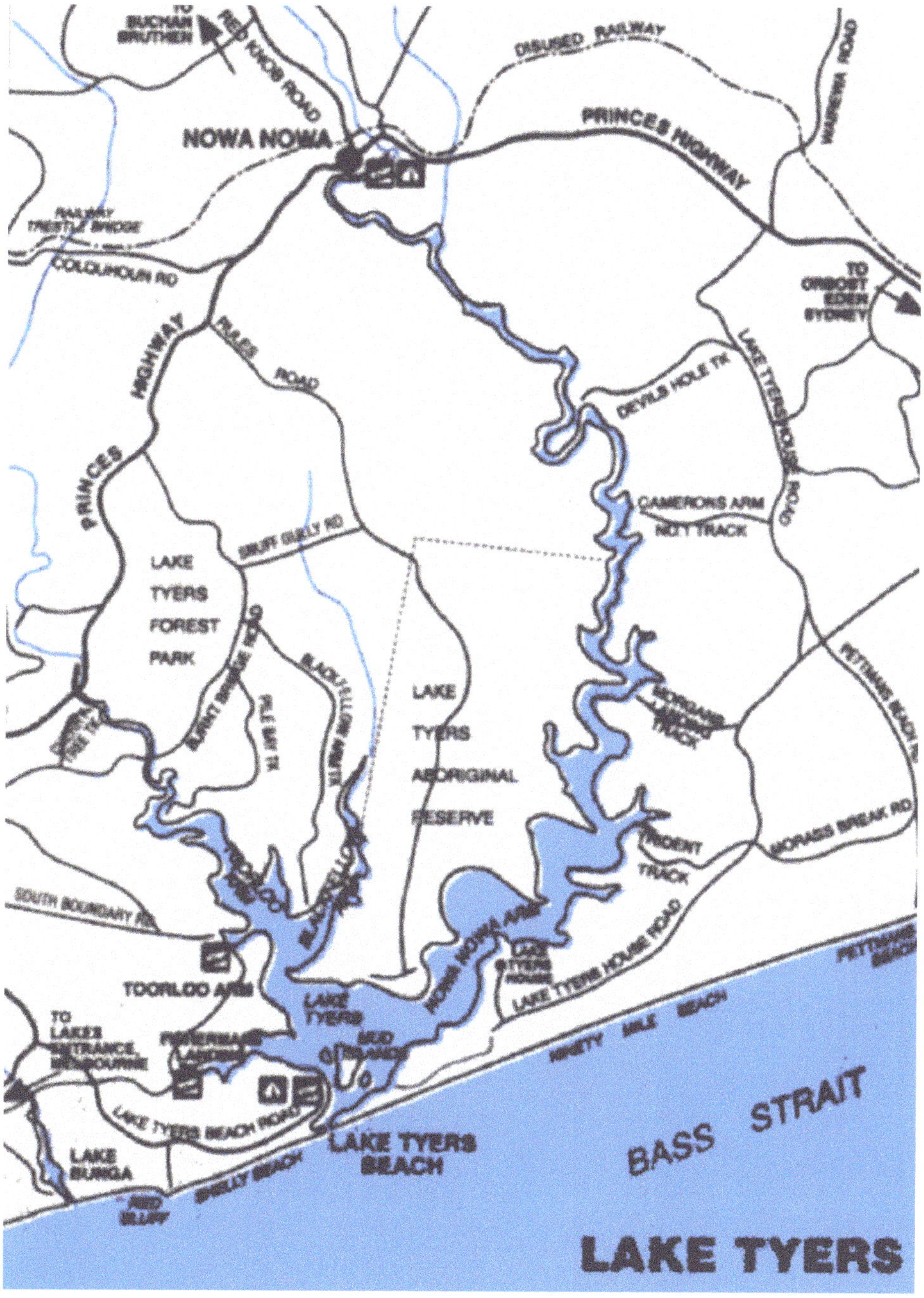

Participants rated their experiences of the current situation across Jim Ife's six aspects of community life: social, cultural, economic, political, personal and spiritual and underpinning these the state of the environment (Ife 1995) using the State of Community indicator.

Snapshot

FLOAT began during the 3 years of drought, prior to devastating fires and COVID pandemics. Socially, culturally, environmentally, personally and spiritually people indicated positive development that created a groundswell of trust and involvement with people who shared a common love of the lake. Environmentally there was energy and greater involvement that erupted into increased distress when natural and built environment was damaged due to policies, vandalism or ignorance. Politically people remained frustrated, despite years of working to engage constructively. This connection between people has continued to nurture personal and community ventures that invest in and celebrate local art, a healthy catchment a vibrant culture leading to employment. In this time of environmental and health crises opportunity to listen to each other and tackle complex situations was established.

8.3.3. Capital indicators used to reflect on impact of the FLOAT

project an arts+science+environment floating art studio on Lake Tyers www.float3909.com/almanac

Socially

Social involvement is the interaction within communities. How would you rate your ability to have positive opportunities for involvement, the energy, time and resources to participate productively?

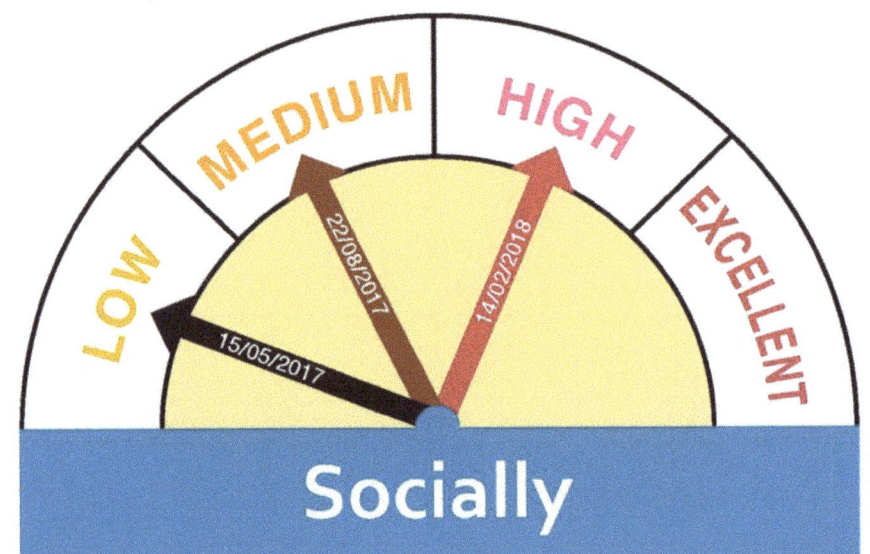

Increase in social activity

At the beginning of FLOAT individuals had an interest in the lake but lacked a way to know other people or collaborate on projects. The weekly gatherings at Tavern Tuesday and involvement in the Almanac invited people to share observations on changes in the landscape and community life. Connections and friendships blossomed as more and more people were welcomed at the gathering. Everyone was listened to. Some husbands came tentatively with a wife who painted, then mentioned that they wrote 'some poetry' or 'painted fish' or 'etched on glass'. The welcoming culture of the group led to them sharing their work.

Connections and friendships blossomed

For example:
https://www.youtube.com/watch?v=_pBImEAV31I Doug Esler
https://www.facebook.com/photo/?fbid=10159018333301704&set=a.99331996703/ Bill Payne

The ripple effect of the group becoming more vibrant with each personal success led to friendships and trust between participants.

Float almanacers

Low. 15/05/2017. *Work outside of community in Bairnsdale on 3 days of week. Carer of young children, so much of social involvement is around the children's activities.*

High. 22/08/2017. *FLOAT has been so enjoyable to attend each week, and also additional activities. More involved in school volunteering, as I have left work to retire.*

Excellent. 2018. *I feel connected to my community and am willing to get involved with community groups. FLOAT has been welcoming and instrumental in encouraging wider/inter group participation. I have a strong connection with school and sporting club and realise the more involved the better I feel about myself and the community. As a carer of younger children it is important to encourage and model the importance of community to them.* (Karen Murdoch)

Medium. *Long been a bit of a loner, travel my own path. Gradually coming out of my shell after a life of introspection and insular pursuits. (Phil later wrote and recorded a poem On being an Almanacker in a collection Stories of the Lake (2019) ruralcommunities.com.au › on-being-an-almanacker* https://www.youtube.com/watch?v=VHJpTRAvVbc. (Phil Evans)

High to Excellent. 17/4/2017 *Heavily involved with Australian Native Plant Society East Gippsland. Only engage with few groups so I can commit fully. A few good friends and family.*

Excellent. 10/9/2017. *FLOAT has been a revelation in broadening the people I know with the local and wider community. People I knew vaguely I know so much better* (Frank Flynn)

High. 28/02/2018. *During the year we have had the opportunity to meet and get to know many members of the local community. Involvement in activities and events has led to friendships and connections* (Leanne Flaherty and Bill Payne).

Politically

How would you rate your current political involvement? That is your ability to participate in decisions that impact on your life at all levels: community/local/regionally/state/national or international levels.

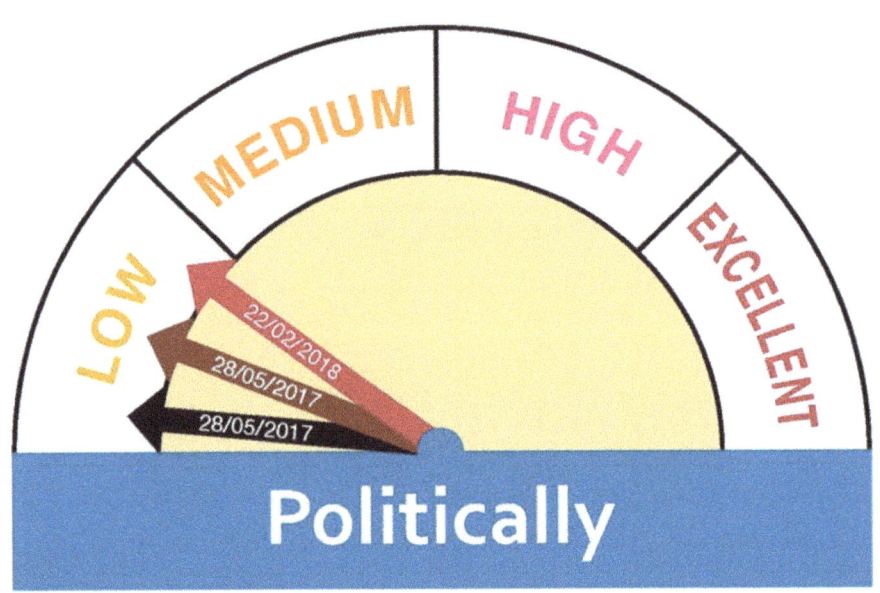

Bigger has not been better for East Gippsland Shire with its average of 2 people per sq. kilometer. The reality of a few regional centres and small scattered coastal and hinterland communities does not fit the 'level playing field' modelling of centralised competitive tendering policies currently legislated into every layer of government. The local government's capacity to act democratically in the interests of citizens challenged under these policies. The once resource-rich East Gippsland shire has increasingly become an area of distress and the majority of natural resources are now owned by overseas companies. Local government and institutions are permeated with corporate language of clients and customers rather than citizens. From a community perspective there is frustration at the absence of community engagement with decision makers that could lead to mutually beneficial partnerships.

A distrust of politicians, political systems and their capacity to act for the public good was a consistent response. In the absence of any planning scheme to regulate coastal development, preference for coastal views and short-term profits resulted in clearing and over population of a sensitive eco-system.

Support came for short-term projects but little long-term engagement or engagement with decision-makers. Community groups continue to 'clean up' rubbish, weeds, care for bird and marsupial breeding sites and monitor the health of the lake. For those seeking to care for a relatively undamaged catchment this is a distressing and frustrating state of affairs where everyone loses as inappropriate development impacts on the lake. The flow on impact on recreational activities, fishing, accommodation, habitat and distress to local Aboriginal communities is of concern.

Float Almanacers

Medium. (29/05/2017) *I find that politicians in general are pushing their own agenda which in most cases is to the detriment of the community.*

Medium. (29/8/2017) *I am questioning more and more about our democracies. What's happening to it? Politics is overwhelming at times, sifting through the bullshit to get to the truth.*

High. (14/02/2018) *Being in FLOAT has enabled me to hear and understand political issues, particularly those impacting the environment. However, there is a strong voice in the group who all want environmental change for the better and are prepared to be politically active particularly in areas of mining and protecting our precious landscape* (Helen Crossley).

Concerns were expressed in relation to local government pandering to developers and business at the expense of constituents.

(9/10/17) Rampant rorting and flouting of building codes, National government – shame over refugee treatment, and lack of leadership on racism (Raylee Flynn)

Low. (02/6/2017) *Policy and planning often seem to drown in a quagmire of bureaucracy and incompetence* (Leslie Wallis).

Low. *Single blocks are now being sub-divided.*

Fire versus forest
Loss of vegetation, habitat for birds, lyrebirds at Lake Tyers Beach, Echidna – small marsupials. 'Ownership of commons' where I live. Gardens encroaching, invasive plants thrown over the bank and take off. Throwing garden waste over is common practice it kills vegetation and 'improves' the view.

No action taken by council despite letters, phone calls, notifications to councillors and bureaucrats. Worked with others to no avail.

Over fishing
Cats and dogs at Lake Tyers Beach!! (Raylee Flynn)

Low. (22/08/2017) Politics do matter to me, but I get very disillusioned at the dishonesty and greed: economics being their major focus (Karen Murdoch).

Medium. Float engaging constructively across all these issues but not well supported within region.

Economically
How would you rate the current state of economic activity in your community? Including levels of employment, circulation of money/goods locally and rate of reinvestment or depletion that impacts on your life. Do you observe a balance between current resources in the area and options for the long term?

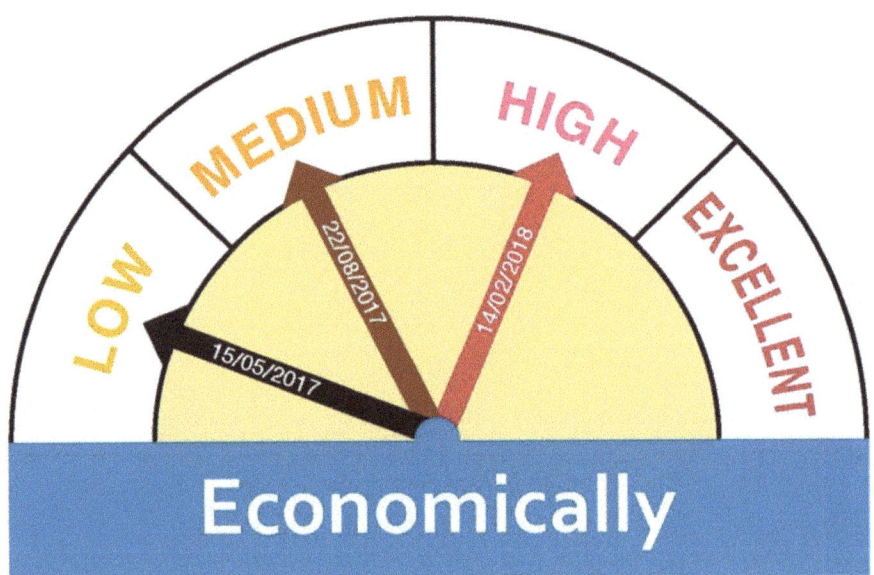

Economic activity increased
Weekly FLOAT gatherings at The Tavern, with 20 to 50 people, many of whom stay for lunch and benefit a seasonal business. Visiting artists stay in local accommodation and the

demand for real estate is becoming competitive. The Lake Tyers Hall committee, FLOAT and *Stories of Influence* (https://ruralcommunities.com.au/stories/) support each other with raffles, attendance, ticket sales and art auctions. Gippsland Solar committed a solar unit to FLOAT vessel for a reduced amount and an Art Auction at the Tavern made up the required amount ($7,000).

Hobbies have turned into art forms and businesses as individuals become more confident in their abilities, to the delight of the group. Fashion shows of textile artists on the FLOAT which feature designs inspired by the lake now have independent web pages: *Floating threads* https://www.floatingthreads.com.au/ and *Frocksmith* http://www.frocksmith.com.au/.

Artist in Residence Lichen Kelp from *Seaweed preservation society* inspired a grand feast at Tavern in partnership with *Sailor's Grave Brewery* featuring seaweed beer, *Seasalt Bakery* featuring seaweed bread and each dish on the menu featured seaweed. Sold out event.

FLOAT almanacers

Low. (15/5/2017) *Community in Lake Tyers Beach and Lakes Entrance have little money to spend on more than basics. Business seems to be struggling and closing down –which effects employment options/tourism etc.*

Low. (22/08/2017) *Economic issues are all consuming, a priority it seems to all government decisions. Something I do not agree with or like (Karen Murdoch).*

Medium. (14/2/2018) *Within the area a number of businesses are closing in the shopping centre. Times are changing and the internet is an option for people to make purchases now. Within the community, I do not hear 'doom and gloom' stories. The community is buoyant and appears positive in regard to economic development. FLOAT has demonstrated other economic options that value the environment. A different view of how the economy should work.*

Medium. (29/05/2017) *I belong to a socio-economic group that is becoming increasingly marginalised.*

Medium. (29/08/2017) *I'm becoming more aware of the struggle for regional communities in terms of budget allocations* (Helen Crossley).

Hobbies have turned into art forms and businesses

High. *(14/02/2018) The FLOAT project has been extremely positive and hopefully has opened the eyes of those who 'control the purse strings'! FLOAT on a SHOESTRING was a successful venture and hopefully will advance to bigger and better community involvement and job prospects.*

Personally and spiritually

How would you rate your ability to 'have a life' that has personal expressions of creativity and spirituality? To what extent are their opportunities to reflect on what guides your daily journey, your inter-action with others and your sense of place in the world?

FLOAT celebrated personal creativity, aware that each of us contributed to the confidence and motivation to take another public step.

Ripples

Our creations, show the fragile beauty of the world.
Words, invite connection.
Our worlds expand as we walk, talk, paddle and listen together,
Observing and interpreting
Being in this natural gallery (Sheil 2018)

FLOAT almanacers

Excellent. *(9/4/2017) (Personal) I have pulled my finger out and taken my photography seriously, and learnt to smile a lot. Pretty happy with where I am. I know who I am and what I believe* (Frank Flynn).

Low. *(02/06/2017) Being a visual artist I find great fulfilment and enrichment on many levels.*

Medium. (2/10/2017) *I feel happy with this creativity sustains me, my spirituality nurtures me through the natural world* (Leslie Wallis).

Med to high. (28/02/2017) *The project, through the personal interests and studies of others opened up environmental stewardship.*

High. (12/9/2017) *Sense of peace. Very comfortable. FLOAT has brought me a whole new sense of self and belonging.*

Excellent. (5/12/2017) *Being involved in the FLOAT Almanac group has increased my confidence in my opinions, my ideas and my direction in life. While my sense of place in the world is not perfect, the past year has supported my growth towards finding a solid ground for my soul* (Carolyn Crunden).

Low. *– a bit 'broken' after breast cancer, brain surgery x 3, radio therapy for a rapidly growing non-cancerous tumour in last 6 years.*

Lapsed Catholic. Absolutely appalled by church. Non church funeral. Grew up on a farm but anti-nature. Now more connected to natural environment. Watch smell and observe. Blown away by sun rises and sun sets which I ignored for 50 years

Excellent. (10/7 /2017) *Important social interactions as what started as a morning activity extends over the afternoon. Don't feel so alone/ frustrated/afraid to express my views* (Raylee Flynn).

Interest in presentation by Sylke Fromberg from Germany on The European Celts and their relationship to nature packed the Tavern, workshop at Fisherman's landing and Lake Tyers Beach Hall.

Environmentally
How would you rate the current state of policy and planning in regard to environmental issues impacting on your community? Are processes open and accessible? Is there an ability to share knowledge and be involved in decisions and actions for care of the environment?

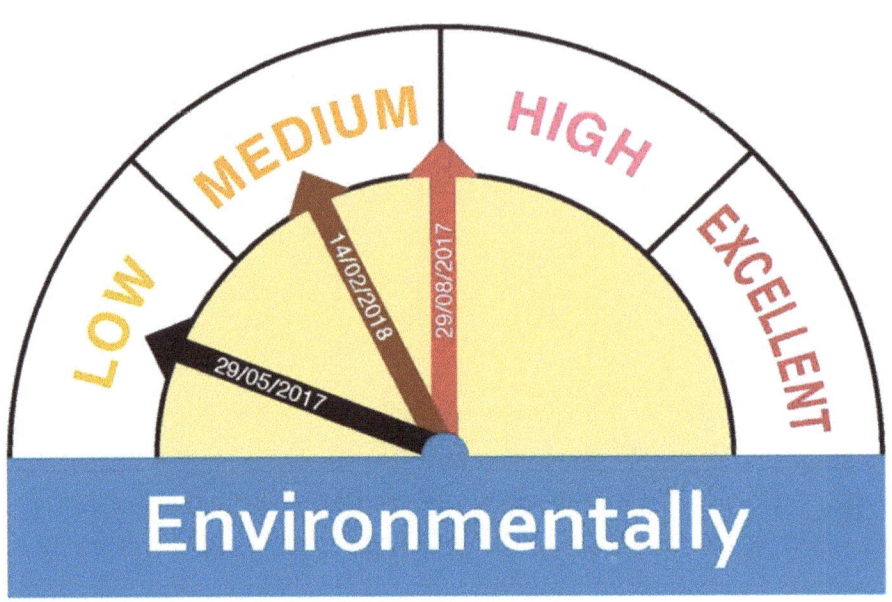

Environmental development increasing

Respected and committed environmentally aware elders with a long history of active involvement in interpretation, planting and protection of the catchment came to FLOAT hopeful but not optimistic. Over time, they began to relax and smile as families with young children came to Coast Action weeding and planting days. FLOAT welcomed discussion on the impact of deer on habitat, the geological evolution of the estuary and its relationship to the Gippsland Lakes along with Indigenous storytellers sharing stories of estuary management. People were introduced to insight of old words and language. Environmental beauty and vulnerability featured in the myriad of creative arts and literature. Community members are more hopeful without being ignorant of limitation of coastal planning legislation.

Float almanacers

Medium. Feb 2018 *Policy and planning in regard to our environment has been absent. The pristine environment is not recognised as the valuable asset it is by government departments. Threats are always around the corner as unsuitable planning and projects are considered, without thought of long-term affect to community and environment. FLOAT supports the appreciation of the environment through experiences and art, knowledge and understanding. FLOAT has connected various groups to work together, communicate with each other and support each other: re environment* (Henk Van Leuwen).

Low. (02/06/2017) *There seems to be an awareness generally of our environment and its impact on decisions, protection and repair, how to find information and pertinent bodies to approach. Landcare is an exception* (Leslie Wallis).

High. (29/05/2017) *This is why I moved here! I love the environment, history, people, cultures and opportunities.*

High. (29/08/2017) *There is a fairly broad platform to share and gather knowledge providing one takes time to investigate.*

High. (14/02/2018) *I have listened to many discussions about the environment, been on some beautiful walks and experienced nature as it should be – left alone to exist in a clean and safe environment. I have seen beautiful images, witnessed the change of seasons and the most exciting thing from all of this is the move to make Lake Tyers Heritage Listed. This would never have happened had it not been for FLOAT and to me it is the 'icing on the cake'. An environmental legacy for future generations to respect, care for and enjoy* (Helen Crossley).

Excellent. (5/7/2017) *Almanac people were involved in recent rainforest working bee.*

Med to High (5/12/2017) *Care, respect and protection of our environment is important to me. Being involved in the ALMANAC PROJECT has improved my local knowledge and given me stimulation to become involved in looking out for opportunities to support decisions which support our environment* (Carolyn Crunden).

High. (28/02/2017) *Could be effective focused on focused issues. I remain hopeful* (Rob Ward).

Through trial and error with 3D printing Rob created a weather station to monitor changing conditions on Lake Tyers. He has since made this available globally. https://www.facebook.com/FLOAT.3909/posts/big-float-shout-for-rob-ward-who-made-this-for-the-almanac-project-and-exhibitio/1824427800956170/

Culturally
How would you rate the state of cultural activities in the community? The private or public celebrations of creative life in song, dance, festivals, art, artisans, food and recreation? How would you rate the balance between local ownership and realistic resourcing in all its dimensions?

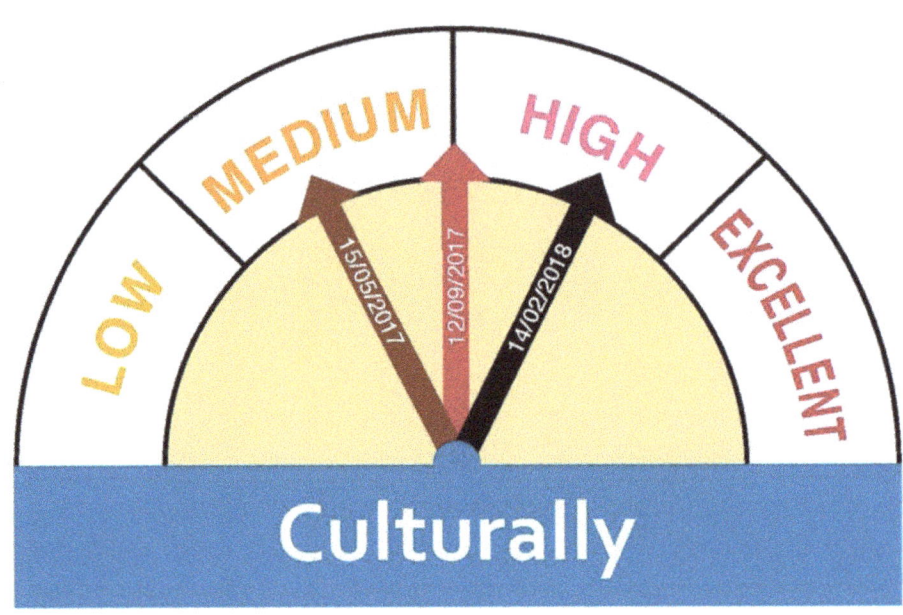

Cultural development increasing

Jochen Kruse, artist and calligrapher, came to Tavern Tuesday regularly. He is quite deaf and spent the time observing and drawing folk at the table, delighting people with page by page emergence of his universal children's story *When Gargoyle saw Schiltzor.* Schiltzohr – German for wallaby with slit in its ear from tangling with wire as it broke into his garden hungry for food during the drought of 2017. The pair go on adventures that include the Notre Dame Cathedral fire – an international almanac.

When Gargoyle saw Schlitzohr - book by Jochen Kruse - foundry www.ifoundthefoundry.com › shop

Josephine Jakobi – our lady of the lake, is a textile artist whose work explores the changing salt and fresh water interchange in the estuary of Lake Tyers. Her exhibition 'Halocline' was the culmination of living beside and on the waters of the estuary for a year. Josephine Jakobi: Artist Insight. A …www.facebook.com › eastgippslandartgallery › p

An active Tavern Tuesday contributor, Josephine's work attracted and supported other textile artists including Glenys Mann, well known organizer of textile workshops internationally. Josephine and Glenys teamed up and held workshops at Bungalook Studios. The event generating an investment in culture, attention to the environment and an income for both artists. Josephine Jakobi 'Voice From The Estuary' – biophiliarts www.biophiliarts.com › post › 2017/10/25 › josephine-.

Masterclass with Glenys Mann… 29 Feb - 6 March 2020 www.fibrearts.jigsy.com › masterclasses

Float almanacers

Medium. (15/05/2017) *Culturally there are various opportunities in the areas around Lake Tyers to get involved in creative events*

Medium. (22/08/2017) *Closer connection to Lake Tyers area and recognizing connections* (Karen Murdoch).

Medium. (18/01/2017) *Quite low as I am still 'new' to the area and settling in, finding the opportunities and getting involved in what's going on locally.*

Medium to High. (12/09/2017) *FLOAT is bringing a new look to cultural development in the area. NO ONE SIZE FITS ALL approach, MORE ALL WELCOME BRING WHAT YOU ARE*

Med to High. (5/12/2017) *There is more starting to happen but in a slowly building way which in the long run feels like it will be sustainable in the future* (Carolyn Crunden).

High. (29/5/2017) *I am enjoying the opportunities to explore different cultural avenues.*

Medium to High. (5/12/2017) *I have found that there is plenty of cultural activities in the community and opportunity to develop further if needed.*

High. (14/2/2018) *The exhibition demonstrated individual creative abilities coming together in a fantastic community setting. Overall it was empowering I've learnt a lot about cultural processes, development of relationships and issues attached to the processes. Being able to advance myself creatively within a community arts project has been fabulous experience and one that will stay with me. I am sure others will be inspired to continue their creative endeavours as I intend to do. It has made me realise that there is a purpose to art in more ways than one. I would never have had the opportunity to develop relationships in the community had it not been for my creative choices and achievements.*

FLOAT has opened up so many opportunities to celebrate /experience cultural activities. It has brought art to the forefront. Indigenous culture was evident (showcased) by the corroboree and the whole community were inspired and emotionally affected by what they saw/ felt. FLOAT encourages cultural development in all its facets and personally I am enjoying the journey (Helen Crossley).

the richness of community life became evident generating action.

As people shared thoughts and insights the richness of community life became evident generating action. People invested in the local economy, culture and environment and in social activities. While the Almanac culminated in an art+science+environment+culture exhibition at Lake Tyers House in February 2018 the foundations of custodianship of the catchment continue.

Change at all these levels is the desired outcome of transformational learning. A shift in understanding and practice reinforced with reflection. New stories are shared, not of frustration, division and isolation but of connection, optimism, action and involvement, located in the landscape.

New stories are shared,

Questions

What are your experiences of group learning that resulted in new personal endeavors?

What changes resulted from this experience?

For yourself, and for others?

Are you aware of a turning point for yourself in regard to this experience?

How did this come about?

9. REFLECTION

We shame ignorance when instead we should shame the systems that create and even rely upon ignorance. Ignorance is a fault of society, not the individual.
(Harry Saddler, Float diary 2019:5).

9.1 Rationale (why)

Regional community development is concerned with a balance between people and the places they live. In European terms, the bio-region provides the reference point. In Indigenous cultures it is the country. A critical feature of regional development is the inclusion of those traditionally excluded from decision-making and for those accustomed to taking control to share the responsibilities. With this change new opportunities and potential will become evident as individuals and groups become aware of reciprocal ways of working. Partnerships will emerge that benefit all. Such a transition will benefit from organizational shifts away from fragmented portfolios or hierarchical structuring towards a culture of including community at decision-making tables.

Partnerships will emerge that benefit all.

Moving from theory to practice can become task orientated, and collaborative ways of working to strengthen community and include new people and organisations can be overlooked. Planned-for periods of reflection provide opportunities to stay focused on the original visions, or to become aware of how these could be extended as understanding and occasion permits.

9.2 Implementation (how)

'Yarning …is structured cultural activity that is recognized even in Research circles as a valid and rigorous methodology for knowledge production, inquiry and transmission. It is a ritual that incorporates elements such as story, humour, gesture and mimicry for consensus-building, meaning making and innovation. It references places and is highly contextualized in the local worldviews of those yarning'.
(Yunkaporta 2019:130-131).

Involvement needs to be embedded as a process. Small group discussions are a key feature of groups as diverse as Black Lives Matter (en.wikipedia.org › wiki › Black_Lives_Matter)

Yarning circles in Indigenous communities (Yunkaporta 2019:131), in Citizenship Schools and the Civil Rights movement in America (https://www.nche.net/hm0214westhoff), and in Spain study groups were an essential beginning to co-operative ventures in Mondragon.

Journals also remind us of a stage of unknowing,

9.2.1. Journals. Community members are encouraged to keep individual journals to maintain a record of their reactions and thoughts on the processes and outcomes of being a member of the group. This opportunity for writing and reflecting on situations of interest provides time to formulate ideas that can later be shared. Journals also remind us of a stage of unknowing, before we were introduced to other ways of understanding our own past and options for a different future. Our stories are significant whether they affirm those experiences or give insight into impact of past policies that had not been shared in the past.

9.2.2. Strategic questions constantly invite reflection and involvement from diverse life experiences. As people speak connections can be made and new opportunities for ways to work together become apparent.

9.2.3 Involving wider community. The strategies within Collaborative Engagement introduce ways of working that strengthen community interaction. While the work begins with study circle participants, these skills, knowledge and attitudes extend into the community. Organising a public event to involve the wider community is an important step.

9.2.4. Celebrate, continue learning. Groups are encouraged to plan regular periods for acknowledging their achievements and to put in place ways of working to improve areas of concern. An annual event is a good opportunity to do this, as it enables a timely response to concerns rather than a blow up due to frustration when issues are not acknowledged or given attention. Celebrating what has been achieved raises awareness of what is possible when people work together as well, as personal confidence.

9.3 Outcomes

Concerned to raise awareness of the beauty and vulnerability of the gorge

This leads to that. In 2014 concerned that despite successful campaigns by the Nowa Nowa community to prevent damage to the ancient Nowa Nowa Gorge by blasting to install a gas pipeline (Duke Energy 2000) or drilling to install an optic fiber cable (Telstra 2010) a proposal to mine iron-ore by Eastern Iron threatened the catchment once again. It seemed that only locals, both Aboriginal and non-Aboriginal, valued this ancient landscape and its largely undamaged catchment (Blakeman 2019). Concerned to raise awareness of the beauty and vulnerability of the gorge and lake without dividing a community the Centre for Rural Communities invited people to share and record stories of their life on the gorge. Singer/songwriter Jan Wositzky contributed a night time performance and the community were enthusiastic about 'doing it again'.

http://storytellingguildvic.blogspot.com/2014/08/gorgeous-yarns-with-jan-wositzky-nowa.html

The event became *The Stories of influence*, an annual gathering of storytellers sharing hidden histories that had been hidden away under the bed in reports, diaries and letters or in hearts and minds. *Stories of influence* evolved and grew each year as people spoke of stories that some knew well but had not been told in public arenas. Wayne Thorpe spoke of *'A story of Bung Yarnda (aka Lake Tyers)'* that told of the need for the catchment to open and close naturally to feed the plants, the fish, birds and people. https://www.youtube.com/watch?v=aaykiOzgaTs

Over the next 9 years stories shared by Aunty Eileen Harrison and Carolyn Landon: *A Koorie Woman's Life*, Bruce Pascoe's *Dark Emu: black seeds agriculture or accident*, Jan Wositzky's performances of William Buckley as well as stories in song by Uncle Herb Patten, by Todd Cook, in textile by Aunty Doris Paton and art by Ray Thomas and Leann Edwards changed our awareness of impact of policies on this community and others.

The film documentary on *The Warrigal Creek Massacres* by Swinburne film team https://www.youtube.com/watch?v=FiPWjgx7nQ0– and the personal experiences of families impacted resulted in the formation of Reconciliation East Gippsland to take steps to raise awareness of this not so distant history. By the following year three other writers/families shared their stories of personal involvement as perpetrators or survivors. https://ruralcommunities.com.au/stories https://www.facebook.com/storiesofinfluence

The group became active in working with Uncle Max Dulumunmun Harrison to hold healing ceremonies for the land on Brodribb River, Millie Creek massacre site and to raise general awareness of the past practices and impact of policies. A humbling journey of celebration of survival of culture that we have been welcome to share. There are other stories of 'listening to the land' in later chapters.

Stories of influence evolved and grew each year

Questions

Are you aware of the benefit of opportunities for reflection and planning within organisations with which you are involved?

Was this an opportunity to raise issues of concern?

Was this an opportunity to acknowledge work and achievements during the year?

What strategies did your organisation use to involve people in this event?

In your opinion was the event worthwhile?

Why was this?

FURTHER REFERENCES

Alexander, J., and Cannata, S., (2019) *Art beat of the country: a time when art became the response to hard times on the land.* ebook: https://lifestoriesmentor.com.au/featured-book/art-beat-of-the-country/ https://www.eastgippslandartgallery.org.au

Bailey, A., Barker., J., Brinkley, C., Brown, D., Butler, C., Grey, S., Penny, L., Sheil. H., Webb, M., (1996) *Hearing the voices of rural women: More than one way*, Report of the Rural Women's Network, Office of Rural Affairs, Horsham, Victoria.

Belenky Field, M., McVicker Clinchy, B., Rule Golderger, N., Mattuck Tarule., J. 1986. *Women's Ways of Knowing: The development of Self, Voice and Mind.* Basic Books, New York.

Business council of co-operatives and mutuals. https://www.facebook.com/bccmau/

Bruce, L., (2005) 'Evaluation and Change', *New Community Quarterly*, Vol. 3. No. 4, Summer: 2005: 26

Caling, T., (2005) 'Bruthen and District Study Circle', *New Community Quarterly: Vol. 3 No 4 – Summer 2005:31-38*

Franklin, M.A., Short, L., and Teacher, (Eds)(1994) *Country women at the crossroads*, University of New England Press, Armidale.

Foley, G. 1999 *Learning in Social Action: A contribution to Understanding Informal Education.* Zed Books. London.

Garlick, S., (1997) 'The ebb and flow of Regional Development Policy and Practice in Australia: an overview and future possibilities,' *Regional co-operation and Development Forum*, Canberra, November, pp 24-34.

George Floyd protests in Australia, Wikipedia en.wikipedia.org › wiki›George_Floyd_protests_in_Australia

Heaney, T. W., & Horton, A. I. (1990). *Reflective engagement for social change.* In J. Mezirow & Associates, Fostering critical reflection in adulthood: *A guide to transformative and emancipatory learning* (pp. 74-98). San Francisco: Jossey-Bass.

Ife, J; (2019) 'Reflection on an election: a personal essay', *New Community Journal* Vol.17. (2) Issue 66.p 61-67.
https://permaculturewest.org.au/resources/archives/rowell/jill-jordan-on-community-building/

Knowles, M., (2016) Malcolm Knowles' 6 Adult Learning Principles | Darlo Higher ...
darlohighereducation.com › news › malcolmknowles6a...

Larsson, S., (2001/2010) 'Seven aspects of democracy as related to study circles', *International Journal of Lifelong Education*, Vol. 20. No.3. (May-June) pp.199-217.
Seven aspects of democracy as related to study circles ... www.tandfonline.com › doi › abs

Learning Circles Australia (1998) *News of learning circles Australia: Not just talk.* Australian Association of Adult and Community Education Inc.

Maloney, M., (2020) https://www.earthlaws.org.au/about-us/aela-team/michellemaloney/
www.earthlaws.org.au 2020

Mathews, R., (2017) *Of Labour and Liberty: Distributism in Victoria 1891-1966.* Monash University Publishing, (e-books).

Mathews, R. (1999), *Jobs of our own: a stakeholder society,* Pluto Press, Sydney

Macfadyn, P., https:www.flatpackdemocracy.co.uk

Peavey, F, (1990's) https://commonslibrary.org/strategic-questioning/

Rose-Bird, D., (1997). 'Indigenous Ecology and an Ethic of Hope', *Environmental Justice: Global Ethics for 21st Century Conference,* Melbourne University.

Rose-Bird, D., (1996) *Nourishing Terrains*, Australian Aboriginal views of Landscape and Wilderness, Australian Heritage Commission, Canberra. https://www.academia.edu/4539641/Nourishing_Terrains_Australian_Aboriginal_views_of_Landscape_and_Wilderness_Australian_Heritage_Commission_Canberra_1996_

Rose-Bird, D., (2004) *Reports from a wild country: ethics for decolonisation*, University of New South Wales Press, Sydney.

Sheil, H., (2015) *Building Community Futures through Co-operation*, Centre for Rural Communities, Nowa Nowa https://ruralcommunities.com.au/publications

Sheil, H. (2014) Education has a critical role in community being the answer, *International Association of Community Development Conference*, Glasgow University. https://ruralcommunities.com.au/wp-content/uploads/2016/05/Helen-Sheil-Education-has-critical-role-paper1.pdf

Steinem, G., (2018) *Power in progress, Guidelines for difficult conversations*, Fessler, Quartz at work. https://qz.com/work/1467935/gloria-steinem-says-these-are-the-best-guidelines-for-difficult-conversations/

Sullivan, Kath https://www.weeklytimesnow.com.au/news/politics/joan-kirner-remembered-as-architect-of-landcare/news-story/62719cb857cf5b682eff0b290adee0a6

Tacey. D. (1995) *Edge of the Sacred*. Transformation in Australia. Harper Collins. Australia.

Vella. J. (1994) *Learning to Listen, Learning to Teach: The power of dialogue in Educating Adults*. Jossey Bass Publishers. San Francisco. https://www.youtube.com/watch?v=fFYI_Qo8wpY

Yunkaporta, T., (2109) *Sand Talks: How Indigenous thinking can save the world*, Text Publishing Company, Melbourne.

Who's counting? Marilyn Waring on Sex, Lies and Global Economics https://www.youtube.com/watch?v=WS2nkr9q0VU

Waring, M., (2018) *Still counting: Wellbeing, Women's Work and Policy making*, Bridget Williams Books Ltd (BWB Texts), Wellington www.bwb.co.nz.

CHAPTER 5

180

CHAPTER 5
BIO-REGIONAL APPROACH

This is why we're trying to encourage our fellow Australians, our brothers and sisters out there, to get to know where you live, because it's place-based. The land is alive, the rivers are alive, the living systems are alive, the birds and the fish - everything communicates. Don't see yourself as a human being as elitist and above other living systems. This is the gift of Indigenous People across the world, saying we want you, because your DNA is embedded here. We want you to get to know your country, to feel your country, to heal your country, because it's all our country.

Dr Anne Poelina https://www.regennarration.com/episodes/084-regenerative-songlines

FOCUS OF THIS CHAPTER

1. A bio-regional approach
2. Role of community development worker
3. Finding out
4. Working with government
5. Learning about learning
6. Networking
7. Rural communities, regional groups, peak bodies
8. Communication: social media and platforms
9. Establishing structures and financing projects: regional economics
10. Rural trusts and foundations

    Further references

1. A BIO-REGIONAL APPROACH

Simply put, [bioregionalism] means learning to become native to place, fitting ourselves to a particular place, not fitting a place to our pre-determined tastes. It is living within the limits and the gifts provided by a place, creating a way of life that can be passed on to future generations.

Judith Plant in https://cascadiabioregion.org/what-is-bioregionalism

Regional workers are well placed to create and resource opportunities for people to 'meet' and speak of their situation in public forums. Engagement that begins by fostering the inclusion of inter-generational knowledge of people and the landscapes they occupy makes visible the unique characteristics of community life that can inform organizational planning.

Communities cannot tackle the situation in isolation.

Communities may have existing structures that can benefit from introducing or revisiting inclusive practices. Establishing a co-operative culture strengthens community relationships and is especially valued when many are are experiencing grief in regard to what they love being damaged or destroyed, whether by nature or a way of life. Predictable natural disasters of drought, fire, flood, plagues of locusts and mice overlaid by isolation to minimize the spread of pandemic viruses have limited contact. Small groups, on-line contact, social media, local media radio and television all provide opportunities to discuss how best to live in and heal damaged landscapes and populations. The outcomes will not be known in advance but attention to each of the strategies within Collaborative Engagement for Transformation creates a welcoming, receptive and reflective organisation people trust. Mallacoota and District Recovery Association is a good example madrecovery.com/

Communities cannot tackle the situation in isolation. As they are the site of impact of multiple decisions made by public and private sector organisations mechanisms to factor in the quality of community life are critical. Linking communities with resource people and information expands options and reduces isolation. These shifts towards working in partnership with communities facilitates local knowledge being present in regional planning.

Examples include: The Network of Neighbourhood Houses that connects houses through regionally resourced organization. The Network employs workers in rural communities and provides basic operating costs. Landcare is another well-known example and historically the Country Education Project and East Gippsland Access Project. Rather than compete for limited rural funding community hubs formed an alliance between Mallacoota, Orbost, Lakes Entrance, Swifts Creek, Buchan and Bairnsdale to access a range of community and youth related funding.

By pooling funding, local workers were employed with primary responsibility to community based committees. These workers covered training, education, adult literacy, youth information and employment, community development activities and counselling (McDonald 1991:214, Sheil 2002:23). Other regions had similar collaborative approaches. While communities experience common issues, local solutions can accommodate differences in population size, culture, resources, knowledge and experience of working collaboratively.

2. ROLE OF COMMUNITY DEVELOPMENT WORKER

A recently released report produced by the Mirboo North & District Community Foundation and the Mirboo North & District Community Bank, found 92 per cent of residents agreed with the statement that people around here are willing to help their neighbours, compared to the state average of just 74 per cent.

https://mirboodistrictfoundation.org.au/our-impact/vital-signs/

2.1 Introducing and affirming the value of democratic processes is a primary role of the community development worker. In chapter 1 the different stages of parenting were discussed to draw attention to the changing needs of individuals as they moved towards maturity and independence. Workers employed by large organisations have the dual educational role of involving and educating their organisations on inclusive ways of working that begins with investing in local knowledge, planning and local ownership.

2.2 Developing skills to work and plan collaboratively follows the establishment stage of listening and respectful dialogue. Learning to listen takes practice, learning to encourage involvement by others takes practice (Vella 2002, https://wvnds.wordpress.com/2008/03/04/learning-to-listen-learning-to-teach-jane-vella/). Practicing these ways of working, supports the transition from an individual with concern about a particular issue, to that of group member prepared to work on a common activity. Each time people speak, they name their situation, clarifying both their understanding and options. It is an evolving journey of personal and community development.

Learning to listen takes practice, learning to encourage involvement by others takes practice

An important issue for workers is to be aware of the ways people connect with information and relate it to their situation. People benefit from having time to draw on their past experiences and talk through what they value, as well as seeking out information and ideas.

2.3 Trust develops as members practice respectful ways of working together creating a foundation for moving from reacting to externally set agendas, to thinking and dreaming of how life could be. Visioning is a time for the worker to step back, to not participate in the regular meetings of the group. Like the learning to drive example; the goal is for the new driver to reach a stage when your support and the practice culminate in independent travel. This is an expression of confidence in the group to support independent thought and action. Direction and decisions at this stage belong to the group, not the worker.

Direction and decisions at this stage belong to the group, not the worker.

2.4. Timing. Be flexible approach in regard to the timing of introducing community members to further information, or new contacts. In the initial period of groups chose to concentrate on establishing a legitimate presence in the community. The group members will initiate contact when they are ready. It is a matter of timing.

2.5. Support. While you may live in the district your role is a facilitative role. It is not healthy if the group becomes dependent on your involvement. Social justice organiser, Gloria Steinem recommends the principles of *Black Lives Matter* as a way to have difficult conversations.

It is not healthy if the group becomes dependent on your involvement.

Lead with love

Low ego

High Impact

Move at the speed of trust.

Alicia Garza, Patrisse Cullors and Opal Tometi

It takes as long as it takes or move at the speed of trust in recognition that people are at different stages due to damage of past events. This is especially relevant following trauma of disasters. The work is about supporting the skills and development of confidence for the long-term involvement in community decision making. https://qz.com/work/1467935/gloria-steinem-says-these-are-the-best-guidelines-for-difficult-conversations/

2.6 **An ongoing presence.** As groups move towards initiating action they may require assistance establishing legal structures and holding public forums to involve the wider community. The worker can support community groups access information, knowledge and resources to transition towards taking on responsibilities as decision makers.

Questions

When might you support groups move from a learning to an action phrase?

What groups exist in the community that the group could work with?

What experience of legal structures do you have: Incorporated Association, Co-operatives,

Trading or Non-Trading with, or without shares, Partnerships, Associate Members or under the Auspice of a larger organisation?

How familiar are you with the legislation under which the organisation operates and the practical requirements of fulfilling these obligations?

Name (3) three practical ways you could support groups be aware of new responsibilities without overwhelming them with detail?

3. FINDING OUT

I believe that in almost all situations women relate firstly to the personal. This gift of women-kind has been greatly underestimated and undervalued, yet it is a valuable contribution to public debate and decision-making and deserves to be supported and encouraged.

(Mitchell in Franklin et. al. 1994:141)

3.1 More than information

Stories shared between communities of ways people worked to be better prepared for future disasters are more than information. These stories break a sense of isolation and raise awareness of options without imposing an external solution. The stories can raise hope and confidence in community led change. The process affirms recognition that rural and regional community members know what they are experiencing and can make good decisions for their future. Stories within 'the kit' include the strategies and resources utilized including tasks that can be approached with a sense of fun.

The stories can raise hope and confidence in community led change.

The 21st century is known as the Information Age with rapid adoption of new technologies to problem solve situations. This scope of information through print, radio, television, libraries, digital platforms, government departments, community based organisations and corporations can be an asset or overwhelming. Information has often been prepared in response to a specific situation that may have changed. As communities take on more responsibilities the values and goals reshape social, political and cultural relationships. The opportunity to discuss proposals with other communities provides a trusted sounding board.

As discussed in the introduction, the strategies within the *Model of Collaborative Engagement for Transformation* were developed from analysis of the Rural Women's Network (1986-2000) and the Rural Women's Program (1985-86). Networker Jenni Mitchell reported that people constantly stated that: *"They could not find an answer to their question"*, (Mitchell Op. cit). They observed that there was a gap between values held by those asking the questions and prepared answers that failed to resonate. In dealing with new situations people initially find it difficult to convey their concerns, or be able to explain the nature of a possible solution. At this stage people speak about what is currently of concern, of what happened. Their distress at not being able to meet the health needs of their families or community, or to have a venue to meet in, the breakdown of communication systems, the loss of bird life and habitat of all that they valued.

that there was a gap between values held by those asking the questions and prepared answers that failed to resonate.

For workers, being aware of this discrepancy is an important insight. Simply providing 'information' through 'expos' or pamphlets rarely results in changed understanding for individuals or agencies. Personal interaction allows people to become aware of situations and resources in a meaningful way. What was required was not more information, rather information in ways it could be heard at the time from sources that are trusted, strengthening relationships.

Questions

Within your community can you identify key contact people or organisations?

Who do you ask when you want local information?

What qualities are basic to this relationship?

Is this a resourced contact, or an informal one?

What could be learnt from this awareness?

3.2 The reality is often complex

Human beings don't live in economies. We live in families, neighbourhoods and communities.
Building community encourages people to be part of something much bigger than themselves.

https://davidsuzuki.org/what-you-can-do/how-to-make-a-difference/

Community life involves the rich daily interaction with people who have different life experiences, different ages and interests. It is inter-generational. A healthy community has a vibrancy of diversity in a similar way to a natural eco-system. The challenge for the worker is to foster points of connection drawing on knowledge, skills and resources in communities.

A shared community concern to improve safety from fire is an example of people holding different views on how to be better prepared informed by their experiences and information they access. Some want cleared land and advocate burning around communities.

This may lead to consideration of timing, of cool burns, hot burns, pre-planned burns, cultural burns, who by, when, the skills needed, and the condition of soil, are often overlaid by license to log after fires, leaving areas drier. There may be concern that the removal of logs by industry groups and confused responsibility of Vic Roads and local government, lack of training of crews and attention to risk and emotive language of 'killer trees' can escalate fear, that adds to distrust and stress. There is concern that the practice of regular hot burns on remaining habitat contribute to rising temperatures through increased production of carbon dioxide, loss of carbon storage in trees and plants, leading to loss of top soil and land unable to regenerate cover thus contributing to the problem not mitigating. The continuing loss of habitat for species that reduce leaf litter as well as those critically endangered by past practice and recent fires are on-going concerns.

Providing ways to intersect this knowledge with departmental planning cycles, budgets and resources benefits from skilled facilitation and a willingness to adapt practices towards the shared goal of improving future situations.

Negotiation and decisions for future direction require local involvement.

It is within communities that this complexity of situations and local knowledge of habitat, history and opportunities to mitigate situations can be best understood. Creating opportunities for agencies to resource and inform, to collaborate on points of shared responsibility rather than direct and control a shift can occur within the funded responsible agencies. This encompasses land and water management organisations such as Department of Environment Energy and Climate Action, their Forest Fire Management crews, Indigenous organisations, the Country Fire Association crews as well as between local branches and urban hierarchies engaging with communities.

The inclusion of local knowledge and the time to establish agreed upon roles and responsibilities improves outcomes that lessen trauma and share available resources. In this process other points of view on issues of burning or not, who by and in what manner can become more informed and less volatile. Negotiation and decisions for future direction require local involvement. Resources to facilitate this engagement as a constructive and legitimate step enables all parties to actively participate. This is also relevant to inappropriate developments that become battle grounds between private or public developers and community groups that can prove expensive to all parties.

This was the situation in the coastal community of Mallacoota in the lead up to the 2019 – 2020 fires. Relationships between community members and local government were strained after long drawn out confrontation over the design, location and installation of an access boat ramp at Bastion Point, Mallacoota. Divisions in the community and trust in legal and democratic practices were severely diminished. Concerns of who makes the decision, who lives with the long term consequences and values used to balance the environmental social and financial impact of such a decision are on-going. Local Government played a major role in discussions and implementation of the boat ramp, rarely facilitating comprehensive involvement of local people in collaborative forums. They also bear the on-going costs. This fraught relationship with local government led to establishment of an independent organization being incorporated following the fires. Mallacoota and District Recovery Committee (MADRA).
https://www.abc.net.au/radio/programs/am/mallacoota-takes-bushfire-recovery-into-its-own-hands/12441670

https://www.edenmagnet.com.au/story/6417250/bastion-point-dredging-woes-continue-although-surfers-are-taking-advantage-of-the-sand-buildup/

Collaborative engagement strategies offer a way for communities to work through these issues and be heard equally, ensuring local knowledge of tidal conditions and all values inform public decision making. *Republik of Mallacoota* https://www.imdb.com/title/tt19387600/ documents Mallacoota residents experience of their journey of community led recovery. Disaster recovery policies all advocate involvement of communities, alongside agencies and government departments prior to disasters.

3.3 Local ownership

Local papers, community radio and responsibly monitored social media are a bountiful source of community activities. Contributors are familiar and trusted identities. During the fires impacting on Mallacoota the community radio sharing accurate information reduced trauma and assisted safety.
https://www.eastgippsland.vic.gov.au/media-releases/2021-australia-day-award-winners-announced

Disaster recovery policies all advocate involvement of communities,

Local media can also be a great source of historical information as well as showcase assets and events of local importance. The Mirboo North Times Newspaper supported campaigns to protect the local swimming pool and improve access and signage in Lyre Bird Forest Walk.Disaster recovery policies all advocate involvement of communities, This may be the kindergarten or school, Community Health Centre, Bush Nurse, or TAFE College. Historical societies, Neighbourhood Centres, Government Offices and Tourist Information Centres vary from place to place. Local Government offices can direct you to Citizen's Advice Bureau who can assist with information on everything from aged care options to free tax advice. In communities without these services the information network frequently works through a group such as Landcare, general store, pub, local church or a respected citizen.

Bruthen Landcare Regeneration – Fairy Dell Recovery project
Fairy Dell is home to many native animals and bird species, and significantly, it is the southernmost place on the planet where the Leichardt Fern (Cyathea Leichardtiana) also known as prickly tree fern is found.
(Tambo Rambler August 2020, Issue 253:1-3)

In 2019 Bruthen Landcare was about to fold. People had retired and moved away. New members were needed. The AGM saw 23 new members sign up and discovered a healthy bank balance. Research of past projects identified two sites close to Bruthen, the Old Station site and one near the Tambo River walking bridge and river junction. Both were in need of restoration work the community was keen to act on. Then the fires hit impacting on homes and properties, national parks and reserves. Fairy Dell, a warm temperate rainforest reserve, approximately 10 kms from Bruthen was severely impacted. A popular site for locals and visitors with picnic tables, toilets and well maintained walking tracks was closed for safety reasons.

Following the fires support came from East Gippsland Landcare Facilitator and Conservation Management Networker who provided insights into government organisations and funding sources.

Bruthen Landcare worked with the Conservation Management Network to regenerate the reserve and repair fire damage infrastructure. An application for a bushfire recovery grant from Landcare Victoria for Fairy Dell a walk, plant and weed identification workshop was held with permission from Parks. *'The site while still blackened was covered in leafy green plants and small ferns. Most trees had bright green epicormic shoots growing back which is really promising. To our delight a couple of the Leichardt Ferns also survived the fires'.*

Future work involves removal of trees fallen on the tracks, rebuilding of bridge, toilets and seating…. along with weed removal. Parks Victoria are involved, Bruthen Landcare and the Emerald Link. The partnerships are positive and give hope…. (Tambo Rambler 2021).

The partnerships are positive and give hope….

Questions

Who were the key partners in this negotiation?

What roles did each play?

What information did each party contribute?

At this stage how would you regard the process and participation?

Are you aware of local/regional issues in your community that have featured in the media? Who raised the issue, and who is involved in determining solutions?

Has this been an informative process?

Can you identify blockages in communication?

What other parties could be useful in working towards a solution? How might this be approached?

4. WORKING WITH GOVERNMENT

The Local Shire Office or Post Office may have a directory of organisations in the area. The office of your local parliamentarian, and government departments can be an excellent source of information. Peak Bodies hold a wealth of historical knowledge and practical resources. Some have funding to provide information to regional areas, while others are staffed by volunteers, many of whom are generous with their

information and experience. Known as the Third Sector or the Civil Society they have a different agenda to Governments or the market place, forming partnerships with either.

Working with government involves being aware of changing policies and practices. Portfolio responsibilities can change departments especially with changing governments. For example youth related services in Victoria are primarily located with Department of Education, however the health department and Department of Human Services also have youth focused activities while local government offers some services. Relationships between government departments at State and Federal level also alter with changes to funding arrangements and Compulsory Competitive Tendering requirements. A practical way to deal with this is to establish what you currently know about all three levels of government relevant to community interest.

Third Sector or the Civil Society they have a different agenda to Governments or the market place,

Questions

Who are the local councilors in your Shire?

Who is the Chief Executive Officer, and the responsible person for an area in which you have an interest? Eg. Planning, civic engagement, finance, arts, environmental health…

Is there a regional organisation such as a Regional Arts Council, Reconciliation Victoria, or Community Recovery Association? Who is the contact for this organisation?

By knowing this information you can contact the democratically elected representative, the bureaucratic staff, peak bodies and interested community members. These are strategic people to invite to a local meeting or informal gathering to familiarise them with your issues and to become aware of current polices, funding opportunities, contacts in other regions and the cycle of planning and budgetary time frames.

For issues that come under regional, state or federal jurisdiction being aware of the responsible minister, and relevant contact in their office as well as bureaucratic staff are all important steps.

Questions

Do you know the State Member for Upper House (Member of Legislative Council) and Lower House (Member of Legislative Assembly) in your area? (This applies in all states except Queensland.)

Are they responsible for any one area: do they hold a portfolio on environment or planning for example?

At a Federal Level there will be your local Federal Member, and a Senate representative. As these members are absent for lengthy periods it is useful to get to know the office staff who advise and keep them up to date with constituents issues. Remember though these members, even if ministers deal inside a policy and bureaucratic framework and it is important to be aware of with current policy of the party in power at the time. The opposition policy may provide leverage on an issue of concern. From a departmental point of view make a contact in the bureaucracy, a name to phone and address correspondence.

Remember these members, even if Ministers deal inside a policy and bureaucratic framework

You may like to visit www.aph.gov.au to check or extend your knowledge in regard to this topic.

5. LEARNING ABOUT LEARNING

There is a generation of people across all ages and walks of life, right around the world, regenerating the systems we live by – the economy, food, health, energy, politics, the sciences, sports, the arts and more - and doing so with a more holistic focus, better weaving these systems together to form a more effective and artful tapestry of human and other life on this planet.
Charles Massey 2020 –RegenNarration

Change frequently involves unlearning and rethinking

Change frequently involves unlearning and rethinking in ways that lead to regeneration of the environment and enrichment of community life. You are not alone in this endeavor. There are useful resources, programs and research available that can inform community choices. For instance action research texts offer a step by step guide to involve people and find out about a given situation. Yoland Wadsworth's resources (2010, 2011) are valuable and practical, using cartoons and humour to focus in

on more bizarre attitudes. The recent insights offered by Lynne Kelly, on ways of remembering within oral societies that give insight into rigourous practices that accurate knowledge over generations that encompassed the complexity and inter-related nature of life (Kelly and Neale 2020). Lynne Kelly as Western knowledge archivist and Maude Neale Indigenous archivist collaborated to write *Songlines: The Power and Promise* (2020). The text and subsequent exhibition offers unique insights into Indigenous traditional knowledges, how they apply today and how they could help all peoples thrive into the future. Both approaches invite involvement and can open our minds to different ways of understanding our place in the world.

Encourage groups to find out what educational resources can be accessed locally. Make enquiries through local schools and libraries, adult education centres, regional Technical and Further Education institutes or Regional Universities. Access to professional pathways in skills and knowledge is continually merging and being renegotiated across institutions and regions. In Victoria, the Adult, Community and Further Education board resources Learn Local programs and pathways with partner organisations that includes Neighbourhood Houses, Community Hubs, TAFE colleges and Universities. ([https://www.vic.gov.au/learn-local-sector).](https://www.vic.gov.au/learn-local-sector) Discovering how to access these may be a role the worker undertakes In the process understanding of potential future partnerships may become apparent.

5.1 Schools

Schools rely heavily on involvement from families, community and industry groups. They may welcome the opportunity to reciprocate by providing access to school facilities and expertise, consolidating their role in the community. Be considerate and involve staff with responsibility for opening, closing and cleaning premises.

5.2 Adult Education Centres and Neighbourhood Houses

Once you begin to 'find out' communities are rich in skills and knowledge.

Adult Education Centres and Neighbourhood houses are resourceful hubs of adult learning for practical skill development and array of programs. Groups running local papers may organise writing workshops and computer classes with the local adult education centres. Once you begin to 'find out' communities are rich in skills and knowledge.

Check the local papers and source a program guide for further information. Many centres are receptive to ideas for new programs. Be aware that they run to tight budgets and timelines. Become familiar with planning sessions, what is on offer as well as who to contact.

5.3 Technical and Further Education Institutes (TAFE)

Technical and Further Education Institutes operate over a large geographic area. They have excellent libraries. Some have an arrangement where for a small fee community members are registered and may borrow books and other resources. Enrollment in programs opens up options of mutual benefit.

Regional institutes face the challenge of meeting the same minimum numbers as urban classes and welcome innovative arrangements with other organisations. With increasing use of 'blended programs' (on-line and regional residential or face to face sessions) access is expanding.

For a range of qualifications students need practical experience. Natural Resource Management Courses, Community Services, and regional medical residencies can all complement a community need for assistance. Regional Universities may have programs like Education for Sustainability Tasmania: a UN- recognised Regional Centre of Expertise – a new kid on the block. . https://www.youtube.com/watch?v=SkLUOovOVlM received recognition for community engagement.

TAFE Institutes can target training for particular needs such as submission writing and communication units and may be a partner in accessing funding.

Questions

Are you familiar with educational resources in your community?

Is there access to the local school for community members, either in existing classes or for new programs such as computer classes, possibly offered through the adult education provider?

Do you know who to talk to about access?

Does your local Technical and Further Education Centre offer outreach programs?

Who is the contact for these?

Are you aware of TAFE Curriculum at your regional institute that may be of assistance either as a resource to the community, or for professional development of members of the study group?

The qualifications are identical

5.4 Open Universities Australia.

Open Universities Australia allows you to study locally accommodating work and family commitments. The qualifications are identical to students who complete their studies on campus. There are no entry requirements and students can access a range of support services. Students receive specially developed study materials, plus some courses have television, radio and online resources.
https://www.open.edu.au/online/degrees

5.5 University of the Third Age

U3A, the University of the Third Age, is an international movement providing low cost educational opportunities for retired people in a relaxed and informal environment. Its main purpose is to promote and practice lifelong learning. No prior qualifications are required; no degrees are awarded. For further information contact your local Adult Education Centre as U3A operates autonomously across multiple sites in Australia and Internationally.

5.6 Regional Universities

Universities focus on teaching and research. A regional campus can provide excellent pathways in learning for individuals, access existing research or educators with skills and knowledge relevant to regional issues. For example: Grampians Natural Disaster Research was a coordinated response to the landslide events of January 2011 in the Grampians National Park. Federation University Australia were engaged by Northern Grampians Shire to investigate the social, economic and environmental impact of the events in which floods precipitated over 190 landslides, causing significant impact to the environment and communities surrounding the Park. https://researchonline.federation.edu.au/vital/access/manager/Repository/vital:7606 The report draws on diverse expertise to look at risk and resilience of current and future disasters.

The Parks office for the Grampians, traditionally known as Gariwerd is located in Hall's Gap National Park. It was surrounded by mud and land flows during the flood. The recovery management team headed up by Dave Roberts began a massive effort not only to repair damage and reinstate access but to appreciate the causes of devastation and re-craft landscape infrastructure to work with water flows and ensure sustainability. They worked across government portfolios and educational institutions to better understand the complexity of this landscape. Deakin University conducted bio-diversity assessment of aquatic fauna populations, a bio-scan of Grampians National Park was carried out by Melbourne Museum, and contractors were employed to deal with emergent pest plants, animal populations and threatened species associated with impact of flood and storm damage on 11 sites. Several threatened species projects were completed in conjunction with students from Deakin University, Arthur Rylah Institute surveyed and mapped the extent of chytrid fungus and produced a report on extent and recommendations for implementation of Cinnamon Fungus and spread post Grampians flood events.

They worked across government portfolios and educational institutions

The Parks team worked with five Traditional Owner groups, Aboriginal Affairs Victoria and contractors to assess 67 indigenous sites – two not previously registered. Rehabilitation of damaged sites, artefacts and scar trees was carried out with Traditional owner's and future protection sites planned. Sites of European significance were repaired and upgraded. Visitor sites and campgrounds were repaired and upgraded, a new camp ground was constructed. Road bridges and crossings were repaired or replaced. There had been previous episodes of fire and flood and the parks team were already tired. It was a massive effort in diplomacy, collaboration, research and hard work over long hours in difficult conditions. The outcome in regard to waterways and storage, walking tracks and roadways, camp grounds and visitor centers and care of country and relationships is a credit to this team. They launched a 2011-2013 Vintage to celebrate.

It was a massive effort in diplomacy, collaboration, research and hard work

Best described as a troublesome period, this Vintage took some crafting and careful consideration to eventually become what will go down in history as a 'Top Shelf' drop.
If the texture first appears cloudy and gravelly, it will be due to the source of the water where this wine began - Bellfield. You'll get used to the bits of sandstone as we've masterfully mix in other ingredients including left over power barrow tracks, bits of flaking metal from Mackenzie Falls bridge topped off with a hint of sweat from the left arm pits of the walking track team. Aged craftily in salvaged timber from Silverband falls log jams, the wine promises plenty and rarely disappoints. The bouquet may seem a bit rough around the edges, but a bit of spit and polish will reveal the inner gems of this Vintage. Described by some connoisseurs as persistent, this wine is best shared with good friends and colleagues who have lived and breathed the ups and downs of this Vintage. It's not often you get to leave behind such a big legacy, however this Vintage will be remembered long into the future by the remains that are visible in the surrounding Landscape.
  ...Bottoms up....
Dave Roberts, RIC. 2013. Grampians National Park Flood Recovery Program. Parks Victoria.

Many universities have departments focusing on sustainability, or social and environmental themes that welcome community partnerships, placements or involvement that can be mutually beneficial. University of Tasmania – Sustainability Living is one example. https://www.youtube.com/watch?v=SkLUOovOVlM

Questions

Do you know who is head of the faculty in an area of interest in your community? Environmental Science, Business and Marketing or Journalism for example.

What is the decision making body for the regional institution?

Do you know any of the people on this board?

Is there a public relations officer or marketing manager you could contact and involve in your project?

6. NETWORKING

It is personal, it is based on trust and it is about change.
(Jenni Mitchell 1996 in Bailey et. al. p14)

Regional networks facilitate collaboration on shared concerns.
The worker can assist by organizing a regional forum where people can speak of their situations and access information and options. Respecting local knowledge and local ownership are critical aspects of planning. For example in relation to Regional Tourism, facilitation can support communities work through issues of local management to find a balance between developments that generates employment opportunities and those that invest in environment stewardship. Involving community groups in the planning or hosting of such an event signals their central role to representatives of peak bodies: both private industry and community group's responsible authorities (local/state/federal government or agencies) and politicians that can resource initiatives.

Regional networks facilitate collaboration on shared concerns.

Respecting local knowledge and local ownership are critical aspects of planning.

Consider how the following invite involvement.

- Creation of a welcoming environment.

- Have fun. Ensure some lighthearted interaction to allow people to relax.

- Hypothetical, Trivia quiz, Celebrity heads, a storyteller to share stories of experiences within workshops, or from individual conversations. These strategies entertain and inform.

- Involve local groups in catering, promotions, registrations and entertainment. Everyone learns, everyone benefits.

- Displays of photos, plans, information and products can generate conversations.

- Value diverse participation.

- Canvas decision of time, date and location of the gathering.

- Explore availability and cost of child-care.

- Interactive sessions that engage everyone in learning.

- Show casing of local situations.

- Provision of relevant skill development. (Scoped prior to event).

- Inclusion of resource people from peak organisations.
- Opportunity to network through reasonable length tea breaks and lunch time.
- Range of media to publicise the event beforehand, and on the day.
- Provide contact details and relevant material for people to take.
- Seek feedback following the event.

What did people find most useful, what would they change?

Finding connections

Heal country, heal our nation - calls for all of us to continue to seek greater protections for our lands, our waters, our sacred sites and our cultural heritage from exploitation, desecration and destruction.
https://www.naidoc.org.au

Reflection enables the group to continually learn

Many groups issue invitations to annual events. Reconciliation Week activities or National Aboriginal and Islander Day Observance Committee (NAIDOC) activities provide an opportunity to rethink our relationships with each other and the land. You may reciprocate with invitations to speak or come along to your group. *Bruce Pascoe reminds us that in the progress to full knowledge of this country, you will have many questions for Aboriginal communities, but do remember that Aboriginal and Torres Strait Islander people are just 3 per cent of the population and it is exhausting to answer questions from the other ninety-seven per cent.* (Pascoe and Shukuroglou 2020:xiii)

When attending functions inquire whether you can bring another person. This expands awareness of relevant contacts and resources, reduces reliance on one person and shares responsibilities. Organising an annual gathering to discuss how the group/project is evolving is an opportunity to celebrate what they did well and what they would like to change in the future. Reflection enables the group to continually learn, rather than victimise individual people. A network of involved, informed active people gives hope and energy. Networks create forums for local people to be the seekers and processors of relevant knowledge, and is such a different experience to blaming community members for being apathetic or disinterested.

Community members may be exhausted from life events so as a worker it is important to be responsive to this and create ways to nurture and support without creating dependence.

Questions

Are you aware of an issue of common interest in your area?

In planning an event around this issue how might you be most useful in raising awareness of other interested organisations and decision-makers?

Outline steps to take paying attention to your role, and that of the interested community group (s).

7. RURAL COMMUNITIES, REGIONAL GROUPS AND PEAK BODIES

7.1 Rural Communities

Other rural or regional communities are an excellent source of information and support. Community members are usually willing to share their experiences of beginning new ventures, and pass on details of useful contacts. When visiting communities to 'find out' about a particular project, factor in ways to value community members time. Community involvement is often at the expense of people's daily income producing work or family responsibilities. Especially following disasters people are struggling to provide their time voluntarily in an on-going capacity. As a worker, take account of who is at the table in paid and unfunded capacities. Discuss ways this can be minimised, recognized and compensated. Some organisations bring a gift of local produce, provide useful promotion or pay for travel time. Are there opportunities to create local employment?

factor in ways to value community members time

Networking between communities can be mutually beneficial. Following an initial face to face meeting, on- line forums enables people who live at a distance to stay in touch and increases awareness of shared interests.

7.2 Regional Groups

Regional boards focus on industry or departmental agendas. As publicly funded organisations they produce annual reports and have a board of directors. Community groups may be invited to comment or consult, but many have only marginal involvement with regional organisations. Already stretched workers may respond to invitations to attend community functions with a sense that they will be questioned about their practice and their workloads increase. The reality is, that if respectful working arrangements are in place, community members frequently provide seasonal and current information that informs planning and action. During COVID when regional workers were unable to travel these community partnerships became critical for land management partnerships.

Partnerships similar to Landcare facilitate engagement.

With increased appeal of regional life styles it would be timely to expand community involvement

With greater awareness of the increasing vulnerability of eco-systems and regional economies it is becoming evident that central government departments benefit from investing in a two-way flow of information. Partnerships similar to Landcare facilitate engagement. The North East Catchment Management Authority's, *Our Communities our Catchment* uses a place based approach to invite all agencies and community groups to quarterly meetings that raise awareness of activities in the catchment. https://www.necma.vic.gov.au/Projects/Current-projects/Our-Catchments-Our-Communities. In many regions there are regional arts councils, environment groups, local government networks and industry groups. Resourcing community members equalizes relationships and capacity to be 'at the decision making table'. Community group members may find it useful to become familiar with the executive and the roles, responsibilities and activities of regional groups to incorporate local issues in their activities and future planning.

Resourcing community members equalizes relationships

Regional festivals and focus

They like a good festival in Margaret River, preferably with a cheese platter and a glass of red. The climate and soils favour food production – it's an incredibly rich agricultural area if you combine that with the beaches and the surf then it's understandable that the region boasts comfort and ease. He reminds us that the region has always produced abundant food quoting dairy entries by Lieutenant George Grey in 1841.
(Pascoe and Shukuroglou 2020:236).

Regions may become known for their food and culture through the people who with commitment and passion produce and celebrate our wonderful cuisine. Food and wine festivals involve coastal, hinterland and urban communities. Regional and state guides to farmers markets and annual festivals that circulate money regionally are investing in regional regeneration. Land that is cared for continues to produce food, unlike mining or other extractive industries that fail to reinvest in regional futures. Awareness of changing conditions have motivated a movement towards RegenNaration www. regennarration.com

Nature based and cultural tourism is growing as *Australia realizes this sector's contribution to the development of more diverse, sustainable and resilient regions.* Outdoor activities kept many sane and fit during the pandemic. The appeal of walking groups, kayaking, rail trails for bike riding and nature based tourism on land or the water, coast or mountains is expanding.
Nature Based Tourism in Australia - Ecotourism Australia https://www.ecotourism.org.au

Art and literary festivals are networked by state and regional organisations in recognition of the social, economic and cultural richness they generate. Regional Arts Victoria and Regional Arts Australia http://www.rav.net.au › contact-us

Pascoe and Shukuroglou's *'Loving Country: a guide to sacred Australia (2020),* and Marcia Langdon's, *Welcome to country: a travel guide to Indigenous culture* (2018) invite involvement in local economies and culture. A growing interest in Indigenous culture provides ways to invest in locally owned ventures.

These relationship to the land invite consideration of investment, a shift away from importing finance and industry for extractive industries that in the long term leave communities poorer with environmental damage to mitigate. One supports growth and development for the long term, the other depletes an area then moves to a new location to repeat the practice.

Questions

Is there an Area Advisory Committee or Regional Development Group in your area?

Do you know the executive officer?

Are you aware of the role and funding of this organisation?

Can you name 5 other regional groups that may be of relevance to community organisations?

7.3 Peak bodies advocate and resource local activities

Citizens and their movements - non-profit organizations or CSO (Civil Society Organisations) operating at every level of human societies from global to local, are now recognized as distinct sectors separate from markets and governments.
(Henderson. 1999:53)

Peak bodies co-ordinate and promote work often carried out by diverse industry or community based organisations. For example Australian Women in Agriculture Inc. is a peak body for local Women in Agriculture groups, while the Foundation of Australian Agriculture Women Inc. supports the professional development of women in decision-making impacting on rural communities. https://extensionaus.com.au/VRWNetwork/tag/women-on-farms/ https://awia.org.au/resources/

The Victorian Local Governance Association (VLGA) https://www.vlga.org.au resources women in local government, celebrates partnerships with reconciliation initiatives within local government, communities and schools. The Helping Achieve Reconciliation Together (HART) awards showcase collaborative ventures across the state and link to national cultural opportunities and celebrations such as Girraway Ganji Consultancy an Indigenous owned YouTube Channel. https://www.youtube.com/channel/UCQ--N9r7-SxvArqLA_qs8tg

Rural Councils Victoria established in 2005 with a vision to create rural communities with sustainable economies contributing to the health, character and live ability of Victoria. With the impact of recurring disasters this peak body is well placed to present a regional development perspective https://ruralcouncilsvictoria.org.au/

The Municipal Association of Victoria represents all local governments https://www.mav.asn.au/

Organisations such as:

- Society for the Provision of Rural Education (SPERA) network and support the role of rural education, https://spera.asn.au

The Country Women's Association (CWA), advances the rights and equity of women, families and communities in Australia through advocacy and empowerment, especially for those living in regional, rural and remote Australia. They have an established presence and are influential in raising issues that may otherwise be marginalized. https://www.cwa.org.au

Service clubs such as Rotary https://my.rotary.org and Lions https://lionsclubs.org.au have rural branches and promote local partnerships. Make contact with local branches and share information on your project. The Brotherhood of St. Laurence and the Young Women's Christian Association (YWCA) have a long tradition of working in partnership with community organisations

Regional groups such as Birdlife Australia https://birdlife.org.au have state and regional branches Industry groups also have regional, national or international peak bodies to facilitate promotion of products, markets and changes in the industry.

The Australian Centre for Rural Entrepreneurship ACRE is an active educational and professional development resource for rural communities to build a resourceful and enterprising culture and economy. https://acre.org.au/

Find out, organisations will welcome your involvement.

Questions

Are you familiar with peak bodies relevant to an area of interest in your community?

In what ways could the group be a resource for the local community?

Technology is both an asset and a risk.

8. COMMUNICATIONS: SOCIAL MEDIA AND PLATFORMS

Technology is both an asset and a risk. Establishing access to centres where people can be informed in how to protect their data, to avoid scams and come to learn of constant upgrades and options is a bonus for any community. Schools, libraries, neighbourhood houses, University of 3rd Age are all accessible.

Attention to personal contact, listening to people's concerns, providing opportunities for practice and relevance are extremely important. Available time is an important component to consider.

The pandemic and need for isolation motivated increased uptake of on-line communication within organisations. An upside of this was that more rural people participated in forums, the downside was that less people met face to face in communities. It varied from sector to sector but many organisations reported centralist decision making remained dominant. As people are choosing to live in regional areas it is timely to revisit this approach.

Questions

Are you aware of on-line forums or platforms relevant to issues in your community?

If so, join or subscribe and become familiar with the opportunities this offers.

Your group may be interested in being included on a website of relevance to local activities?

8.1 Keeping everyone in the loop.

People of different ages and interests communicate using different mediums. Always check on the preferred form of communication. In organizing an annual event I find that I personally phone some people, group email, facebook, Instagram, write letters to others and then meet face to face with working groups. Involvement is an important part of the process. Articles in school newsletters and local media, make contact with potentially interested people.

Always check on the preferred form of communication.

Questions

What ways does your group communicate?

How might you personalize information for particular groups?

Can you share local communication as well as networking that you found useful?

9. ESTABLISHING STRUCTURES AND FINANCING PROJECTS: REGIONAL ECOMONICS

Projects and enterprises that reinforce local knowledge networks and common causes in a community are the beating heart of a regenerative economy. They build trust as they create local communities of practice and idea exchanges, nurturing the collaborative skills critical to any self-sustaining community that can respond nimbly and adapts to changing circumstances. Regen Tottenville – in Field Guide to Regenerative Economy.
http://fieldguide.capitalinstitute.org

The sequenced approach encourages groups to establish a vision for their community prior to considering the task of funding projects. If community members have spent time working through their dreams and plans for and with the community it is more likely to stay on track and not be distracted by funding for other programs.

Groups are encouraged to begin with small projects

Groups are encouraged to begin with small projects while building their own skills and potential and trust in each other. In the beginning a project may operate under an umbrella

organization. If in time the group takes on new responsibilities it can then choose an appropriate legal structure. The kit gives examples.

Valuing all work

Everyone should have the opportunity to contribute to their community in a way that is meaningful for them.
(Valuing Volunteering 2018).

funding tied to criteria that frames urban lifestyle as the benchmark

Rural people invest time, energy and resources in their communities and environment for the benefit of all Australians. It is important that money granted for regional development be negotiated in this spirit rather than using the language of disadvantage and funding tied to criteria that frames urban lifestyle as the benchmark. This may be relevant in times of crisis, but not long term development. When there is no involvement in decision making, funding can lead to a hand out mentality that becomes internalised, undermining confidence. To some it is the stamp of failure.

The current competitive lottery of submissions to government, with unclear guidelines, political attachment to the ballot box and no evaluation of impact, breeds suspicion and confirmation that government departments are out of touch with community led change. While communities frequently need assistance in group skills, inclusive planning and support to implement projects, relationships with government departments and welfare agencies also benefit from changing their practice towards working with community groups. Money deposited in their bank account and a photo opportunity still leave communities operating in isolation. Ongoing regional support and resourcing maintain involvement.

unpaid work is constantly within rural areas, facilitated by paid urban workers

It is now acknowledged that volunteering becomes burdensome when demands exceed the energy, time and skills of the volunteer. If the unpaid work is constantly within rural areas, facilitated by paid urban workers the imbalance leads to exhaustion and resentment. Distributive regional employment programs that employ local workers resourced by central organisations offer a reciprocal and practical model that is able to work responsively within communities. Regional organisations benefit from broad involvement and understanding of working with people at a range of levels in constructive ways.

Organisations such as Red Cross, or Brotherhood of St. Laurence may provide guidance and support.

In Australia the volunteer or unpaid sector was valued at $290 billion in 2021. The significance hits home when compared to the mining sector that contributed $121 billion to the GDP at this time. A figure decreasing by 1.4% in the last year, unlike volunteering which just keeps growing.

https://www.ethicaljobs.com.au/blog/value-of-volunteering-in-australia-tops-290-billion

There is global interest in creating visibility and resourcing for this sector. New Zealand has introduced the *Living Standards Framework* (LSF) to track what matters for New Zealand's well-being now and in the future: across people, place and generations (https://www.treasury.govt.nz/information-and-services/nz-economy/higher-living-standards/our-living-standards-framework (Dec, 2019).

the volunteer or unpaid sector was valued at $290 billion in 2021.

The Living Standards Framework increases visibility of the benefit and costs of economic expenditure on the whole population and the environment. The ongoing monitoring of changing directions provides a platform to factor in constant challenges of disasters, pandemics and climate change in a systematic rather than reactionary approach.

Understanding the impact of finance is conveyed in a report *Building a better working world*, (Ernest and Young: 2014) that uses the term 'Sticky Money' to indicate the multiplier impact of regionally owned co-operative and mutual organisations. The paper conveys experience of the closure and return of financial services in rural communities in Australia.

The Barossa Community Co-op Foodland uses its revenue to source produce from local suppliers, employing local people and providing rebates to members. Suppliers, employees and members then re-spend part of their earnings, salaries and rebates with local shops and service providers. For every $1 dollar spent in The Co-op an additional 76c of value is created for the local economy. The multiplier impact or 'Sticky money' generates further benefits through the co-operative principle of co-operatives supporting other co-operatives. Barossa Pizzas a locally owned family business was invited to sell their pizzas in the Foodland Co-op and supported to make the transition increasing local employment and income generation (op.cit).

Mechanisms to track the impact of 'Sticky Money' were sourced from the United Kingdom's Total Value Framework, Local Multiplier Framework of Co-operatives (2013). The framework makes visible the re-investment of profit, customer/member satisfaction, levels of economic and democratic participation, employee well-being, investment in communities and environmental impact (op.cit).

9.1 Regenerative economies

An ability to walk the balance beam to 'get things done' in order to 'keep things going' (efficiency) on the one hand, while taking risks and exploring new paths (building resilience).
https://reallyregenerative.org/regenerative-economics

Regenerative economics provides a framework for community involvement and regional reinvestment. It is a shift away from practices that benefit distant shareholders frequently at the cost of the source community and their environment. Regenerative economics draws on elements of cooperatives that values all members irrespective of financial contribution or employment. Membership reframes relationships between paid and unpaid workers and management.

Regenerative economics principles inform activity and expand language and practice towards transforming and healing damage from extractive and exploitative economic practices.

Two sources of guiding principles are

1. **Capital Institute** – https://capitalinstitute.org
   Regenerative systems are always engaged in this delicate dance dependent on harmonizing multiple variables instead of optomising single ones (Capital Institute – https://capitalinstitute.org).

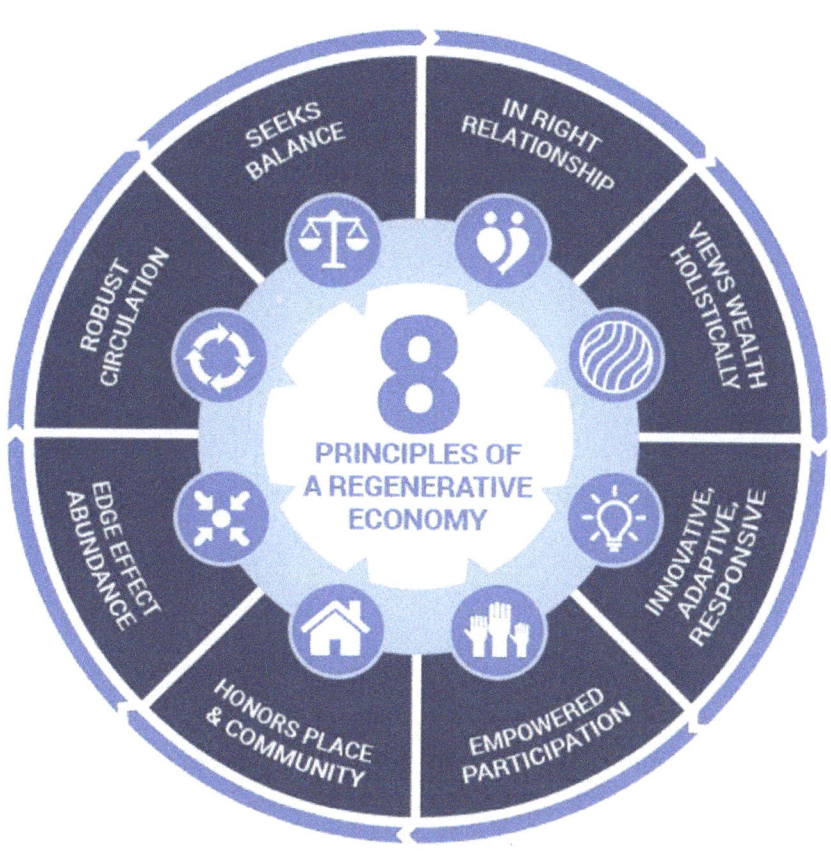

The Mondragon Co-operatives in the Basque region of Spain demonstrate the value of this principal.

2. **17 Rules for Sustainable Local Community**: (Wendell Berry **https://sustainabletraditions.com)** (May 2017)

Wendall's questions, are those community members would ask if they wanted their community to cohere, to flourish, and to last.

Always ask how local needs might be supplied from local sources,

1. *Always ask of any proposed change or innovation: What will this do to our community? How will this affect our common wealth.*

2. *Always include local nature – the land, the water, the air, the native creatures – within the membership of the community.*

3. *Always ask how local needs might be supplied from local sources, including the mutual help of neighbors.*

Look into the possible uses of local currency, community-funded loan programs, systems of barter, and the like.

4. Always supply local needs first (and only then think of exporting products – first to nearby cities, then to others).

5. Understand the ultimate unsoundness of the industrial doctrine of 'labor saving' if that implies poor work, unemployment, or any kind of pollution or contamination.

6. Develop properly scaled value-adding industries for local products to ensure that the community does not become merely a colony of national or global economy.

7. Develop small-scale industries and businesses to support the local farm and/or forest economy.

8. Strive to supply as much of the community's own energy as possible.

9. Strive to increase earnings (in whatever form) within the community for as long as possible before they are paid out.

10. Make sure that money paid into the local economy circulates within the community and decrease expenditures outside the community.

11. Make the community able to invest in itself by maintaining its properties, keeping itself clean (without dirtying some other place), caring for its old people, and teaching its children.

12. See that the old and young take care of one another. The young must learn from the old, not necessarily, and not always in school. There must be no institutionalised childcare and no homes for the aged. The community knows and remembers itself by the association of old and young.

13. Account for costs now conventionally hidden or externalised. Whenever possible, these must be debited against monetary income.

14. Look into the possible uses of local currency, community-funded loan programs, systems of barter, and the like.

15. Always be aware of the economic value of neighborly acts. In our time, the costs of living are greatly increased by the loss of neighborhood, which leaves people to face their calamities alone.

16. A rural community should always be acquainted and interconnected with community-minded people in nearby towns and cities.

17. A sustainable rural economy will depend on urban consumers loyal to local products. Therefore, we are talking about an economy that will always be more cooperative than competitive.

At an international level futurist economists include accounting systems acknowledging 'social and human capital and ecological assets and unpaid work' (Henderson. 1999 p 12). With recognition comes the ability for sustainable development. Currently those working at a local level to not only establish excellent ventures but to educate decision makers on collaborative ways of working experience high levels of burnout.

Following disasters governments at all levels, philanthropic organisations, businesses and the community sector support recovery through a plethora of grants and loans. Communities are leading change and welcome partnerships with organisations, rather than the traditional view of grant seekers becoming dependent recipients of welfare or charity. There are excellent examples of how communities used funding to leverage ongoing support and investment.

Partnerships offer a 'middle way'. They are, for many, the ideal way of being equal decision makers in planning the future of rural and regional communities. Partnerships are a radical shift from hierarchical structures where one well-funded individual manages and assumes major responsibility for decision making. The profile of local involvement transforms into that of valued partner with shared responsibilities. The Bendigo Community Bank partnership referred to in Chapter 2 was initially established with mutual benefits to the organization and to local communities. In the initial stages talk with other communities with experience of how they began, many from humble beginnings that have expanded as skills and finances allowed.

Partnerships offer a 'middle way'.

10. RURAL TRUSTS AND FOUNDATIONS

The Vision
That a Charitable foundation based on a partnership between philanthropy, community, government and business be established and operate using innovate funding mechanisms and organisational structures which will support communities to respond positively to change and build social and economic wealth in rural and regional Australia.

The Foundation for Rural and Regional Renewal, or FRRR (F-triple-R) is a not-for-profit organisation connecting common purposes and funding from government, business and philanthropy with the needs of rural people and places. It collaborates with communities around Australia and strengthens their capacity to turn change into opportunity. https://frrr.org.au/about-frrr Your local federal member's office is a good contact for up to date information. Find out as much as possible prior to entering into any arrangement for funding.

10.1 Government Grants

Accessing government grants can be a bonus, or it can tie groups into intense periods of activity, over which they rarely participate in making decisions. Be aware of terms and conditions of any funding and if there is another agency involved in the delivery of particular programs; these may be brokers, or training institutes who have agendas and requirements different to that of community needs.

Communities can access funding from all levels of government.

Local government has annual funding rounds for grants to community organisations. These are often for capital works and may not fund co-ordination time, or supervision. A community development officer or local councilor within the Shire would be a good contact to determine funding in your area, and when funding rounds are advertised.

State government grants originate from various departments with responsibility for rural and regional issues. These may be to community based organisations or regional groups. State government encourages liaison with local government. The benefits of this vary from Shire to Shire: in some situations community organisations are working creatively in spite of government support and tying them back in to past policy can be a hindrance. However recognition from another level of government for a local venture can lead to credibility.

Visions for communities may involve groups beginning to work together, they may not always depend on accessing grants or fund raising.

10.2 Fund Raising

Some groups choose to raise finance by holding a local event to raise startup capital. These can be fun and involve a wider group of people expanding ownership of a new venture. There are inspiring stories of community resourcefulness where people came together and pooled resources of time, money, equipment and expertise to focus on a particular community project. The target can be the local sporting venue, creation of a wetland, purchase of a hotel, community banking partnerships or setting up a local paper. Rural communities have a history of this resourcefulness as many schools libraries and churches were established with funding from tree plantations, or agisting and raising stock.

Rural communities have a history of this resourcefulness

The start-up capital of the Mirboo North Times Ltd. was raised at a local talent quest and auction. This became an annual event despite the newspaper no longer needing to raise funds. The second year the Cricket Club and Skateboarders organised the event with talent from young people under 21 years old.

In any venture ensure an open and accountable legal structure that will remain community property in the long term. These clauses need to be written into the original documentation of establishing any community enterprise. While this may not seem to be a priority when beginning a venture it is critical for the foundation of the organization in the future. Later confusion and unpacking of poor records can be exhausting and diminish credibility.

10.3 Sponsorship

Sponsorship can be from a large organisation for the purchase of promotional material for a community event, program or facility. Packaging differentlevels of sponsorship visibility during an event is one approach. Sponsorship is for mutual benefit. Terms and conditions of sponsorship need to be clearly agreed by both parties and evaluated to determine any ongoing relationship. Invite sponsors to participate personally for greater involvement and understanding of the event. This will assist in future discussions.

In any venture ensure an open and accountable legal structure that will remain community property in the long term.

- Top level sponsorship may guarantee a high level of visibility. Banners, logos, key tags etc.

- Middle level sponsorship might feature at a lesser number of venues or for particular events.
- Local sponsorship may choose to fund an individual award, or event.
- Anonymity may also be accommodated through solidarity tickets for events or donations.

the people are as important as the product.

Talk through issues of moral concern regarding community organisation's values and the sponsoring organisation. The two can be matched if issues are voiced and group research for relevant sponsors. https://bccm.coop/wp/wp-content/uploads/2020/07/BCCM-Governance-Principles-2020.pdf

10.4 Co-operatives

Successful cooperative enterprises transform a community by establishing economic democracy.
http://proutglobe.org/2012/10/what-makes-cooperatives-successful/

Co-operative legislation varies from state to state, so become familiar with relevant requirements and opportunities. Co-operatives can raise funds through share capital but unlike companies operate on the principle of one vote per shareholder irrespective of number of shares held. Legal requirements for auditing are usually stringent and similar to a company, as shareholders money needs to be managed in an open and accountable manner.

Co-operatives are an excellent structure for democratic decisionmaking but require a substantial time commitment if this is a community venture. Remember to build in support for those who expend time, energy and resources maintaining the smooth functioning and visible presence of the cooperative. Become familiar with the legal requirements. Training for cooperative directors can be available through peak organisations. Training is an investment in the future of your community: the people are as important as the product.

The Co-operative Federation of Australia https://fed.coop/ is an Australian peak body able to resource new and existing co-operatives. Communities with experience of initiating and owning services and industries use this knowledge to meet community needs. The Maleny Community in Queensland has

7 legally incorporated cooperatives and an even greater number of similar social enterprises, which work in most areas of community life. These include: a consumers' coop, a cooperative bank, a cooperative club, a workers' co-op, a cashless trading coop, a cooperative radio station, a cooperative film society, 4 environmental coops, and several community settlement coops'. http://proutglobe.org › 2011/05 › maleny-cooperatives-...

Mirboo North community has a strong foundation of community owned ventures. The Mirboo North and District Community Foundation works in partnership with the Mirboo North and District Community Bank. In a first the two organisations combined to seek community views on how best to invest their resources. The Mirboo North 2020 Report Vital Signs is a snapshot of key quality of life areas: health and wellbeing; education and learning, economy; and environment and a Belonging report, asks people to discuss the issues they care about, what data surprises them, what they could do to make a difference, and whether the data would change the focus of their community organisations. Initiatives supported by the Foundation include the community bus, recreation, education and environmental initiatives https://mirboodistrictfoundation.org.au/community-bus/

While Covid 19 delayed the conversational aspect of this project *"it is also about allowing time for us as a community to adjust our perspectives and develop an understanding how the impact of COVID-19 affects the community's priorities,"* Ms Rogan said. People know they will have a forum to share views and that decisions will not be imposed externally.

The trend of one venture leading to another is also evident in Yakandandah. Both Mirboo North and Yakandandah are stronger by include neighbouring communities. https://bccm.coop/video-social-enterprise-case-study-yackandandah-community-development-company/

The Business Council of Co-operatives and Mutuals is an active peak organisations. Alan Greig is a prolific researcher and networker linking individuals, organisations and sectors. https://bccm.coop able to link groups with expertise and relevant contacts.

Community and Co-operative Energy Rise in Australia (2019) is an area of significant interest and able to link up nationally. See Australia's early co-operative movement by Gary Lewis. (refs).

Activity

Select one of the frameworks and discuss the reality of these principles.

Begin with the criteria that most appeals. Date this and keep it for future reference.

It can be the beginning of your own Regen narration story.

Podcasts on www.regennaration.com hosted by Alan James provide current examples.

Questions

From previous involvement in raising finance for ventures what sources of funding have you sought? How useful did you find these?

For the short term?

For bringing about long term change?

Are there opportunities within the community to begin to reinvest finance, such as superannuation funds, or community banks, or other community owned ventures?

FURTHER REFERENCES

Wild Life Professor Dusgupta (May 2021) Economics of bio-diversity….
Sir David Attenborough. https://www.youtube.com/watch?v=ni8CWoQLC70 UK

Bailey, A., Barker, J., Brinkley, C., Brown, D., Butler, C., Grey, S., Penny, L., Sheil., Webb, M., (1996) *More than one way. Hearing Rural Women's Voices*, Office of Rural Affairs, Horsham

Berry, Wendall (May 2017) 17 Rules for a sustainable local community. https://sustainabletraditions.com

Brophy, H., (1985) *Rural Women's Programme,* East Gippsland Community College, Bairnsdale

Franklin, M.A., Short, L., and Teacher, E., (Eds) (1994) *Country Women at the Crossroads,* University of New England Press, Armidale.

Kelly, L., and Neale, M., (2020) *Songlines: the power and promise,* Thames and Hudson Australia, Port Melbourne.

Lewis, G., (2019) Australia's early co-operative movement, http://globalartscollective.org/gary_lewis.htm

Martin, J., (2015-2019) *Re-visiting the 1986-7 Study of Small Towns in Victoria. How theory and method in small town studies have changed over last 2 decades.* Australian Journal of Regional Studies. Vol 11, No.3, 289-302 https://search.informit.org/doi/epdf/10.3316/ielapa.058383766756095

Massey, Charles https://www.abc.net.au/news/2020-09-28/charlie-massy-regenerative-farming-movement/12438352

Network of Neighbourhood Houses (regional contacts). https://www.nhvic.org.au/pages/faqs/category/networks Networks | Neighbourhood Houses Victoria https://www.nhvic.org.au ›

https://www.nhvic.org.au/pages/faqs/category/networks Community steps up: Echuca - covid response https://www.nhvic.org.au/Handlers/Download.ashx?IDMF=816bda72-dd87-4128-80b6-7aeb86387705

Pascoe, B., and Shukuroglu, V., (2020) *Loving Country: a guide to sacred Australia,* Hardie Grant Travel, Melbourne. (print and audio).

RegenNaration podcast https://www.regennarration.com/story Charles Massey 2020
Regeneration podcasts Facilitator and educator Anthony James

Republik of Mallacoota
https://www.imdb.com/title/tt19387600/

Sailor's Grave
https://www.youtube.com/watch?v=julVYdj0Y-A

Sticky Money
https://bccm.coop/wp/wp-content/uploads/2014/12/Sticky-Money-Report_EY-2014.pdf
https://bccm.coop/

Steinem, G., (2018) https://qz.com/work/1467935/gloria-steinem-says-these-are-the-best-guidelines-for-difficult-conversations/

Wadsworth, Y., (2011) *Do it yourself social research* (3rd edn.) Action Research Press, Australia. (practical guide to social research projects)

Wadsworth, Y., (2010) *Building in research and evaluation. Human inquiry for living systems,* Allen and Unwin, Action Research Press, NSW.

CHAPTER 6

• CHAPTER 6 •
CONTINUING TO DEVELOP

We are required, in this view, to bear the burden of our history, and at the same time to ensure that the outcomes of our exchange are not known in advance. We begin one of the tasks of repair when we refuse to determine milestones, and thus make ourselves available to be surprised by what our fellow human beings, and the world itself may. want of us.
(Rose Bird 1997:12)

FOCUS OF THIS CHAPTER

1. Narrative as a tool for change:

    1.1 personal growth and development

    1.2. challenging existing world view

    1.3 potential for positive change

    1.4 moving forward together

2. Use of media

3. Continuing to affirm

4. Walking away, knowing how, when and why

5. Continuing to connect and learn

    Further references

This professional development manual originated to raise awareness of the interdependency of rural and urban life. As we engaged with rural people it became evident that the strategies of Collaborative Engagement are transferable across sectors and landscapes. As we found out about the reality of life for groups designated as 'other' a recurring pattern emerged. Opportunities to participate in a rich life were limited by discriminatory language, myths (lies) and enforced by legislation for the majority of humans and life on the planet.

The realisation that the same process was used again and again to marginalise

The realisation that the same process was used again and again to marginalise those who were not the elite can unite a groundswell of willingness to reframe thinking. A bio-regional approach offers connections of an understandable scale, centering on place and the unique characteristics of community relationships at that time.

Strategies: Reflection

Planning time to reflect provides an opportunity for new understanding to emerge. Some facilitators will have entered into this field with great hope and a willingness to be surprised by the direction it takes them. Others begin with ideas of what they want to contribute. It is timely to reflect on how your expectations matched reality by revisiting the regular entries in your journal. (Chapter 1). Each time you write you select words to describe your feelings, to record the tough times, the pleasures as people develop and learn around you. These words are the indicators of your personal story of challenge and change. Take a look at that journey. What and who has changed? Is there a new awareness of working with communities as they become more involved in public decision making?

Gaining confidence in the significance of dialogue can be a subtle process of emotional and intellectual maturity.

Questions

Look through your journal and identify situations that confirmed or challenged your understanding of events and the people involved?

How did this influence your work in regional development?

Could you share these stories with other people?

In what ways has your language changed?

How have the stories people share changed?

Are there opportunities to share their stories?

Paulo Freire invites us to enter into a utopian journey informed by dialogue, *'not utopian in the sense that it is unrealizable but in that they unite in a single perspective the denunciation of a dehumanising reality and the annunciation of a possibly more human one, and thus primarily turned towards the future'* (Friere, 1970:11).

Gaining confidence in the significance of dialogue can be a subtle process of emotional and intellectual maturity. *In Women's Ways of Knowing: the development of self, voice and mind*, (Belenkey et. al. 1997) identifies 6 stages of development triggered and affirmed through dialogue that track journeys from silence to confidently constructed conversations not threatened by diversity. With practice you can identify these stages while being aware that regression can be triggered by fear and trauma. As you reflect on your developmental journey become aware of the milestones indicating growing awareness resulting in changed attitudes and practice. This transition from being an isolated individual concerned about the future of the community, to becoming an active member of a group with an agreed upon vision is a powerful shift. Rather than react to externally set agendas, the community is able to engage constructively on how such a change will enhance or threaten community life in the future.

The worker can encourage practices that record stories as a valuable contribution for reflective sessions. This can involve children or others in interviewing people, recording meetings or visits to a site of interest that generates conversation. These initiatives form a basis for your narration. Taking the time to share stories provides opportunities to reflect on the impact of change. As people speak and listen they become aware of the barriers faced and the way expanded awareness transformed relationships within and between communities and agencies. Documenting these experiences invites involvement and affirming the value of including community perspectives. In the process community members and organizations gain insight into the overlapping nature of their roles and capacities.

Taking the time to share stories provides opportunities to reflect on the impact of change.

It is essential to begin locally, not because it is easier, but because this is the location of identity, where there is the opportunity to strengthen values and relationships. The goal is to heal and resource community and in the process transform relationships with agencies and responsible authorities.

1. NARRATIVE AS A TOOL FOR CHANGE

We use language to create the world.
(Postman 1995:82)

Narrative is a powerful tool to more fully appreciate the impact of policies, thoughts and actions. The reader/listener connects their own experiences with the story integrating new understanding. Consider how the growing interest in hearing the songs and stories from marginalized groups raises awareness of a rich and interconnected diversity.

The goal is to heal and resource community and in the process transform relationships with agencies and responsible authorities.

These stages of growth and change are evident in the following conversations, presentations and publications from *Stories of Influence* incorporating collaborative engagement strategies (See checklist Chapter 4).

A story of stories

Veronica Brady, writer, Catholic sister and campaigner for Reconciliation challenged Australians to find a new guiding story to bring happiness beyond the god of consuming things.
(Brady 1996)

We began by finding out more about ourselves, by sharing stories that had been hidden away

This story is of the coastal community where I live searching for ways to protect our precious landscapes and our populations from inappropriate development that damaged both. Again and again. We began by finding out more about ourselves, by sharing stories that had been hidden away under the bed in letters, diaries and reports and in people's hearts and memories on Bung Yarnda (Lake Tyers) in Gippsland, Victoria. The stories were and are challenging, exposing us to the reality of our past and present culture.

The Bung Yarnda (Lake Tyers) catchment includes the Nowa Nowa Gorge that in Aboriginal knowledge has a dreamtime protection story and in European terms is a Devonian rock formation 400 million years old. Just beyond the road bridge, bubbles of gas appear in the water, signs of the fragile crust linking to sulphur springs. You can travel the 25 kilometres of inlets and islands, forests and swamps down the catchment by boat. Sea-eagles and kingfishes are a common sight. At the estuary opening is Lake Tyers Beach, a holiday destination and home to approximately 500 residents. Across the water the Lake Tyers Aboriginal Trust manages a stunning peninsula of land and is home to around 200 people https://laketyersaboriginaltrust.com.au/. On the far side are farms and homes with long associations. They are three distinct communities. This much loved landscape has a rich and contested history that shapes our lives.

This much loved landscape has a rich and contested history

For a time, I lived on the banks of the Nowa Nowa Gorge and was involved in the David and Goliath campaigns this community, black and white, initiated to prevent the ancient gorge being dynamited by companies taking services past us, from Melbourne to Sydney. Initially, a gas pipeline constructed by Duke Energy, a derivative of Esso (1999-2000); then, optic fibre by Telstra (2010) for communication. Elizabeth Bakewell local doctor and resident speaks of the epic nature of this time in *The mouse that roared* (Bakewell 2019) in a collection of words and music inspired by Bung Yarnda. https://ruralcommunities.com.au/the-mouse-that-roared/

Despite a **Ramsar** listing (https://www.dcceew.gov.au/water/wetlands/ramsar) as a significant site for migratory birds, the catchment remains unprotected, and in a planning sense, invisible. In 2014 a license to mine a small but high quality deposit of iron-ore, initially by Australian-owned mining company Eastern Iron, in the upper catchment of the lake valid until 2034, has since been sold to a predominantly Chinese-owned company, Nowa Nowa Iron https://easternresources.com.au/. Gold and copper extraction were added to the license.

The beginning of *Stories of influence...*
Feminist practice begins with asking and listening, providing space for words to be crafted around experiences, recognising that stories do not emerge fully formed. The work of Mary Field Belenkey and colleagues draws attention to the contribution of language to a personal and moral developmental journey, not only for the speaker, but for the listener (Belenky Field 1986, 1997). Jan 'Yarn' Wositzky, professional singer and storyteller, was a regular visitor to Nowa Nowa and offered to record local stories and host a performance in the local Hall in 2014. We named the event *Gorge(ous) Yarns*.

Community development recognises that you cannot learn for someone – but you can learn from them. It was a tentative beginning in our small community to have conversations *Stories on the hill @ Nowa Nowa hall* about our past and present lives.

you cannot learn for someone – but you can learn from them

People came and told of lives lived on the gorge. Josephine Jakobi shared her mother *'Maisie's Byrne's* poem' written in the 1930s on 12 pages of lined paper still held together with a nappy pin. The words told of a bountiful life on the lake (Jakobi: 2019) inviting those walking the roads during the depression to come and share the bounty of this place, lovingly. https://ruralcommunities.com.au/maise-byrne-1930s-poem/ Jan Wositzky sang songs of humour and tragedy. The response was positive. People smiled at each other. We hadn't divided our small community. Will you do this again?

As people shared their personal stories, or gave life to past events in song and theatre we began to find connections across the divides of language and experience that anthropologist Deborah Bird Rose names the hierarchy of multiple absences (1997). This insightful analysis of Western relationships shows how discrimination and dispossession occurs and is reinforced with language that classifies one group of people as present and its opposite as absent, as 'other'. A pervasive framework that becomes internalised when people are marginalised and silenced.

Unpacking language, lies and legislation that create 'the other'. Each of these four ways narratives contribute to change are evident in *Stories of influence* (Sheil 2000).

As people shared their personal stories, or gave life to past events in song and theatre we began to find connections across the divides of language and experience

- personal growth and development from isolated silent individual to connected being,
- challenging existing world-views of superiority of species, culture and gender,
- potential for positive change through the creation of new language and new grand story,
- transformation of new partnerships and new paradigms towards regenerated futures.

1.1 Personal growth and development from silent, isolated individual to establishing connections.

'it was one of the proudest moments of all our lives. ..To be able to show people who we were was wonderful because nothing like this ever happened before. .. I mean to come out here with these cloaks!.. It was just so powerful...' My spirit wouldn't let me give up. Wearing this cloak allowed me to believe in myself. I felt that no one could say I was nothing ever again.
(Harrison and Landon 2011:234).

Eileen Harrison and Carolyn Landon's book B*lack Swan: a koorie woman's life,* (2011), gives insight into the traumatic impact of assimilation policies to move a loving family from Lake Tyers Aboriginal Mission to a distant place and the consequences. Eileen was born deaf, initially crafting her story as pictures, then working with Carolyn as a longer story emerged. Despite the memory triggering painful emotions Eileen spoke quietly and courageously of the difficult but liberating experience of painful memories surfacing as she read public records of her family.

Art and story are a powerful combination. Every piece of Eileen's vibrant art displayed on the walls in our humble Nowa Nowa Hall sold that weekend. They connected with her story and people hugged and thanked her as they too shed tears. She is now Dr Aunty Eileen Harrison and each year her art and stories educate more people of a rich cultural life. The above quote refers to Eileen's experience at the Commonwealth Games held at the Melbourne Cricket Ground, where she proudly wore the possum skin cloak she had made.

Emerging writer, Megan Webb Hand spoke of coming to *Stories on the hill in 2016* to speak of writing of her recovery from child sexual abuse crafted from 15 years of journals during therapy. By the end of the weekend, she received an offer of an introduction to a publisher who offered to read her manuscript. She left identifying as a writer not a victim.

Art and story are a powerful combination.

Questions

When people have the opportunity to speak publicly of their concerns there is the opportunity for a number of changes to result. What might these include?

For the individual?

For the identified issue/interest?

1.2 Challenging existing world views. Of superiority of species, gender, culture and location.

I went home and thought I have to unlearn what I know, strip it back and start again.
(Murdoch 2018)

Listening to these stories gave insight into histories that had been hidden. Bruce Pascoe lives in East Gippsland and spoke of his book *Dark Emu: Black seeds agriculture or accident* (2014). Dark Emu documents unopened reports from early 'explorers' observing the growing and harvesting of grains, farming of fish and eels, ceremonial practices, challenging the official narratives of this land being unoccupied *(Terra Nullius)*, inhabited by uncivilised people. The invitation to re-imagine our relationship to the land is a love letter to us all.

The responses to this invitation give a glimpse of outcomes informing our future.

- *Dark Emu* is now an opera, performed by the Bangarra Dance Theatre- choreographed by Stephan Page featuring Yuin nation stories and songs.
- *Young Dark Emu: a truer history*. Bruce Pascoe (2019). Magabla Books, Western Australia. Educational resource
- *Black Duck Foods:* https://www.youtube.com/watch?v=MQ3ioWnjZ2M
  New language of Environmental Goods and Services predicted to generate $48bn by 2050 by CSIRO.
- Murnong daisy being used by top chefs in partnership with Aboriginal organisations.
  https://www.sbs.com.au/food/article/2021/07/01/native-superfood-8-times-nutritious-potato-and-tastes-sweet-coconut
- Farmers for Climate Action in partnership with First Nation's people
  https://www.youtube.com/watch?v=ZWOqOSWeJM0
- https://www.crikey.com.au/2021/07/13/bruce-pascoe-has-become-too-big-to-fail-almost-impossible-to-question/

bring a welcome economy in this stripped back, sold-out region.

Harry Saddler, author of T*he Eastern Curlew: the amazing migratory bird* (2018), combined presenting at *Stories of Influence* with a week's residency on FLOAT, the community owned floating art studio (www.facebook.float3909.com). This regional arts initiative brings an engaged network of artists, scientists, environmental activists, biologists, botanists, fishing people, bird watchers to Lake Tyers. The connecting link is the lake.

It is a story of shared responsibilities.

Both *Stories of Influence and FLOAT* bring a welcome economy in this stripped back, sold-out region. Harry walked and talked with locals knowledgeable about the mudflats, the lake, changes in habitat and the impact of 3 years of drought. He shared insights into communities in Northern and Western Australia, in Korea and China and to the wonders and vulnerability of migratory birds. The *East Asian Australasian Flyway* connects habitat and climate, each place home to the Eastern Curlew challenging binary understanding of where this bird belongs. It is a story of shared responsibilities. *The Guardian* reported the story and a recording is circulating through Rotary D9510 online Australia. Harry plans to return to Melbourne and tells others of our region. In his second book, *Questions raised by quolls?* (Saddler 2021) he wrote of how his views of rural people was challenged by our shared concern for vulnerable species and the damage inflicted on First Nation People. Word of the catchment and community spreads https://www.youtube.com/watch?v=f_yOI48i7qY

1.3 Potential for positive change.
New language and a new grand story offering hope.

The response to *Dark Emu, Black Swan* and other 'untold stories' affirmed the significance of local stories. The second time Gunnai custodian Wayne Thorpe welcomed us to Krowatungalang country of the Gunnai Nation (Gippsland), he spoke of a story he was working on *A story of Bung Yarnda (aka Lake Tyers)*. This was published in 2016 and promoted 'on country.' At *Stories of influence* we sat underneath shady gums on the billabong (Gilligan's Island) at Nowa Nowa listening to Uncle Herb Patten playing gumleaf to lead into Wayne's story of how the fresh water flowing down the catchment feeds the plants, habitat for fish, birds and insects as well as humans. The fresh water knew when to invite the salt water, Narkahungdha, to rest under the shade of the big gums in Bung Yarnda. When the lake estuary opens, food is distributed to the ocean. A local story of estuary management with universal significance. http://www.laketyersbeach.net.au/culture.html
https://www.youtube.com/watch?v=aaykiOzgaTs

A Living Bung Yarnda Project to monitor quality and quantity of water in the lake was initiated by Dr. Jessica Reeves, a research scientist who formed a strong bond with Aunty Eileen Harrison, her art and the lake after hearing her story and spending time in the catchment https://www.livingbungyarnda.net.au/. Jessica gained support from responsible land and water management agencies for the project be managed by Lake Tyers Aboriginal Co-operative. The Citizen Science approach complements the growing art+science+environment involvement generated by FLOAT, the local *communiversity*. Lake Tyers is named after Crown Lands Commissioner of Gippsland, T.J. Tyers, of whom local historian Peter Gardner records that *in 1844 [he] was out on a punitive mission hunting the Kurnai who had been spearing settler's cattle* (Gardner, 1988:29); the country's earlier name Bung Yarnda is becoming more widely used.

Dr Aunty Doris Paton comments that, as with stories of children being taken away, it was too painful for Aboriginal people to speak of massacre stories alone.

Questions

Are you aware of changed awareness resulting from shared stories of positive partnerships and resourcefulness from within rural and regional communities?

In what ways does this impact on individuals and groups within communities?

Are you aware of the guiding motivation for people's involvement in change initiated from within communities?

How are these hopes and dreams shared within a group or community?

1.4 Moving forward together
New relationships and new partnerships emerging

At the invitation from the Lake Tyers Beach hall committee *Stories of influence* moved to the Lake Tyers Beach Hall in 2018. Leanne Flaherty (Reconciliation West Gippsland) offered a screening of *The Warrigal Creek Massacres* (2018) a documentary made by filmmakers at Swinburne University, Andrew Dodd and Lisa Gaye led to a Friday fringe event https://www.youtube.com/watch?v=FiPWjgx7nQ0.

In the documentary, Dr Aunty Doris Paton comments that, as with stories of children being taken away, it was too painful for Aboriginal people to speak of massacre stories alone. These are black and white stories. Peter Gardner's publications, including *Our founding murdering father, Angus McMillan and the Kurnai Tribe of Gippsland* 1839-1865 (1987), proved valuable resources. The impact of this screening was profound. People stood, visibly upset saying that they didn't know. Asking why they didn't know. Some began to find out.

By 2109 three European families shared stories acknowledging their ancestors or community's involvement in murders and the impact of steps initiated by First Nation people to publicly acknowledge the past and survival. *Stories of influence* provided a place to share their stories.

- Shocked by the extent of the massacres and how little was publicly known, Shane Rees, president of the local Hall Committee, researched official records to document the official version of cause of decline in Aboriginal populations in Gippsland (Rees 2018). With support of other concerned residents he set up *Reconciliation East Gippsland* (REG). An opportunity to support recognition came about in response to a newspaper article by Uncle Max Dulumunmun Harrison, co-author with Peter McConchie, of *My People's Dreaming, An Aboriginal elder speaks on life, land, spirit and forgiveness* (2012).

  Later in 2019 Uncle Max organised a healing ceremony on the junction of the Brodribb River and Millie Creek involving around 50 descendants of the massacre. Reconciliation East Gippsland was privileged to be included in this peaceful ceremony focused on celebrating the survival of those attending (Pascoe and Shukuroglou 2020:4). Some are heartened by the opportunity to change the public history beyond that of the death of one white man. Uncle Max is writing a new book, *Rivers of Kinship* and continuing to hold ceremonies on damaged country. (Sadly Uncle Max died from COVID in December 2021. Others carry on his healing work).

  > *Uncle Max organised a healing ceremony on the junction of the Brodribb River and Millie Creek involving around 50 descendants of the massacre.*

- Cal Flyn, young Scottish journalist and author of *Thicker than Water: a memoir of family, secrets, guilt and history* (2016), spoke of tracing her great-great-great Uncle Angus McMillan's forays into Gippsland in the 1840s. Cal's writing locates this personal story within a wider context of the good and bad that is within us all and factors that tip humanity into evil, not only in Australia but also in Canada and America. We linked to Cal by zoom in her home in Orkney; a chance for us to connect with her experiences and to speak of the impact of her story in Gippsland.

- Joan and Alan McColl showed the film *Dhakiyaar Versus the King* https://www.youtube.com/watch?v=7fl2HpYihcU an inspiring story of two laws, two cultures and two families (one being the McColls) coming to terms with the past, seeking ways to act responsibly in the present and future. They welcomed the opportunity to share their emotional journey of being forgiven by descendants of Dhakiyaar's family for what their ancestor, a policeman, had done on Woodah Island off Darwin in the 1930s. Now in their 70s, the McColls are distressed that this tribe with a living culture are existing in poverty and extreme hardship under current policies.

In 2019 *Stories of Influence* Saturday night performance included singer/songwriter Todd Cook singing *The Butcher* about Angus McMillan's destructive trail through Gippsland. Working for the Edinburgh Fringe (2012/13), Scottish and Australian musicians spoke of Scots forced to leave their homelands due to British policies and becoming the inflictors of barbarity in their new homeland. As Paulo Freire perceived, the oppressors and their descendants are both impacted (Freire 1987).

Stories of influence was recognised as one of *Melbourne City of Literature* regional presenters contributing to the *UNESCO Cities of Literature* and features on their roadmap.

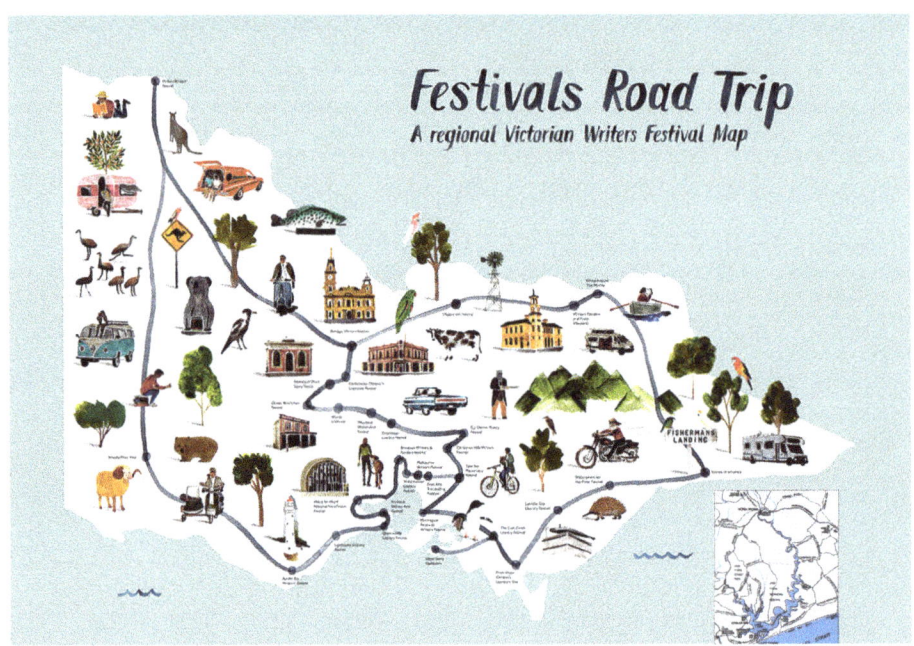

Being connected to the world of words in Melbourne through the Victorian Writers Centre, the Wheeler Centre and the Small Press Network validates the significance of local events. All invested welcome contributions of time, funds and contacts to our rural gathering. Edinburgh is also a City of Literature and as my daughter has made this city her home, prior to COVID I visited regularly. As well as the Edinburgh Writers Festival there is the Scottish Storytelling Centre a hub of performance and celebration of stories. https://www.scottishstorytellingcentre.com/. I take my wee grandsons who enjoy storytelling time particularly when there is music and performance. My daughter is a writer and we visit *The Scottish Poetry library*, where I've gifted local publications.

However, the opportunity to speak with organisers did not eventuate until David Ryding, manager of *Melbourne City of Literature* (MCOL) wrote, introducing me to the directors of the *Scottish International Storytelling Festival* (SISF). A one hour meeting with Donald Smith at the *Storytelling Centre* over a pot of tea was an instant love affair of connections.

When I spoke of the profound impact of *Stories of influence* for both presenters and listeners Donald Smith responded enthusiastically and I sensed this affirmed the foundational principles of the *Scottish International Storytellers Festival* that has an *Earth Charter* and a *Program of Place* that seeks 'earth stories'. Events named 'talking cures' recognise that dialogue within families, communities and across and between nations offers points of connection and pays attention to 'transformative myths' (origin stories) that assist integration with nature, our relationships and our spirituality and the role of artists. The question of whether Indigenous people can be restored to a place of honour and inspiration, an embedded concept is evolving in our community https://www.sisf.org.uk/

A one hour meeting with Donald Smith at the Storytelling Centre over a pot of tea was an instant love affair of connections.

Both *Stories of Influence* and the *Scottish International Story Telling Festival (SISF)* celebrate stories of place, of people with fragments of culture standing strong, of languages that had been silenced, of song and performance. I left in the pouring rain under a black Edinburgh sky during the Festival when buses struggle to run on time – with a warm sense that our tiny gathering 'Stories of influence' on the catchment of Lake Tyers in East Gippsland, had a broader legitimacy and presence.

Donald contributed an article for *New Community* journal introducing me to the *Habits of Mind* that shaped the work of the *Scottish International Story Telling Festival (SISF)*. Patrick Geddes' work on bioregionalism and planning needing to be *'scoped by detailed knowledge of ecological, social, geological, cultural and hydrological conditions of the local region'* resonated with conversations that I hear every week at *FLOAT's* Tavern Tuesday, gatherings based on the democratic approach of study circles where each person is valued for their presence at the table.

> *At these gatherings people speak of their love of where they live, of the impact of changing conditions and damaging policies.*

To learn that Geddes' *Cities in evolution* (1915) led to the *Local to Global* concept inspiring the 1992 United Nations Local Agenda 21 in Rio de Janeiro affirmed the value of both our weekly gatherings and annual sharing of stories. At these gatherings people speak of their love of where they live, of the impact of changing conditions and damaging policies. These regular conversations are deeply personal and inter-generational, taking into account knowledge of past events and seasons, the impact of changing conditions and what it means. The dramatic contrast with language used by our current leaders, choosing words such as 'protestor pests' and 'killer trees' when referring to people and their concerns about species extinction and the climate emergency, is an appeal of the group and generates hope.

Connecting streams

The connecting links between Geddes' work in social planning being underpinned by ecological balance and Jim Ife's community development frameworks seeking to balance 'social, economic, political, cultural, personal, spiritual development, recognising that for all these we depend on the environment (Ife 1995), has synergies. Both recognise that a regional approach demystifies global events offering insights of a manageable scale.

Narrative evolution: embracing the cultural story of landscape restoration.

> *Understanding of one's own culture and experience was, he [Geddes] believed, the route to personal and social confidence, the way to end internal colonisation, and the key to outward looking internationalism. To achieve this he put the folk songs of working people, nomadic Travelling people, and cultural minorities centre stage.*
> (Smith 2019: 'From Scotland to Lake Tyers',
> New Community Vol. 17 (4) 10-15)

Geddes would recognise a story shared by Martin Potts' story as *'narrative evolution'*. Martin co-ordinates projects by *Greening Australia*. This story originated from Lake Wellington wetlands in Gippsland that were drained by settlers for farming. The approach, a call to action acknowledging the degradation of the land and communities, began by listening to the stories of the land. It is a land with many stories; massacre and burial sites were found; canoe trees and stone artefacts were evidence of ceremony.

A smoking ceremony with dancing and singing was held at every planting. More recent cultural and settler stories emerged. Children were introduced to culture, to habitat planting and to local species of frogs. Reintroducing species able to flourish in this increasingly saline environment slowly brought this landscape to life. Employment is generated and planting undertaken to reclaim wetlands. Those involved learn of the *Yam story* from Aunty Aileen Blackburn-Mongta and the T*urt-Willan Story of the Women's digging stick.* https://www.facebook.com/BegaNews?posts/2238273736199728https://howittandfison.org/document/XM526/5

Reintroducing species able to flourish in this increasingly saline environment slowly brought this landscape to life.

The call to action involved local schools, farmers, cultural groups, responsible agricultural and land management agencies, environmental and cultural groups, plus organisations working on employment, water and habitat. Scientists from six Universities monitor the impact on grasses, blue carbon and biodiversity, along with community organisations concerned with frogs, birdlife, Landcare and Coastcare.

Koorie artist, Alfie Hudson created this painting, depicting the now verdant meeting places to thank Martin. The footprints walking through country are his. It is an emotional story of hope while the community and land wait for rain. A call to action holds and transforms the trauma, healing people and place that Patrick Geddes would have appreciated.

Habits of mind

A call to action holds and transforms the trauma, healing people and place

In Scottish poetry and storytelling, stories of myth, of monsters, of spiritual beings in the landscape in performance are familiar. I am reminded of this quality when listening to Lynne Kelly, author of *The Memory Code* (2016), speaking of artefacts and characters being memory triggers for knowledge in oral societies. As a science researcher, Lynne was impressed that oral cultures 'remembered' vast bodies of complex knowledge on species, navigation, genealogy, plants and history without written records. In response to her constant questioning of how people knew, she was introduced to techniques that demonstrate the extraordinary capacity of our brains at any age. Lynne has since tested these in experiments, not finding a magic formula but the use of imagery, character, repetition, story, music and dance. The story challenges the accepted wisdom of the 'inferiority' of oral societies and is potentially transformative for practice and understanding within our education system. Her second book *The Memory Craft (2019)* introduces the best memory techniques from ancient times and the Middle Ages to methods used by today's memory athletes.

oral cultures 'remembered' vast bodies of complex knowledge

Geddes may have smiled, when in 2019 the concluding panel of writers chaired by National Rural Reporter, Kath Sullivan unexpectedly became a conversation about trees. Jack Whadcoat (oldest/newest writer on the panel) had just published *'It isn't easy being a tree,'* (2019) a slim publication of conversations over his lifetime with an ageing *Mountain Grey Gum* (Eucalyptus cypellocarpa) in his backyard. Harry Saddler, Eileen Harrison and Lynne Kelly all became animated as they spoke of ways their current practice and writing was inspired by trees and their protection.

There are many stories and choice of action is not simple, linear nor universal. But that people meet sharing a common love of the catchment Bung Yarnda (Lake Tyers) and discuss these issues regularly opens our hearts and minds to what we did not know.

Our growing awareness is evolving into a guiding story that Veronica Brady, Patrick Geddes and Hamish Henderson would welcome. Our community is stronger and more connected to face these challenging times of constant health, economic and environmental crises. We are contributing to change.

Questions

In what ways do these local stories of change initiated lead to new roles and relationships within communities and between communities and institutions with a public role?

In your view what opportunities for continuing change are evident?

How might these different relationships be resourced?

Are you aware of impacts flowing between rural/regional and urban areas?

Begin locally and create a safe and respectful environment.

2. USE OF MEDIA

Begin locally and create a safe and respectful environment. Public speaking rates as a highly stressful activity if the speaker is unprepared. By beginning with small groups a worker provides opportunities for community members to become comfortable speaking of their interests and able to more comfortably participate in public forums.

Ensure the information presented is owned by the group even if one person is the spokesperson. If there is a local paper or radio, this is a great place to begin. Make contact with the organisation, become familiar with the editor, journalists, and announcers. Find out how and when the material is required and ask if your group could contribute.

Print media requires the skill of presenting information in a brief but interesting format. This is not always limited to information. It can be a personalised story with a photo, or quote to draw attention. It is important that people contribute stories and information in their own style and language rather than an assumed accepted formula. When writing an article, get another group member to give you feedback. Read articles in the daily papers and take note of the styles that you enjoy reading.

Some issues such as young people leaving the area are recurring and benefit from a current approach. If you can interview a person, or group of young people this personalises the situation and raises awareness of the wider issues and resources if this is the point to your story. This may inspire a journalist to research and feature other related material.

In the daily papers or the regional weeklies, a last minute crisis or feature story can result in your article being dropped. This is not personal, rather pressure on media that sells advertising and competes for space. Try re-sending the article to another source, as a letter to the editor, or have it listed on their website.

Radio, print, television and social media all require different skills and resources. Public forums sharing the reality of local situations offer points of connection and reduce isolation.

Public forums sharing the reality of local situations offer points of connection and reduce isolation.

At a regional or state event make inquiries about when and how to contact local media. Let them know your areas of interest. Journalists and reporters require fast access to people they know can provide a local perspective on issues. The relationship is mutually beneficial.

In regional areas, radio is an excellent way to share stories and information. Many people spend time travelling and listen to their local or regional station. In times of home isolation radio is a critical link. Talk back programs are useful to raise issues, but be prepared and organised in what you want to say. For an interview with a radio station speak to the announcer prior to the show and discuss what questions they will ask you, or send through background information to enable the interviewer to raise the important issues. Provide contact details.

Television requires interesting footage and short brief statements that convey the essence of your story. Programs featuring rural areas will often appreciate contacts to draw attention to a local issue, campaign or festival. Songs and visual recordings of events add depth and richness to a story. Podcasts, participating in panels and contributions to relevant magazines offer significant forums. Contact the relevant reporter and extend an invitation to meet with your group. Regional platforms and community face book pages are other useful forums to explore.

With all media it is helpful to know time constraints the journalists and reporters work to. When are their busy times, when are they looking for stories? Contact information needs to be up to date, and personalised. When sending information always include contact details for your home and business, if you will not be available all the time, include a second person.

Task

If you as the worker have been a resource for a group make time to acknowledge what has been achieved and who will take on roles in the future. There may be wider interest in expanding similar ventures. Prepare a statement to send to all media with the offer of a follow up interview for radio and television. In preparing this press release consider:

Who you are?

Who you are responsible to?

What has been your role in the community?

Why was the position created?

What are the outcomes at this stage?

Are there key people you may wish to feature in the press release?

Is there a key point that you wish to convey?

How could you do this?

Where can people contact you?

How might you build on existing knowledge of the project?

What contacts and information will you need to research to distribute this press release?

Consider how a network can be established to raise awareness of the group and resources (time, finance, equipment, venue etc) essential to its operation.

3. CONTINUING TO AFFIRM

This business of making accessible the richness of the world we are in, of bringing density to ordinary, day-to-day living in a place, is the real work of culture…of enriching our consciousness; increasing our awareness of what exists around us, making it register on our senses in the most vivid way; but also of taking it into our consciousness and of giving it a second life there so that we possess the world we inhabit imaginatively as well as in fact.
(Malouf 1998:35)

Plan an annual event to acknowledge what has been achieved individually and collectively. Celebrations are a public affirmation of the value of the group and to showcase activities. Celebrations bring people together socially to consolidate friendships and networks, without the pressure of 'getting the job done'. Some organisations provide awards to everyone, give flowers or mementos, some celebrate through musical entertainment and food. Guest speakers relevant to the group's interest may further publiscise their work and continue motivation, but essentially this is a time for conversation and relaxation. Informal conversations at these events may lead to new ventures or partnerships.

By the time of annual reflection, relationships have been made, strengthened and trust developed. Members of the group will have the confidence to include others in discussions and planning. Taking this step invites a new cycle of engagement based on sound foundations for the community and region. Linking community activities into resourced networks can both expand options and generate greater awareness of shared interests.

Working towards a more sustainable future requires a change in our practice

Consider ways to induct new members, to ensure a respect for the democratic processes is adopted and practiced by the group. Some groups require interim membership for 12 months prior to holding office to minimize take over by old autocratic ways. Remember the way we work determines the outcomes. Keeping relationships healthy and continuing to affirm the importance of inclusive processes and values requires attention. Working towards a more sustainable future requires a change in our practice that can be challenging. However, working through problematic times will build new understanding and skills, just as celebrating success will affirm the important values held within rural communities. The community may ask for assistance in these events, and the worker may discuss their role and the assistance they can offer. The goal is to support the ongoing development and involvement of the group continuing to learn past the period of support and establishment. In communities with a clear process of engagement on local issues through local media, gatherings, performance or other democratic means I have seen younger people adopt similar actions when troubling issues arise. It was a heartening experience.

Questions

How do groups in your community acknowledge and celebrate their work?

List benefits that have come from public recognition of organisations you are familiar with?

In discussions with people in the groups how significant are these times?

Who for?

What changes result?

4. WALKING AWAY, KNOWING HOW, WHEN AND WHY

Collaborative engagement for transformation strategies provide a way for people to come together, share experiences, knowledge and resources around issues they have in common. A point of connection may be about future of employment for young people, the state of the river or any of a myriad of life limiting or enhancing situations. While people may disagree on other issues, this is a point of shared interest. Whether people's assumptions are affirmed or challenged, the interaction raises awareness of the pervasive nature of paradigms about the present and future (Hicks and Holden 2007:501-512).

The role of the community development worker is to support individuals within the group move from despair to action and optimism.

The role of the community development worker is to support individuals within the group move from despair to action and optimism. Increasing capacity during the visioning stage and gaining community credibility requires the worker to support more community members taking on public roles. Generally members of the group will have the confidence to share their experiences of being in the group and the long term goals they have discussed. From this base alliances with other organisations can be entered into.

Groups that began with achievable projects will have had time increase skills, confidence in themselves and the wider community. While the worker can assist by sourcing information and contacts about legal structures or funding, or plan public meetings, the speed, direction and ownership of these steps need to be determined by the community group. The transition period will vary from community to community depending on past experiences within the community, the resources, energy and networks available.

If the worker was employed to facilitate a study circle or the establishment stage of a group there will be a definite end to this stage. While groups may choose to continue meeting regularly it is significant to acknowledge the changes that have taken place and plans for the future. This is a good time to say your farewells but let them know where to find you, or another worker. Affirm their ability and your confidence in them and encourage their involvement in a continuing network.

the speed, direction and ownership of these steps need to be determined by the community group.

In the analogy of parenting there is the stage of leaving home, when support and contact may be regular and important followed by increasing confidence for individuals to take on new roles and responsibilities. As with parenting this is a time of mixed emotions: great pride and a time of sadness at no longer being an important component of the group. This needs to be acknowledged by all concerned. It can be helpful for the worker to reflect on the difference between dependency and the ability of the group to act on their own in current and future ventures.

Questions

In what ways can the worker encourage the group to maintain an inclusive way of working past the study circle period?

Are you aware of strategies that would assist the group reflect on their personal and community development?

At what stage might this be relevant?

5. CONTINUING TO LEARN

Universities have a responsibility to look after the well-being of the planet, not as stand-alone beacons of knowledge, but as places where the wisdom of communities, eco-systems and the academy create partnerships for a world that is more sustainable and just. The key interrelated challenges of our time such as: runaway climate change, the loss of bio-diversity, the depletion of natural resources, the on-going homogenization of culture and rising inequity, require university leadership.
(Garlick and Matthews 2013)

This introduction to transformative community development is written for people with responsibility for regional engagement. Further options to continue developing expertise and knowledge in an area that is becoming increasingly important in the national wellbeing include:

- Enrolment in Diploma of Community Development. (TAFE and Community Houses)

- Undergraduate course in Community or Regional Sustainable Development.

- Grad. Diploma and Post-Graduate Research in regional development within Universities

- Masters of Environment and Society or Sustainability frequently have community engagement or community development subjects.

This manual is an introduction to resources and skills to engage with *'ordinary people who educate us'* with an understanding that it is from within communities that life affirming values are evident and celebrated.

The professional development manual is both an invitation and a contribution to a dynamic and evolving partnership between tertiary educational institutions and regional communities that are at the front line of change. The approach outlines a process of engagement with rural communities as they develop inclusive community plans and of ways educational institutions can both offer professional pathways and establish partnerships with communities. Education has a critical role in communities and all levels of government taking steps towards a sustainable future.

Education has a critical role

Institutions incorporating a regional framework towards regeneration and revitalisation between institutions and communities will find mutual benefits. New language denotes change. It is of interest that from an institutional perspective that the concept of Ecoversity a vehicle for how education about and for environmental sustainability might be theoretically elaborated and practically applied is being advocated (Garlick and Matthews 2013). Locally the idea of 'Communiversity ' the sharing local knowledge associated with the establishment of a floating art gallery by residents of Lake Tyers is being used. The FLOAT spoken of in chapter 4 is home to creations and reflections of art+science+environment+culture https://www.abc.net.au/news/2021-04-16/lake-tyers-beach-communiversity-east-gippsland/100072886

Task

Craft a story of change in a format of your choice. Print, song, digital, graphic, textile are all welcome. Presenting the story from the perspective of the worker, and from the perspective of change within the community adds to awareness of barriers and the knowledge of opportunities.

We continue to learn.

FURTHER REFERENCES

Bakewell, E., (2019) *The mouse that roared*, in 'Stories of the Lake: recordings of words and music inspired by Bung Yarnda (Lake Tyers)', (Ed) Sheil, H., Centre for Rural Communities, Toorloo Arm. https://ruralcommunities.com.au/stories-of-the-lake-recordings-of-words-and-music-inspired-by-bung-yardna-lake-tyers/

Brady, V. (1996), *Can these bones live?* Federation Press, Sydney.

Belenky- Field, M., McVicker-Clinchy, B., Goldberger-Rule. N., Mattuck- Tarule, J., (1997) (2nd Edn). *Womens Ways of Knowing: The development of self, voice and mind*. Basic Books Inc. New York.

Dodd, A., Gaye, L., Fair, J., Boadle, J., Owsianka, A. & Winnell, B., Sheil, D., (2018) *Warrigal Creek Massacres* https://www.thecitizen.org.au/articles/student-film-shines-lighton-gippslands-bloody-hidden-history

Eileen Harrison - Indigenous Australia
https://ia.anu.edu.au › biography › harrison-eileen-17792

Flyn, C. (2016) *Thicker than water. A memoir of family, secrets, guilt and history,* Harper Collins. London.

Freire, P. (1987) *Literacy reading the word and the world,* Routledge and Kegan Paul. London.

Gardner, P. (1990) *Our founding murdering father, Angus McMillan and the Kurnai Tribe of Gippsland* 1839-1865 Ngarek Press. Ensay.

Gardner, P. (1983) *Gippsland Massacres, destruction of Kurnai tribe,* West Gippsland and LaTrobe Valley Education Centre. Warragul.

Garlick.S., (1997) The Ebb and Flow of Regional Development Policy and Practice in Australia: An overview and Future Possibilities. *Regional Cooperation & Development Forum.* Australian Local Government, Canberra.

Garlick. S., & Matthews, J., (2014) 'University responsibility in a world of environmental catastrophe. Cognitive justice, engagement and an ethic of care in learning', *University engagement and environmental sustainability,* pp 9-20. Warragul.

Geddes, P. (1915) *Cities in evolution* London: Williams, London. https://evolutionaryurbanism.com/2017/02/27/cities-in-evolution-patrick-geddes/

Jakobi, J., (2019) *Maisie Byrne*, 'Stories of the Lake: recordings of words and music inspired by Bung Yarnda (Lake Tyers)', (Ed) Sheil, H., Centre for Rural Communities, Toorloo Arm. https://ruralcommunities.com.au/maise-byrne-1930s-poem/

Mathews, I., (2019) *Winning for women,* Monash University Press, Melbourne.

Martin, J., (2006) 'Study of Small Towns in Victoria re-visited', Centre for Sustainable Regional Communities, in Henshall, *Towns in Time Analysis 1981-2001,* Essential Economics.

Pattern, Herb (Uncle) 02/06/2022 *Uncle Herb Pattern reflects on a life of gum-leaf playing*, Coster, J. and Lucas, R., (ABC radio) https://www.abc.net.au/news/2022-06-02/uncle-herb-patten-entertaining-gumleaf-playing/101118740

Postman. N. (1995) T*he End of Education: redefining the value of school.* Vintage Books. New York.

Rose Bird. D., (2000) *Indigenous Ecology and Ethic of Connection.* Global Ethics and Environment, edited by Nicholas Low, Taylor & Francis Group, 2000. ProQuest Ebook Central, http://ebookcentral.proquest.com/lib/rmit/detail.action?docID=169837.

Shoemaker. A. (Ed) 1994. *Oodgeroo. A Tribute.* Australian Literary Studies, University of Queensland Press.

Stories of influence https://ruralcommunities.com.au/stories

Sheil, H. (Ed) 2019. *Stories of the Lake. Recordings of words and music inspired by Bung Yarnda (Lake Tyers.* Centre for Rural Communities Inc. Toorloo Arm.

Smith, N., & Sheil, H., (2006) Study of small towns revisited, Swifts Creek, *Towns in Time Analysis 1981-2001*, Henshall, https://ruralcommunities.com.au/towns-in-time-2001

Thorpe, W., (6th July, 2019) *Bung Yarnda – Camping Place* recorded by Rachel Lucas https://www.youtube.com/watch?v=z_HIY7Yq6Gs

Thorpe, W., (2017) A story of Bung Yarnda, https://www.youtube.com/watch?v=aaykiOzgaTs

www.ingramcontent.com/pod-product-compliance
Lightning Source LLC
Chambersburg PA
CBHW041658040426
R18086800002B/R180868PG42333CBX00012B/3